Wakefield Press

A BRIEF TAKE ON THE AUSTRALIAN NOVEL

Born of an Australian mother and a French father, Jean-François Vernay grew up in New Caledonia's multicultural community which shares some of Australia's characteristics, including a convict heritage and a complex history of settlement. Using Peter Carey and Christopher Koch as a starting point, he has been researching Australian fiction for 20 years and has published widely in the field, both in French and in English. Dr Vernay is an energetic critic, editor, creative writer and cultural commentator. His fiction and nonfiction books have appeared in France, Australia and in the United States.

By the same author

Water from the Moon: Illusion and reality in the works of Australian novelist Christopher Koch, New York, Cambria, 2007.

Plaidoyer pour un renouveau de l'émotion en littérature, Paris, Complicités, 2013.

A Brief Take on the Australian Novel is a revised and expanded edition of *Panorama du roman australien des origines à nos jours*, Paris, Hermann, 2009.

A BRIEF TAKE ON THE AUSTRALIAN NOVEL

JEAN-FRANÇOIS VERNAY

Originally translated by

Marie Ramsland

and revised by Jean-François Vernay

Wakefield Press
16 Rose Street
Mile End
South Australia 5031
www.wakefieldpress.com.au

First published 2016

Cover designed by Michael Deves
Cover art © Prudence Flint, *A Fine Romance #21*, 2005, oil on linen (135 x 97 cm)
Edited by Margot Lloyd, Wakefield Press
Text designed and typeset by Wakefield Press
Printed in Australia by Griffin Digital, Adelaide

National Library of Australia Cataloguing-in-Publication entry

Creator:	Vernay, Jean-François, author.
Title:	A brief take on the Australian novel / Jean-François Vernay.
ISBN:	978 1 74305 404 8 (paperback).
Notes:	Includes index.
Subjects:	Australian literature – History and criticism. Novelists, Australian.
Dewey Number:	A820.9

Contents

Inserts

Teaser

According to cognitive scientists, emotions and intelligence are interrelated and equally important in many situations, especially in decision-making processes such as choosing a good read. And yet marketing strategies want consumers to believe that books, very much like happiness pills, are made available only on prescription: critics are there to tell you which book to buy or not; TV and radio book shows guarantee a quick, though sometimes efficient, airing for selected latest releases; literary festivals tend to feature writers with the highest profiles who, perhaps, do not need to generate further publicity; while literary prizes like the Miles Franklin Award also contribute to this winner-takes-all logic, and the dutiful consumers, spoilt for choice, are meant to take their pick – but chance and personal taste no longer have anything to do with it. The prescriptive trend is so common a practice that, as part of the National Year of Reading, a 2011 campaign was devised to compile a list of books that would aptly encapsulate the 'Australian experience'. Once again the winners are ... anyone but the readers.

While I was researching Australian fiction, people started asking me what they should read. This is a tricky question because you need to provide an answer while carefully avoiding establishing a canon. Bearing in mind that any recommendation would reflect my own tastes, I tried to conceive a neutral space like a virtual giant table on which would lie any appealing Australiana-packed novel, for avid readers to make their own choices. This project presented itself as the horizontal counterpart of the vertical library bookshelf, in which pre-selection, classification and exposure were of the essence.

In writing this book, I also wanted to convey the oft-neglected 'pleasure of the text': the kind of cultural enjoyment one may not derive from science books. For it is the privilege of the literary text to enable readers to experience its *jouissance* – a French word which carries a primary meaning of 'orgasm', but which Roland Barthes uses to encapsulate the highest form of enjoyment and sensual pleasure. I am grateful to my publisher for allowing me to share my emotions with other readers, as I feel there is no better way to enhance the pleasure of the text.

Melbourne, 23 December 2015

Sneak Preview

Jean-François Vernay's 'brief take on the Australian novel' begins one step back, with a 'draft definition' of Australian literature. This is quite proper, not because the author's definition is provisional, but because 'Australian literature' itself continues to be subject to redefinition, and Australia's fictions too. The shape is not settled – and I do not mean to say 'yet', as if one day in the future it will have found itself. It is not a question of adolescence, but rather something inherent in the appeal and interest of Australian writing that it continually breaks away from definitional grabs. To adapt Ranajit Guha's title, *History at the Limit of World-History*, Australian literature can be considered to be at a double limit of world and literature. *The World Republic of Letters*, for example, Pascale Casanova's lofty survey, mentions Australia only in passing, as an item in Commonwealth lists. And before the European idea of Australia came into being, the *literature* of the country was oral, visual, performative – Aboriginal – or else a matter of speculation. Even if we restrict literature to what is written in a conventional sense, and agree on a notion of Australia as the largely English-speaking society inaugurated with the British invasion of 1788, it is still the case that Australian literature exists at the limit of world literature. While many works can be identified as 'tied in some way ... to things Australian' (the flexible definition Vernay borrows from D.R. Burns), no single characterisation is generally accepted as adequately or permanently descriptive of Australian literature as a whole or as an entity. Indeed, the label 'Australian' is commonly resisted by Australian authors themselves. Robert Dessaix, for example, is quoted as saying at the Adelaide Writers' Week in 2010, 'Do any of us write as Australian writers? I know I don't. I write as *moi*.' Sydney-born Australian novelist Steve Toltz commented recently that he was more comfortable writing in the northern hemisphere.

This is paradoxical, since Australian literature as a category would seem to be readily delimited, not only by its island-continent geography of place, but also by its marked temporality (in English, at any rate), from colonial commencement in 1788 to the present shifting, always advancing moment. Yet within those apparently clear outlines, there are many different versions of how texts and their authors and readers relate, adding to or departing from the larger field. In essaying his spirited, wide-ranging, highly informed and suitably opinionated survey of Australian fiction, Vernay acknowledges that he must face the reaction of interlocutors who 'seem unaware of [the] existence' of Australian literature. It appears that those writers, editors and critics who have been part of the internal dynamics of Australian literature over many years have failed to construe their production for external perception. The situation arises *despite* the international success of many individual authors from Australia. It's as a contribution to changing things that this new book is so fresh and valuable.

This 'brief take' (actually a response to years of reading and research) charts an incomplete quest through a terrain in which the many varieties of Australian novel line up in historical continuum as they respond to changing creative possibilities, divergent in their individual striving for achievement, yet also asking to be read against broader social and political contexts, patterns of literary tradition and innovation, and the shared thematic concerns that Vernay outlines.

His guiding principle is to see Australian literature on its own terms rather than, as is often the case, as a subsidiary of the Anglophone subset of world literature, to be placed according to the favoured methodologies of Anglo-American academia (often, ironically, translated French theory). This requires him to separate Australian fiction from its British beginnings, tracing its differentiation through the inventive agency of authors as they take steps of their own, according to inward and outward necessity – migration, dispossession, marginalisation, experience without precedent, political commitment, and a determination to be heard, to be published, to gain recognition and reward. Vernay's is a decolonising project that brings a vitalising perspective to Australian literary studies.

Starting with various 'firsts' for Australian fiction, the panorama proceeds through an impressive range of authors, in which obscure figures join well-known names, high mixes with low, and commercial or genre fiction challenges the literary. Marcel Aurousseau appears beside Miles Franklin; Walter Adamson, Don'o Kim and Antoni Jach with David Malouf and Eva Hornung. There's a series of close-ups on key authors and works, such as *Clara Morison* (1854) by Catherine Helen Spence, praised for its embodiment of 'the possibility for women to free themselves [from] patriarchal chains'. Vernay adduces scholarship, especially from outside Australia, that sees the local through new eyes. His approach is original, even polemical; the style relaxed, and sometimes pointed. 'There is a certain loquaciousness among Australian writers,' the author notes as a puzzle to be investigated, an 'abundance' linked perhaps to 'an anxiety of not belonging'. There is much to argue with here – one doesn't have to agree with every claim or interpretation – and the sensation of being provoked within a coherent overall analysis is pleasurable, a prompt to reconsider.

The use of pseudonyms in colonial Australia, the scope for hoaxes later on, 'cultural cringe' and expatriation, war, historical fiction, representations of Aboriginal experience and the work of Indigenous authors, literary multiculturalism, and the changing publishing environment (in an extended postscript) are among the topics covered. Central to the discussion is a conception of Australian utopias and dystopias that is developed from the country's original status for settlers as a penal colony and the consequent understanding of society as prison, 'an institutionalised tyranny', in the creative imagination of successive generations. Quoting Emile Cioran, Vernay notes the totalitarian idea within utopia, thus also potentially dystopic, where the communitarian demands compliance in 'a paradisal space ruled by a coercive administration'.

In this view, Tasmania, particularly through its rendering in the fiction of Christopher Koch, provides an emblematic topos of the island-prison, where insularity induces boredom, paranoia and a desire to escape the constriction of a policed and policing collective. The argument extends outwardly to white Australia's often pathological relationship with a surrounding world where 'all exogenous elements' (Asian, migrant, even Indigenous, conceptualised as outcast) must be kept out, 'as overcompensation for a deep fear of annihilation, a direct consequence of the porous nature of frontiers'. It extends temporally to a contestation of narratives that underline Australia's dependency and defensiveness (and fear of being defenceless), as demonstrated in the many novels 'that correct or denounce official versions of Australian history'. It extends inwardly, psychologically, to a gendered drama of masculine and feminine, within and between individuals, in a world that calls for imaginative transformation. These dimensions connect for Vernay in 'the idea that Australian history has its roots ... in repressed violence', one expression of which is a 'theme of loss lived out as a traumatic experience that gives rise to a feeling of abandonment'. Koch's conflicted male protagonists are exemplary in their response, searching for 'an "otherworld" that is sublimated, imagined or idealised', a 'secret alterity', a heightened, alternative way to live.

Koch clusters with Malouf, Peter Carey, Gerald Murnane, Janette Turner Hospital and, from a later generation, Christos Tsiolkas, among those foregrounded in this view. Vernay quotes from Tsiolkas's novel *Loaded*: 'He ran to escape history. That's his story.' Is that also the story of Australian fiction, Australia's story's story? The conclusions drawn here are discerning, balanced and open to ambivalence. For Australian novelists suspended between a national frame and the desire to transcend it, there is 'an advantage for every disadvantage', writes Vernay suggestively, and always more than one way of looking at the same thing.

The outside gaze illuminates what the insider cannot see, especially when that gaze focuses on what most distinguishes the inside, what makes it what it is. Alexis de Tocqueville's enduringly prescient *Democracy in America* was the result of a nine-month tour in 1831–1832 in which the author appreciated the paradoxes of his subject and was able to see its idiosyncrasies and shortcomings as part of a larger whole. D.H. Lawrence diagnosed 'the withheld self' in the settler Australian psyche after an intense few months' visit in 1922. Vernay's observations are more deeply grounded in scholarship than those of Tocqueville or Lawrence, yet like theirs are enlivened by enthusiasm, sensitivity and passionate engagement. He participates in the quarrels and triumphs of Australian literature. He adds his verdict. Whether this 'brief take' is absorbed in its French or English versions, whether in the classroom where it will be so useful, or elsewhere as a general introduction, a debt of gratitude is owed to Jean-François Vernay for contributing this generous intervention to the love and the labour that is the Australian literary enterprise. Readers of Australian literature will enjoy his company.

Nicholas Jose

Trailer

The original version of *Panorama du roman australien des origines à nos jours* set out to inform the French reader of a literature that was still relatively unknown despite the efforts of a few publishing houses in France, such as Actes Sud, P.O.L., Gallimard, Albin Michel, éditions de l'Aube, Autrement, Plon, Presses de la Renaissance, 10/18.

At the outset, I had to choose how I would present this vast topic. A thematic presentation would have grouped works according to selected affinities, but would have limited the overall depiction of the evolution of the novel. Another approach would have been to present twenty of the most talented authors, but this approach would have sidelined many writers who did not deserve to be left out. Or, I could have chosen to present the main stages in the development of the Australian novel that correlate directly with the main periods in the country's history:

1787–1850 The transportation of the first British subjects as felons, that led to the first descriptions of Australia by government officials, travellers and emigrants (convict literature, realism, diaries, accounts, documentaries, etc.)

1850–1914 The discovery of gold that coincided with an increase in the size of the Australian reading public and the establishment of an extensive pastoral society (Arcadian theme, local colour, nationalism, etc.)

1914–1945 The two World Wars and their interwar period that eventually influenced the economic expansion of the country (urbanism, modernism, etc.)

1945–present Growth, development and international competition, inciting a national consciousness as the country faced global issues (heterogeneity, hybridism, confusion or syncretism of genres, etc.)

In the end, I chose a more personal approach which I believe is more in keeping with the major pivotal and evolutionary stages of the Australian novel.

Since the 1970s in Australia, film has rivalled literature in terms of popular success. Thus I thought it appropriate to borrow a cinematic vocabulary to portray the richness of Australian fiction and to use film as a metaphor. And so this *Brief Take on the Australian Novel* is interspersed with three types of inserts. 'Close-ups' draw attention to (significant) themes, authors and books; 'low-angle shots' acknowledge great novels or novelists that dominate the Australian literary landscape; while the 'panoramic views' survey themes or the careers of important authors.

The analogy between cinema and literature allows the development of parallels between writers and actors. The rise of the 'celebrity writer' or media-exposed author – because of a controversy, their topicality, or popular and critical success – makes us think of the excessive exposure in the media of film stars. The obligation to promote their finished work leads to appearances on television, radio programs, press conferences, interviews, and attendance at award ceremonies in the hope of success. An artist's life is not a long tranquil process – if it ever was.

My deepest appreciation goes to publisher Michael Bollen and his Wakefield Press team, including the designer, Michael Deves, for their support and expertise in realising *A Brief Take on the Australian Novel* along with my associate producers, translator Dr Marie Ramsland, as well as subeditors Professor Nicholas Jose, Margot Lloyd, Dr Christopher Ringrose and Gertraud Widera, for bringing this project to fruition. I am grateful to guest author Dr Noel Henricksen for sharing his uncompromising views on

Christopher Koch's works in the Special Features section. I also wish to express my heartfelt thanks to Nicholas Jose for giving readers an insightful sneak preview of my cinematic project and to Prudence Flint, whose inspirational artwork is featured on the front cover.

No more talking.
Silence and ... ACTION!

Director-cum-scriptwriter
Jean-François Vernay

Prologue

Australian literature: A draft definition

What is Australian literature? This is a question that has at some point troubled most writers, academics and well-educated people in Australia. While many definitions have been offered, none has ever been entirely satisfactory. They have, nevertheless, been divisive and fed numerous controversies.

There are some who think that, because it is written in the English language, Australian literature should be considered as a branch of British literature. How wrong they are! Are we to conclude from this that there is no such thing as American, South African or New Zealand literature – to name three examples – as these countries were originally part of the British Empire? Others consider the concept of a national literature to be absurd. They believe there is only one literature – a 'world literature'.

Some Australian critics recognised that when literature was first produced in the Antipodes, it was riddled with flaws, since it was at its bumbling beginnings. Others were quick to use an organic metaphor, describing Australian literature as a plant or a young shoot that needed time to grow. This 'national immaturity', which several literary historians invoke, gave way in time to the rise of a quality literature. But before ascertaining the important works of this literature, we need to define it.

So what constitutes 'Australian literature'? Is it sufficient for a work to be about Australia? If this were the case, then we would have to include authors like D.H. Lawrence, even though his depiction of the country was limited to two novels, *Kangaroo* in 1923 and *The Boy in the Bush* co-written with Mollie Skinner in 1924. This would be ridiculous when we know that his stay in Australia lasted four months only, from May to August 1922!

Must the writer be born in Australia? This would impose regrettable limitations as it would then deprive Australian literature of its most illustrious authors, such as the Nobel Prize winner Patrick White, who was born in London of Australian parents and educated both in Australia and in the Old Country. Nevil Shute and Arthur Upfield, who both came to the Antipodes in adulthood, would also be excluded. Contemporary examples of such migrant writers would include Peter Skrzynecki, born in Germany of Ukrainian and Polish ancestry, and Austrian-born Renate Yates who grew up in suburban Sydney.

For a book to be acknowledged as belonging to Australian literature, must the writer be an Australian national? This prescription would exclude an author like Paul Wenz, who remained a French citizen, publishing all his novels in French with the exception of *Diary of a New Chum* (1908).

To be Australian, must the work be written in Australia? Many renowned contemporary writers would thus be penalised. David Malouf spent time in Tuscany; Peter Carey chose to live in New York – not to mention those who left the country to live as expatriates in the 1920s and 1930s due to cultural stagnation in the reconstruction period after the Great War and in the Great Depression. Are these writers (such as Christina Stead, Martin Boyd and Patrick White) any the less Australian?

Must the book be written in the English language? Novelists like Giovanni Andreoni, who has lived in Australia since 1962 and writes his stories in Italian, as exemplified by his autobiographical novel *Martin Pescatore* (1967), would in that case find themselves excluded from Australian literature, despite their contributions.

If the defining traits of Australian literature derive from theme, author's origin and nationality, geographic location or mode of expression, we see such a definition here as being too inclusive or too restrictive. Therefore a combination of these five criteria is excluded. However, one could agree with the approach of critic John K. Ewers, who considers any writing, 'poems, short stories, novels, plays, etc., which have been conceived in the minds of the writers who have reacted to the conditions of life in Australia', as part of the Australian literary heritage. D.R. Burns' definition is also worth mentioning: 'there isn't anything explicit ... to be called a rule. But the work should be tied in some way, or its author should, to things Australian'.

If we define Australian literature in these terms, some guidelines are required if we are to assess its relationship to the social life of the country and to world literature.

Iconic themes in Australian literature

The Quest

Quest, which has been an Australian preoccupation ever since the *Terra Australis Incognita* myth, has multiple facets: the quest for a southern continent, an El Dorado, a safe haven, an unexplored country. It wasn't until modernist literature (1920s–1950s) that the physical voyage became an allegory of the psychic journey – in other words, a journey of introspection. The physical and symbolic voyage of Heriot in search of the archipelago of the dead in Randolph Stow's *To the Islands* is an example of this. It is not so much the success of the undertaking that is important (indeed, this is less frequent than the instances of failure) as the discovery of nature that leads the main character to a discovery of the self. To undertake a voyage is, above all, to surrender to disorientation that often involves leaving one's land, which in turn brings about the exteriorisation of identity. When, in *Across the Sea Wall* by Christopher Koch, Robert O'Brien leaves Christine and his native land, his initiation in India, followed by his return to Australia, announces the possibility of change.

Conquest

Territory is the object of profound desire. Its presence often evokes the period of colonisation and the appropriation of land by the colonisers under the pretext of *terra nullius*, which is at the heart of the guilt felt by European immigrant groups. Territorial conquest is obviously an object of migration. Spatial conquest also places Australians on the defensive and gives rise to political intrigues represented in various ways as, for example, dystopia, adventure, or crime. Narratives about invasion, such as Eric Willmot's *Below the Line* (1991), use the motif of conquest to inform us about the psychosis of the Yellow Peril.

Voyage

Australia's history has been marked by voyages, especially by sea. The wreck of the *Batavia* in the seventeenth century has inspired many novels, including *The Bellarmine Jug* (1984) by Nicholas Hasluck, *The Company: The Story of a Murderer* (2000) by Arabella Edge and *The Accomplice* (2003) by Kathryn Heyman. There followed the voyage of exploration of Lieutenant (Captain) Cook in 1770 and the arrival of the First Fleet with Governor (Rear Admiral) Arthur Phillip in 1788, the official date of European colonisation. As with the quest motif, the physical voyage is often an allegory for an imaginary journey, one of introspection. Historically, the first Australian writers, whether born in England or native to Australia, did not adopt an Australian viewpoint but that of an exiled Briton. The figure of the archetypal Australian expatriate emerged with twentieth-century travels.

Geography

Australia is often thought of as a 'land of terror'. Beside the hostilities of the colonial period – the most obvious being those carried out in Van Diemen's Land (Tasmania) with the attempted eradication of the Aboriginal population – the land evoked the convict period. But it is also linked with the identity of individuals. The relationship between man and the land is deeply embedded in the animistic beliefs of the Aboriginal peoples. A parallel can be drawn with the theory of geographic determinism held by Montesquieu. In addition to this, the country is often personified, moralised or fragmented. The analogy between body and land becomes an obvious *topos* when writers want to suggest that geography is an extension of the human body. Place, the *locus*, has a determining influence on our lives, giving rise to an interest in topography that comes from an attempt to interpret space. Culture is linked with literature; interior space with exterior space; the mind with the body; time with space. Landscape is thought of as a thematic tool (as in the recurring theme of Arcadia) or even an integral component of a genre: the pastoral novel. Landscape is a key element for Australian artists, painters and writers, and for their relationship with a national identity.

In the treatment of space, there are three trends which will become evident in the studies that follow:

- Exploitation of a *country scene*, involving the stereotypical traits of the pastoral scene: wide open spaces, eucalyptus trees, cattle, sand storms, floods ... In a realistic vein, there are many authors who present their vision of the environment through detailed and sometimes romantic descriptions of the landscape, embodied in a picturesque lyricism.
- Treatment of the *urban milieu* with its tramways, neon signs, sky-scrapers, and cinemas. Added to this is the affluence of the metropolis.
- The *beach culture* with its sacrosanct institution of surfing, and its lifesavers, ironmen, etc. Recurrent characteristics of this literature that give an account of the Australian

environment include idiosyncratic language, expression of a democratic attitude, a desire to get to the truth and an ironic sense of humour, which can be seen as a defence mechanism by virtue of its cathartic power.

Topography

Cartography as an act of writing is a privileged aspect of literary geography. Perception leads to conception. It is a textual attempt to grasp the context, to '[read] the country', as Stephen Muecke describes it. During the colonial period, the colonisers very quickly realised that they needed a new vocabulary to express their feeling of alterity and to name new realities. As they were at the exact opposite end of the earth to their homeland, they had to confront new geographical forms, a different climate, a different population and different distinctive administrative structures. We have to understand the urgency they felt in giving names to unexplored space as a means of creating new existences and putting in place reference markers. In the same way that taxonomy shows a scientific understanding of an area, land-naming, after land-taking, was a significant stage in appropriating the environment.

Isolation

An important characteristic of Australian literature is its propensity to embody heroic or symbolic figures, whose distinguishing trait is their marginality, their isolation or solitude. A key element of the Australian psyche involves the feeling of living on the margin of society, with the geographic centre an unwelcoming desert and the focus of identity being somewhere else, in some far-away otherness. There is a diffused feeling of belonging without real appropriation of a place, a land, a people. Moreover, there exists in Australia what can be called the southern hemisphere complex of the exiled, which expresses the frustration of a people of British origins who felt marooned on an island in the southern hemisphere. This feeling is registered, in particular, in language used by some people who unashamedly resort to a vulgar expression to describe their country as 'the arsehole of the world'. Using more moderate language, renowned Australian novelist Thomas Keneally situates Australia, according to his character Phelim Halloran in *Bring Larks and Heroes* (1967), at 'the world's worse end'. For David Malouf and Rodney Hall, the metaphor is similar: their country is situated at 'the far side of the globe/world'.

The Antipodes

The notion of a transported Europe is again important for this theme. Australia is, for David Malouf, a 'Europe translated' (because its artists are too faithful to European literary canons) whereas, for Les Murray, it is a 'Europe transplanted'. In the purest carnivalesque tradition, seasons are reversed, social barriers abolished and the country is experienced as a land of wonders. The discovery of a surprising local flora means that it is compared with imported plants, reassuring the colonisers who regard them as icons of a world that is familiar to them.

Abundance

There is a certain loquaciousness among Australian writers. As a general rule, their novels tend to be voluminous and concerned with communities. There are several hypotheses to explain this. The first is that Australians have never been spatially limited. They are accustomed to large geographical sweeps of land and, as a consequence, are not inclined to deprive themselves of fictional space. Another hypothesis has some authors looking to fill the void of these great spaces with a myriad of small details, as the realists do. The third hypothesis posits a naturalist drive with the writer, as he or she attempts to portray the abundance of life on the continent.

Religion

When perceived as a paradise, Australia is made up of Eden-like settings. However, its Inferno opposite is a vast, nightmarish carceral system. Australia is both an object of fascination (a colourful land of contrasts, of curiosities, and so on) and of repulsion (hostile nature, an arid climate, troublesome fauna) which predisposes Australian writers to persist in ambivalent feelings towards their country. The theme of the garden often comes from the vision of Australia as a Garden of Eden, perceived as an enclosed space: a paradise (from the Avestan *pairidaēza*). This inevitably leads to the contrast between a cultivated garden – the mirror of a civilising and cultural enterprise – and an abandoned garden where chaos and savagery are evident, and where nature reclaims its rightful place. Whereas Europe generally evokes violence, insurrection and anarchy, Australia can inspire an idyllic setting, assured tranquillity and stability.

The Garden of Eden myth endures because it is deeply ingrained in the Australian imagination. It disappears only when it yields to its pessimistic counterpoint, the anti-Eden myth, the apocalyptic vision of hell on earth. This vision has persisted since the Dutch ship *Batavia* was shipwrecked in 1629 and discovered later in 1963 about eighty kilometres off the coast of Geraldton in Western Australia. After the disaster, the survivors were surprised by a mutiny organised on shore at a moment's notice by their companions in misfortune, so as to commandeer the ship's cargo. The mutineers slaughtered 125 innocent people before being apprehended and punished. Two, however, managed to escape death but were condemned to a life of exile on the Australian continent. Thus Australia became synonymous with punishment and prison. These were the first criminals to populate Australia, the first two slithering serpents in the Garden of Eden. So the Fall of Australians could be seen as being brought about by greed and violence. Hence the land was predestined to become a colonial penitentiary for felons and convicts. What was seen as a 'hostile' climate intensified this pessimistic perception of Australia.

Disappearance

The disappearance of any Australian, whether important or not, has almost become a cliché. The explorer, the vagabond and other archetypal figures, claimed by an anthropomorphic nature and a hostile space with treacherous areas (bush, deserts, mountains, quarries and marshes), are part of this theme. More generally, these disappearances reveal the foreigner's unease in occupying a land where they do not and cannot feel at home; they are overcome by an anxiety of not belonging. *Voss* (1957) by Patrick White, *Picnic at Hanging Rock* (1967) by Joan Lindsay, *The Hunter* (1999) by Julia Leigh, *Burning in* (2007) by Mireille Juchau and also *The Lost Dog* (2007) by Michelle de Kretser, are a few examples of this tendency. The lost child is another popular variant, as represented by Gemmy Fairley in David Malouf's *Remembering Babylon* (1993). According to Malouf, the status of the 'orphan in the Pacific' – the avatar of the lost child – reveals the sense of abandonment felt by a people whose British ancestors were subjected to the trauma of being torn from their land. The disappearance of an Australian protagonist overseas, as for example Michael Langford in *Highways to a War* (1995), is another variation of this theme, depicting the anguish felt at the loss of a cherished object.

CHAPTER 1

The Colonial Period: Exploration, Confrontation and Description (1831–1874)

The colonial period was propitious for all types of non-fiction (memoirs, chronicles, annals, letters, personal diaries, accounts). It was a time when colonisers tried to define the geography of Australia and describe the conditions of living in the penal and settler colony.

The birth of the novel in Australia did not occur until the nineteenth century was well underway, even though, soon after the arrival of the First Fleet in 1788, numerous writings tried to tell of the Australian experience to please a mainly British readership. These everyday descriptions, whether fictional or real, nourished or challenged the fantasies of conquering a new world and of establishing a new colony. The colonial writers wrote for a British readership who were keen to know what could be discovered in the Antipodes. Consequently, the stories gave specific details of the native flora and fauna, the exotic setting of the Australian bush, the living conditions of the convicts and, from the 1850s onwards, the thrilling adventures of the gold-diggers. The picturesque inspired many writers (as it did colonial painters who had come from Europe with an intellectual baggage and an artistic training that eventually proved ineffectual in translating the real Antipodes). The prosaic content of these writings was constructed analytically and reflected, through an outsider's observations, the difficulties of life in a faraway colony. While the poets, like the painters, were ready to sublimate the Australian environment and its subjects as exotic objects of curiosity, the novelists tended to paint the picture black, or present the everyday unadorned. As with painting, there was no 'great master' due to the lack of competitive rivalry or interest in vying with other artistic talents. It is difficult to speak of 'literary genius' at this time.

The first Australian novel, *Quintus Servinton*, was published in Hobart in 1831 by an unknown author – it is now attributed to Henry Savery. It was not until 1842, when John George Lang's *Legends of Australia* appeared anonymously, that Australia could take pride in having published its first truly native novelist.

Crime and punishment

The penal system operated from 1787 onwards, when the first convicts were sent out to create the Australian colonies and to serve out their sentences. At that time, the British authorities, who wanted to relieve their already congested prisons, had deportation at their disposal. A petty theft was all it took for some 160,000 Europeans to be taken to the Antipodes where they would start a new life or end it banished for ever from their homeland. It was an onerous imposition for the government even if it was driven by economic logic. A maritime and harbour base had to be established for Great Britain's commercial enterprises in the East (for example, trading in tea, otter skins, linen and hemp). In the early period, more than 60% of the population of the penal colonies was made up of convicts. The rest of the population included administrators, government officials, officers and soldiers, including prostitutes.

As has already been mentioned, the 'first Australian novel' to be published is considered to have been *Quintus Servinton*. Other stories, sometimes with illustrations, such as *Notes and Sketches of New South Wales* (1844) by Louisa Anne Meredith, recount the life of convicts only as a sideline and concentrate more on the experiences of the free colonial society busy discovering the new environment. Some authors, such as Alexander Harris and Charles Rowcroft, were more pragmatic in their aims. For example, the didactic concern of Rowcroft's *Tales of the Colonies* (1843) and *Settlers and Convicts* (1852) by Harris allowed future immigrants to expect difficulties of integration by giving an abundance of advice on how to overcome obstacles and avoid many disappointments when settling in the country.

There were three stock characters in literature of the convict system: the convict, the bushranger, and the 'new chum'. This colloquial term was derived from the prison environment, and goes back to the time of the 'newly embarked convict' who appears in the novel *Ralph Rashleigh*, written in the late 1840s by James Tucker, but whose original manuscript was not published until 1952. In the 1840s, a 'new chum' came to mean a recent free migrant, especially someone who came to the colonies to grow rich from the experience, as portrayed by the main character in Paul Wenz's *Diary of a New Chum* (1908). This character is similar in some ways to the 'colonial experiencer', an Englishman of noble birth sent to the colonies in order to acquire professional experience. Literature of the convict system* gave expression to different perspectives on the conditions endured by the convicts. Sometimes, they were presented as rounded characters with a great deal of psychological detail; at other times, they were just stock characters. Each novelist gave their vision of what was known as 'the system'.

The first Australian novel pioneered convict literature by depicting the prisoners' hellish existence. Henry Savery, who came from Somerset, thought that Australian culture had to break away from the English model. Paradoxically, his story was destined exclusively for the British reading public. The historic novel's subtitle, *A tale founded on incidents of real occurrence*, made no mystery of the obvious autobiographical nature of the work, and this led to the author being identified. *Quintus Servinton* prepared

Panoramic view of literature of the convict system

Literature of the convict system flourished during the colonial period because of its topical subject matter, which was of particular interest to British readers. In substance, it had three aims: to speak about the carceral system, making it understood and exposing its evil nature; to evoke melodramatically the life of its escapees; and, conversely, to recount the lives of those convicts able to start a new life by being offered redemption in the colony. More generally, convict literature can be divided into two opposing viewpoints: anti-abolitionist and pro-abolitionist. The anti-abolitionists thought that mere deportation to the Antipodes was too soft a punishment for the villainous. They argued about this lack of severity and pointed to the paltry results from forced labour; in other words, they imagined that the convicts enjoyed an almost enviable existence. In contrast, the pro-abolitionist authors were disposed to do away with this system of servitude. Their novels depicted a colony characterised by violence and deprivation (including the disastrous undertaking of wiping out the Aboriginal population), emphasising the evils of imprisonment and the difficulty of successfully integrating in a coercive and harsh world. This population of convicts, thugs and harlots branded future generations with infamy – the shame known as 'the stain' ingrained in the Australian psyche.

The abundant source for literature of the convict system dried up at the beginning of the twentieth century because the reading public had changed: the ever-increasing number of native-born Australians did not want to be reminded of their origins. However, in the 1960s and onwards, when Australia was gaining in confidence, this historic period of the early days of servitude once again provided inspiration for notable writers, including Thomas Keneally with *Bring Larks and Heroes* (1967) and *The Playmaker* (1987); Jessica Anderson who produced *The Commandant* (1975); Patrick White with his novel *A Fringe of Leaves* (1976); David Malouf and his *Remembering Babylon* (1993); Peter Carey with *Jack Maggs* (1997); Christopher Koch with *Out of Ireland* (1999); Richard Flanagan with *Gould's Book of Fish* (2001) and Kate Grenville with *The Secret River* (2005) as well as *The Lieutenant* (2008).

the ground for literature of this period and its archetypal pattern of condemnation–expiation–liberation. This fictive biography, at the crossroads of colonial and picaresque novels, opens with the meeting of an anonymous author recovering from an illness and the source of his subject matter, the sixty-year-old Quintus who entrusts him with a manuscript about the first forty years of his life. The author fictionalises the eponymous character, whose life is told from its very beginning (*ab ovo*). Most of the action takes place in England, with the last quarter of the book set mainly in Australia. The protagonist Quintus lives a prosperous life in England; he murmurs sweet nothings to various women until he falls in love with Emily Clifton, whom he marries. Later he is found guilty of forgery and the use of forgeries – crimes that entail arrest and the death penalty which he avoids *in extremis*. By a lucky twist of fate, his sentence is commuted to deportation. His exemplary good behaviour allows him to atone for his sins in Australia in the company of his wife Emily and their son Olivant. The couple experience highs and lows as he carries out his sentence before being granted freedom in his early forties, as had been predicted. Eventually, he returns to Devon in England where he spends the rest of his life in tranquillity. This moralistic story can be read as an allegorical religious fable and does not speak highly of the British Empire. Rather, it denounces the emerging society that was based on a system of bondage controlled by an imperial power.

Caroline Leakey's *The Broad Arrow* (1859), published under the pseudonym of Oline Keese, is typical of what some call the 'anti-system' novel. It starts with an unjust act, for the heroine Maida is in prison having been wrongly convicted of killing a child. She is deported to Van Diemen's Land, where she is condemned to a life of servitude working for the Evelyn family. She dies after being the victim of countless humiliations. Based on Christian values, this pro-abolitionist melodrama reinforces the ideology that saw convicts as more sinned against than sinning.

After reading *The Broad Arrow*, London-born author Marcus

Andrew Hislop Clarke was inspired to begin the novel that would eventually crown him with glory, *For the Term of His Natural Life* (1874).* He had left England for Australia at the age of seventeen. Abolitionist in the same way as Leakey, he fought against the wretched conditions of the convict system. An author of plays, novels and short stories, he was inspired by Sir Walter Scott, James Fenimore Cooper and Nathaniel Hawthorne. Marcus Clarke was particularly appreciated for his irony and satire and his ability to depict characters with striking verisimilitude. It is not an exaggeration to claim that Marcus Clarke establishes the convict genre within the literary canon with his anti-system novel *For the Term of His Natural Life*, an enormous literary success that over the years has eclipsed the remainder of his literary output. This well-documented novel owes much to Victor Hugo's *Les Misérables* (1862) and *It Is Never Too Late to Mend* (1856) by Charles Reade. A whole series of stories followed in the tradition of *His Natural Life*, such as *For Her Natural Life* (1876) by Eliza Winstanley, *Moondyne* (1879) by John Boyle O'Reilly, and later *The Escape of the Notorious Sir William Heans* (1919) by William Gosse Hay.

Fear of an alien environment: Between discovery and exoticism

Travellers, government officials, notables and emigrants flooded Great Britain with circumstantial descriptions of Australia and its non-native population. In order to gain any credibility and to be read at the time, Australian authors had to remain faithful to the literary template set by the imperial government, at the risk of being taken for epigones writing 'in the style of ...'.

It should be noted that the first Australian writers, whether they were English- or Australian-born, did not adopt an Australian viewpoint, but a British expatriate's perspective. Well-written British novels were quite rare except for those written by a few authors like Henry Savery, Marcus Clarke and Henry Kingsley. These writings used a rich vision-related vocabulary

Low-angle shot of *For the Term of His Natural Life* by Marcus Clarke

For the Term of His Natural Life or *His Natural Life* (1874) is the nineteenth-century novel *par excellence* of the genre inspired by the convict system. The action takes place in the first half of that century (1827–1846), starting in England and ending in Australia. It tells the story of the tragic fate of Richard Devine, condemned for the term of his natural life for a crime he did not commit. He is deported to Tasmania to live in exile. In his new life, he changes his name to Rufus Dawes to protect a family secret. When he is accused of murder, he has to betray his mother's secret in order to free himself from his predicament. *For the Term of His Natural Life* recounts the tribulations of an unfortunate man who, from one misadventure to another, is unjustly sentenced to serving out his punishment at the penal settlements of Macquarie Harbour, Port Arthur and Norfolk Island. The reader sees Rufus evolve in a picaresque manner from one escape to the next in the middle of a sadistic, sordid world where corporal punishment, homosexual rape and even cannibalism are the fate of prisoners in the system. The protagonist ends up discovering the person responsible for the theft of which he was originally accused. By a cruel twist of fate, just when Rufus Dawes envisages a better life with his beloved Sylvia, who fled with him to Norfolk Island, their boat is caught in a storm and is wrecked, causing them to drown. In the first version, the hero suffers a less tragic end. He is the embodiment of the humanistic convictions held by the author, who was convinced that mankind could survive independent of the Divine.

This novel's Dickensian plot, based on too many coincidences, was severely criticised for its lack of realism, despite the entertaining quality of its briskly moving action. Marred by a melodramatic tone, it has, nevertheless, since its original publication in serial form (in the monthly *Australian Journal* from March 1871 to June 1872), been consistently successful, including musical and cinematic adaptation (a silent film in 1927, reconstructed in 1981; a musical in 2003 and a televised mini-series in 1982).

and were characterised by themes of exoticism linked to travel and discovery. Some productions, especially numerous poems of the time, were written in the romantic style.

Confronted with a new environment, novelists either did not attribute any charm to it and tended to emphasise its diabolic nature by means of hellish descriptions, or gave it a seductive, picturesque beauty that was completely artificial. It is true that, as a general rule, the gaze of the nineteenth-century European observer did not brighten when confronted with the uniformity and aridity of the Australian bush. Some were even disappointed that the animals could not be domesticated to alleviate the tedium of Australian life. It is obvious that this existential ennui stimulated the start of the picaresque adventure novel.

The picaresque tradition is continued with *Ralph Rashleigh* (1952), which was subtitled *The life of an exile* and supposedly written by the convict James Tucker. Both memoir and picaresque novel, it records the adventures of Rashleigh, a convict who finds himself involved in a gang of bushrangers and whose imprudence is reflected in his surname (rashly).

The colonial romance

Appropriated from a British tradition, the colonial romance is an avatar of the period, at the crossroads of the realist novel and romanticism. In short, the hero or heroine in search of an ideal encounters a path full of potential pitfalls. Published mainly in London, often in three-decker form, this literary subgenre was highly popular with women writers engaging lightly with the game of love and chance while being deeply interested in the question of origins. The British reader deliberately ignored the lack of credibility of these stories, filled with repetition to emphasise their documentary value. They were taken for touristic guides to Australia.

Henry Kingsley began the genre with *The Recollections of Geoffrey Hamlyn*. It was later taken up by Rolf Boldrewood with

Robbery Under Arms and by Mrs Rosa Praed. From all the evidence, Henry Kingsley's perception was Eurocentric and phallocentric. He depicted Australia as an El Dorado where his English characters looked to rebuild their fortunes, which they were able to enjoy once they returned to their native country. *The Recollections of Geoffrey Hamlyn* (1859) shows the influence of the Australian dream in the minds of the British. Like most novels of the period, it starts in an English county and takes a long time to arrive on Australian soil. The writer recounts the prosperous and happy life of foreigners in a land of plenty and promise. This idyllic vision of colonisation is seen in descriptions of the happiness derived from living the rustic life characterised by the daily rhythm of farm activities: raising cattle (which was at its height in the 1830s), shearing sheep, branding beasts and so on. Confrontation with Aboriginal groups and brigands – incarnations of evil – justified the colonisers determined to enjoy the fruits of their labour.

The expatriate English writer Rolf Boldrewood, whose real name was Thomas Browne, enjoyed great success with his legendary tale of the bush, *Robbery Under Arms* (1888)*. This marked the beginning of the bushranging novel. Like Boldrewood, Rosa Praed wrote in the tradition of the colonial romance begun by Henry Kingsley, while belonging chronologically to the nationalist literary stream. Born in Queensland and drawing on her own life experience, she evoked a woman's life and the world of the Australian farm in some forty novels published mainly between 1880 and 1916. *Policy and Passion* is her most popular work. *Paving the Way* (1893), a novel of colonial South Australia by Simpson Newland has proved to be an enduring success.

Fraught with naivety, these novels foreshadowed the realism used by the *Bulletin* writers and contributed to the rise of a national consciousness by highlighting the specific nature of Australian culture.

Close-up of *Robbery Under Arms* by Rolf Boldrewood

It is curious that Thomas Alexander Browne, 'Rolf Boldrewood', a former grazier who became a police magistrate in the gold mining town of Gulgong, and eventually goldfields commissioner, conceived this story within a pastoral setting at a time when Australia was emerging as essentially an urban nation. It was probably the hanging in 1880 of the well-known Australian Robin Hood, Ned Kelly, that provided the motive for writing *Robbery Under Arms* (1888) in the style of Sir Walter Scott. The story, full of romantic idealism, exemplifies the difficulty writers experienced in understanding the reality of the country.

Its narrator Dick Marston, son of a convict and guilty of organised crime, recounts from his prison cell his past exploits as a bushranger. Influenced by their ex-convict father, Dick and his brother join a gang led by Captain Starlight, a notorious criminal who eventually dies in a gunfight. Their initiation into crime begins in South Australia, where they sell a herd of cattle they had stolen in Queensland. Going from crime to arrest, interrupted with a short period of adventures in the goldfields, Dick's epic journey ends when he is involved in a shooting match which costs him his freedom. His downfall is however caused by a woman, Kate Morrison, who could not bear to see him with a rival, Grace Storefield. Kate takes her revenge by collaborating with the authorities, a step which hastens her husband's imprisonment. At first he is condemned to death; then his sentence is commuted to twelve years in prison, at the end of which he asks Grace to marry him.

The story was inspired by the life experiences of the most famous Australian bushrangers, such as Ben Hall, Frank Gardiner, John Gilbert and Daniel Morgan, who had become symbols of rebellion. By defying authority and the law, they won the heart of Australians who enjoyed the bushrangers' rebelling against the repressive system. The squatter, a pejorative term initially used to describe people who 'occupied a tract of land' and ran sheep and cattle 'obtained, generally, in very nefarious ways' (G.A. Wilkes, *A Dictionary of Australian Colloquialisms)*, was the sworn enemy of the bushranger.

Feminine writing and feminism

It would seem that, ever from the birth of the Australian novel, a degree of gender equality existed, since the book published after *Quintus Servinton* was *Woman's Love* (1832) by Mary Leman Grimstone (who was born and died in the nineteenth century). Because this work had been finished in Hobart four years earlier, well before the publication of *Quintus Servinton*, it deserves to be recognised as the first novel written in Australia.

It is not necessary here to dwell on a self-published novel like *The Guardian* (1838) by Anna Maria Bunn, though it is worth noting that, despite their difficulty in finding publishers at this time, women felt a deep need to express themselves or to find in writing a way out from their often painful existence.

Mary Vidal published a novel with some Australian content, *The Cabramatta Store* (1850), and another *Bengala* (1860), but both were written in her native England where she had returned. In *Clara Morison* (1854)*, Catherine Helen Spence, a Scottish-born suffragette, recounted the tribulations of a determined and accomplished woman who chose her destiny rather than allowing herself to be submerged by life's circumstances.

Ada Cambridge, who began publishing her stories in 1875, sits between the colonial period and the next phase of Australian writing – having blended colonial romance with the concerns of female fiction. Author of twenty novels, she is also the first female Australian poet worthy of the title. Her reputation was affected for a long time because of her having specialised in romances, of the style written by Rosa Praed. Indisputably, her forte was her description of the Australian landscape. But her weakness lay in her banal plots that relied mainly on syrupy love stories. More recently, feminist criticism has recognised Cambridge's primary concerns, including the denunciation of the iniquitous treatment and servile conditions of Australian women in Victorian society. The most politically committed of her novels are: *A Marked Man* (1890), *The Three Miss Kings* (1891), *Not All in Vain* (1892) and *Materfamilias* (1898).

Close-up of *Clara Morison* by Catherine Helen Spence

Often quoted as 'the finest novel of colonial South Australia', *Clara Morison: A tale of South Australia during the Gold Fever* (1854) is another narrative of the immigration experience – the novelty being the historical context of the gold rush period. True to the time, the story has at its centre an eponymous female character who is witness to the historical events that take place in the colony. The strongly autobiographical aspect of this work written in the Victorian tradition permitted the author to assert the authenticity of her story to her English publisher.

Set in 1850s Adelaide, the narrative tells of the sad fate of a young educated woman, Clara, who comes to South Australia after her father's death because her insensitive uncle no longer wished to support her. Deprived of her aristocratic status, like Cinderella she becomes a domestic servant before she meets a cousin willing for her to join his family. After a few adventures, she gradually adjusts to the colony and marries Charles Reginal, a respectable gentleman, after he breaks his engagement with his fiancée.

While another writer would have chosen to depict exciting adventures and dangers such as bushfires, outlaws, convicts on the run or the gold fever, Catherine Helen Spence emphasises the private realm of colonial domestic life, family-related topics and introspection.

Through a feminist lens, Spence sees the possibility for women to free themselves and to break patriarchal chains. She praised the intellect at a time when the discovery of gold had enhanced the materialistic values of men. Women's fortitude allowed them to realise that marriage was not the magical solution to their needs. Frederick Sinnett was the first critic to highlight the quality of *Clara Morison*, a novel which represents a milestone in the history of Australian literature and which is often regarded as Catherine Helen Spence's *magnum opus*.

CHAPTER 2

'A literature born of the land': The Emergence of a National Consciousness (1875–1900)

From being regarded in some quarters as a land of imprisonment and exile that evoked hell, Australia was transformed into a land of promise and freedom with the possibility of a new lease of life in an Antipodean Garden of Eden. At the end of the nineteenth century, Australia was seen by European socialists as a New Jerusalem. This paradisal vision of Australia, symbolised by the topos of *Australia Felix* escaping from the ills of the corrupt Old Continent, contained the potential for the shaping of a quasi-perfect society. The migrants wanted this country to be brand new, to allow them to reinvent their lives, as it were, from the ground upwards. But this did not take into account the imaginative power of certain writers wanting to keep alive the memory of a Europe they held dear and were unable to leave behind.

So the dramatic decline of the novel, which started towards the end of the nineteenth century, was the result of three inescapable obstacles:

Writers outnumbered readers.

Australians were more interested in British literature than in the native production.

The novel tried to fight for first place with poetry dominated at the time by Adam Lindsay Gordon, Henry Kendall and a few others.

It was not until the end of the nineteenth century that Australian literature stopped being viewed as part of British literature and found its own place on the international scene. The generation of expatriate writers was followed by a generation of native-born Australians who contributed to the emergence of a national consciousness. One of the repercussions of colonial subjugation included an exaggerated nationalism viewed as the 'swing of the pendulum' – an appropriate expression coined by the famous Melbourne-based critic A.A. Phillips. This literary nationalism mirrored the political urgency to establish a federated nation.

While Australia had been presented as a land of confinement as early as its annexation, writers who set themselves up a century later as the bards of nationalism were confined to the land-related narratives. Hence Tom Inglis Moore's central thesis in *Social Patterns in Australian Literature* (1971) arguing Australian fiction to be a 'literature born of the land'.

In the 1890s, the tendency was for brevity which resulted in the popularity of the short story and the short play. Novels often appeared in serial form in the press before being published as books. As a general rule, they sold well, especially works for children like Ethel Turner's *Seven Little Australians* (1894). This great classic of children's literature tells the story of seven small rascals belonging to the Woolcott family (General, Baby, Bunty, Nell, Judy, Pip and Meg) who lead their stepmother on a merry dance and make it difficult for their father to exert his authority. Adventurous and forever teasing, this group of siblings flourishes in the bush by vying with one another in mischievousness. With the exception of this book, writings of the period tended to be more politically inspired with socialist messages of hope for a country of equality.

'Bohemians of the *Bulletin*' and its outcasts

Established in Sydney on 31 January 1880 by J.F. Archibald and John Haynes, the *Bulletin* gave prominence to the best writers of the time, all the while urging its readers to be published in their pages, thereby giving them an opportunity to make themselves known. By promoting Australian writers, this weekly was in part responsible for the rise of a national consciousness, albeit sometimes in an exaggerated form. Anti-imperial diatribes were not unusual and some people were more than ready to demonise Aboriginal people. This reaction was more the result of anxiety projected on an unknown world than actual hostility. In most stories, the household is viewed as a peaceful haven needed to protect Australians against nature and an Indigenous population perceived as fundamentally malevolent. The *Bulletin* gave more than their due to modest folk (like drovers, small farmers, adventurers, to name a few) as well as outsiders and pariahs of all sorts: vagabonds, swagmen, down-and-outs and outlaws. The paper published the top names of the period in all forms: novels, poetry, plays, short stories and so on. Following the tradition of novels in the Victorian era (1837–1901), the plots were segmented into serials so as to encourage faithful readership and to popularise the stories. Apart from Miles Franklin, its collaborators were mostly men: Vance Palmer, Louis Stone, Norman Lindsay, Brian Penton, Joseph Furphy and Steele Rudd. Thus, the 'Bohemians of the *Bulletin*', to poach the title of one of Norman Lindsay's works, were born in opposition to the colonial romance. They would make nationalism rhyme with realism.

Following the example of Louis Stone and Barbara Baynton, Arthur Hoey Davis, alias short story writer Steele Rudd, collaborated with the *Bulletin* from the 1890s but had to wait until the next century before publishing a novel. He conducted his own magazine publication before writing three novels that presented his life story recycled as fiction. The most sought-after Australian prize for short story writing bears his pen name.

The pariahs who did not adhere to nationalistic philosophy were mainly women. Rosa Praed, Ada Cambridge and Jessie Couvreur wrote outside the 'Bohemian' group, all producing work in the tradition of the colonial romance. Couvreur's first publication *Uncle Piper of Piper's Hill* (1889) appeared with the *nom de plume* of Tasma and brought her literary success that her successive books never equalled. Its analysis of a lower-middle-class family, the Cavendishes, is a satire on British mores in the Antipodes.

The 1890s are often described as the golden age of Australian literature – an era of great literary potential. For some, like Arthur Jose or critic H.M. Green, it embodied an optimism that favoured romanticism; for others, it was a dismal period that neglected the rising generation of great writers, such as the short-story writer Henry Lawson and the poet Andrew Barton (Banjo) Paterson, and emphasised the better-known names of Marcus Clarke and Henry Kendall. Writers were concerned with three main themes: country life, describing the urban scene, and contrasting the city with the bush.

Diehard realism

In opposition to romanticism, realism was to be debated in no uncertain terms by what was called the *Bulletin* debate.* According to Henry Lawson, laudatory literary representations of life in the bush were influenced by the flawed perspective writers had on the subject. Those who adhered to the opinions of Lawson opposed dominant Eurocentric perceptions which tainted the Australian landscape with some form of Romanticism. Banjo Paterson, Lawson's opponent, conceived the bush in a much more exalted way since he saw it as a symbol of freedom – an idea that could indeed have been a projection of his own desires.

Realism, with its ordinary characters and its taste for real life experience, was *de rigueur* for the most illustrious novelists of this period, such as Joseph Furphy and Miles Franklin, who

Close-up of the *Bulletin* debate

Even though urbanisation in Australia could not go unnoticed at this time, novelists were more passionate about representing the less-populated bush. It goes without saying that novelty and mystery are always winners. This ideological battle which consumed a lot of ink and involved many writers remained famous as the *Bulletin* debate (1892–1893). It broke out in this context and takes its name from two key figures in the Australian literary scene of the period – Henry Lawson and Andrew Barton ('Banjo') Paterson.

At the core of the controversy was the bush, an important source of inspiration for Australian writers, and for some, an environment that most characterised the Australian way of life. In a poem called 'Borderland' published by the *Bulletin* on 9 July 1892 (and republished later with the title 'Up the Country'), Henry Lawson presented a harsher image of the Australian outback. His pessimistic vision reflected in essence his political concerns for people of modest means, victims of social oppression.

Paterson replied two weeks later under the conservative banner, 'In Defence of the Bush'.

He advised Lawson to confine himself to the urban scene, to which he seemed better suited. The tit-for-tat debate went on and on for some time. For Henry Lawson, it meant sticking to the social reality of the bush. Describing it warts-and-all was intended to give readers a more precise idea of Australia's natural setting. The harshness of this almost gritty realism, very much in line with the inglorious economic situation of the 1890s, contrasted with the romantic vision of the bush in fashion up until that time.

The 1880s prosperity had waned at the beginning of the next decade, the lean period, when more than a quarter of wage-earners lost their jobs. Economic activities were affected more in the country than in the city.

endeavoured to reproduce reality meticulously. A lesser-known writer, William Lane, strengthened by his populist concerns, published *The Workingman's Paradise* (1892) subtitled *An Australian labour novel*, using the pseudonym of John Miller. Money from its publication assisted union members who had been imprisoned after the Queensland shearers' strike the previous year. Advocating socialism, this novel emphasised the poverty-stricken conditions of the ordinary working-class folk in Sydney, using detailed descriptions with a focus on the most sordid aspects of life. The irony of the title originated from the embittered author's incapacity to reconcile his utopian aspirations with reality.

This diehard realism was savagely criticised at the end of the 1950s by Patrick White, who, through his caustic turn of phrase, revealed its monotonous nature.

Mythology of the bush

In spite of a natural world often judged hostile and unrewarding, writers of this period turned away from the urban environment and culture, instead reconstructing nature and the rural world. The choice of the bush could either be seen as a retreat or as a reclusive existence that provided an alternative to the disenchantment and constraints of urbanisation. Increasingly, these rural regions were no longer synonyms for hardship and desolation, but places of reflection and communion with Mother Nature. The bush soon came to be associated with the grotesque and the carnivalesque because of its surprising endemic fauna and flora: koalas, kangaroos, wombats, platypuses, possums and other marsupials, and abundant species of eucalyptus, among other species.

Such is Life (1903)* by Joseph Furphy is unquestionably the most effective literary representation of the bush in this period. In contrast to the pessimistic and sordid vision of an author like Barbara Baynton with her novel *Human Toll* (1907), Furphy saw in the bush a land full of promise. To use John McLaren's expression

Low-angle shot of *Such is Life* by Joseph Furphy

Completed in 1897, this manuscript was not published until 1903. The title is borrowed from famous bushranger Ned Kelly, a phrase he uttered just as he was going to be hanged. *Such is Life* is a quaint, dense and irony-packed novel that brought the tradition of stories about the bush into the twentieth century with its stockmen, teamsters, boundary riders and free selectors.

On 4 April 1897, Furphy wrote to a friend that he had just finished a novel that was set in the Riverina district of New South Wales and the northern part of Victoria, a work he described as 'temper, democratic; bias, offensively Australian'. The opening sentence, 'Unemployed at last!', sets the book's ironic tone, but the rhythm of the adventures that follow is syncopated by an authorial voice that is at times disturbing and also by digressions, repetitions and philosophical conjectures that give the prose a contemplative tone.

When it was published, the book was thought to be the true story of a person named Tom Collins, with a deliberate confusion of author and fictive narrator certain to catch some readers off guard. For the first time, an author was speaking to an exclusively Australian readership using vernacular speech and contemporary slang expressions that make reading his work today arduous.

Underestimated by literary critics during his lifetime, Joseph Furphy was recognised posthumously through the efforts of Nettie and Vance Palmer, Kate Baker and A.G. Stephens, who praised him highly.

Contemporary criticism tends to see *Such is Life* as a postmodern novel ahead of its time. Evidence of this is its fragmented storyline, the metafictional allusions, the use of pastiche and the fact that it parodies the colonial romance as illustrated in the works of Henry Kingsley, Rolf Boldrewood and Rosa Praed. These are only a few characteristics of its complex narrative structure.

from *Australian Literature*, Furphy's philosophy could be: 'if we cannot have a heaven, we need not build a hell on earth'.

Following the example of *Such is Life*, *My Brilliant Career* was written just prior to the nation's re-shaping as the Commonwealth of Australia (officially declared on 1 January 1901) and published soon after. The finished manuscript of 1899 was rejected by local publishers before being taken up (with the assistance of Henry Lawson who was briefly in London) by Blackwood & Sons, a Scottish company in Edinburgh. This autobiographical work brought the author some admonition from her own family circle. The book – the title of which originally indicated a degree of uncertainty, as Stella Miles Franklin wanted it to be *My Brilliant (?) Career* – gave her early notoriety. With this small masterpiece, Miles gained the respect and admiration of the big names in Australian literature like Henry Lawson who, captured by its outstanding authenticity, wrote a preface for the book, and Banjo Paterson, who became infatuated with her. In substance, the story relates the activities of an adolescent, Sybylla Melvyn, who rebels against life on her parents' dairy farm in the bush which she considers too humdrum. Rejecting all forms of domination or enslavement, she is reluctant to succumb to the charms of Harold Beecham, a dashing young squatter who embodies the classic Prince Charming as portrayed in the literature of this period.

Miles Franklin* counted heavily on the success of her novel to prepare the way for a brilliant literary career, but fate had it otherwise. Because the book was published overseas and not in Australia, its short-lived success brought her little income. She decided to write a sequel to the novel that was initially rejected by publishers in 1910, but published in 1946 under the title *My Career Goes Bung*.

The general theme of stories of this period was the difficulty of living in a world packed with promises of a brighter future, a future that turned out, in the end, to be unrewarding. While the bush was the yardstick against which Australians measured mateship, it

Panoramic view of Miles Franklin

Born on 14 October 1879 near Tumut in New South Wales, the eldest of seven, Stella Maria Sarah Miles Franklin enjoyed a childhood on her parents' farm at Brindabella where she was educated by a private tutor before starting school in her adolescent years. At first, she tried to evoke in her writing the world of the British aristocracy, and then wrote *My Brilliant Career* which acquainted her with celebrity for a few years.

After a bad patch, Franklin left for the United States to familiarise herself with the working class. When two of her novels published in London did not have the success anticipated, she turned her attention again to political issues, like the status of women and the anti-conscription movement in the First World War. During her second stay in Australia (1927–1931), she came upon the idea of fictionalising her family's story in a saga about pioneers located in the Monaro region. It was finished in 1933 and published as *All That Swagger* (1936). She published six novels using the nom de plume of Brent of Bin Bin: *Up the Country* (1928), *Ten Creeks Run* (1930), *Back to Bool Bool* (1931), *Prelude to Walking* (1950), *Cockatoos* (1954) and her posthumous publication *Gentlemen at Gyang Gyang* (1956). *Like All That Swagger*, these novels, concerned with outdated nationalism, commemorated the great era of the first colonists and once again brought her prestige as a writer. Franklin believed that only the life experiences of a writer could create worthwhile literature and that an interest in Australia was not necessarily synonymous with provincialism: 'more than ever, we need this understanding of ourselves', she emphasised in a letter to the then Prime Minister J.B. Chifley.

When she died on 19 September 1954, Miles Franklin left a nest egg to finance a literary prize in her name which today has unequalled prestige. The first person to receive this prize was Patrick White for his novel *Voss*. In a similar philanthropic gesture, White later changed his Nobel Prize money into an award that would reward under-appreciated writers – a subtle homage to Miles Franklin who suffered from chronic lack of recognition.

was no less an obstacle for marital relations, which often collapsed in this hostile milieu. Those who wrote in the Lawson tradition (Lawson was justly nicknamed 'the apostle of mateship') tried to justify egalitarianism, democracy and brotherhood. These values, useful for surviving in the bush, took into account the necessity to overcome any difficulty when faced with extremely harsh living conditions.

At times, the depiction of the bush was a way to preserve emotional ties with the land. Rosa Praed kept her connections with her native country this way after leaving Australia at the age of twenty-four with her husband, to live in England. This is doubtless the reason her novels concentrate largely on Australia with typical characters like James Tyson in *Mrs Tregaskiss* (1895) or Sir George Bowen in *Nùlma* (1897), descriptions of the region where she was born and the omnipresent bush.

Paradox of paradoxes, there were attempts to make an essentially urban population along the Australian coastline believe that the true Australian spirit emanated from the outback. Novelists wanted the average city dweller to identify with the bush, bush life being the flavour of these years because of its distinctive characteristics. Writers slowly and methodically succeeded in achieving a uniquely Australian quality, a fact the *Bulletin* highlighted on 18 December 1935: 'Gradually, the Australian scene and peculiar qualities of the Australian character are being re-created into a local literature, and with every fresh book in the tradition the task for subsequent writers becomes a little easier.' Having said this, had local colour become an imperative for writers, their creative freedom would have been constrained.

Iconoclasts like Leon Cantrell have generally debunked the accepted mythological ideas about the bush. In his work, *Writing of the Eighteen Nineties* (1977), Cantrell claims that solitude, failure and betrayal at this time were much more frequent than success and proof of egalitarianism or mateship. According to Cantrell, these years were branded by loss and detachment, as well as disillusionment about economic stagnation. Evidence of this can be read between the lines of these jaundiced literary views of life. It might be argued that writers, who initially met difficulty when trying to develop a unique identity within an urban context hardly conducive to creativity, were then forced to turn to the more distinctive outback in order to pave the way for a national consciousness.

The adventure novel and its nomadic figures

The adventure novel was particularly in vogue from 1880 to 1900. It drew its dramatic intensity from adversity experienced by characters that had to be flexible to overcome the diverse obstacles they encountered (a natural world considered treacherous and an Indigenous population believed to be hostile). Two archetypal figures appear in the tales of exploration of this period: the taciturn bushman and the lucid battler with a particularly combative temperament. For historian Russel Ward, Australia's history is encapsulated in the battler who succeeded in making a singularly hostile environment his home by wisely resigning himself to his destiny, with the support and complicity of his mates.

The gold rush brought many European adventurers to the Antipodes at the beginning of the 1850s. Most writers did not explore this theme immediately, except for Catherine Helen Spence with *Clara Morison*. It was only in the final years of the nineteenth century that adventure stories reflected this godsend by reviving optimism with the promise of an appealing future.

The adventure novel suited a series of stock characters, be they main or secondary ones. It is interesting to note that these characters came from the Australian countryside and shared an inordinate taste for wandering. Among these cultural icons, we can cite the swagman, the bushranger (famously inspired by Ned Kelly), the drover, the sundowner and the fossicker – sifting through disused quarries that had already been exploited in the search for minerals. In *The Australian Legend* (1958), Russel Ward drew attention to 'the noble frontiersman' who was the dominant figure of this period.

Although marginal, a series of adventure novels was published in the last two decades of the century. The stories involved New Zealanders and were set against the background of the New Zealand Wars of the 1860s. Although criticised for some of its erroneous cultural references, *War to the Knife or Tangata Maori* (1899) is a classic of this genre written by Rolf Boldrewood.

How can writers of this period be defined? Should we see them as chroniclers of society, pioneers of literature or myth-makers? All three titles seem appropriate. Some commentators found that all these more-or-less realistic stories evoking the nomadic life of their characters within a rustic environment were singularly lacking in originality. Having said this, some voices were heard later in the 1950s denouncing the fallacious character of this so-called homogeneity. In actual fact, it would seem that the fault was attributable to critics who were unable to grasp the nuances or the subtleties present in this literary output.

CHAPTER 3

The Ebb and Flow of History: Detachment and Engagement (1901–1950)

After Federation, a sharp contrast in Australian literature was noticeable: detachment, by authors hiding behind pseudonyms or living elsewhere as expatriates, in opposition to engagement, expressed through a neo-nationalist or populist trend and through the grounding of numerous narratives in specific historic moments.

In the first half of the twentieth century, a substantial number of stories published in serialised form in literary journals and newspapers were highly successful, and resulted in sequels, such as Henry Handel Richardson's trilogy published as *The Fortunes of Richard Mahony* in 1930. Eleanor Dark produced a literary triptych with *The Timeless Land* (1941), *Storm of Time* (1948) and *No Barrier* (1953). One success led to another, and the trilogy of Vance Palmer gained many followers. *Golconda* (1948), *Seedtime* (1957) and *The Big Fellow* (1959) trace the professional rise of Macey Donovan, a unionist who becomes a top politician. *Landtakers* (1934) by Brian Penton was originally to be the first part of a trilogy, but he had to be content with a companion novel, *Inheritors* (1936). From 1928 to 1956, Miles Franklin made the most she could of this trend with her heptalogy that took up the pioneering spirit prominent in her most memorable novel *All That Swagger* (1936). This fashion for multiple volumes continued into the second half of the twentieth century with writers like Nancy Cato with her trilogy about the Murray River: *All the Rivers Run* (1958), *Time, Flow Swiftly* (1959) and *But Still the Stream* (1962). Martin Boyd began his tetralogy about the Langtons with *The Cardboard Crown* (1952), followed by *A Difficult Young Man* (1955), *Outbreak of Love* (1957) and *When Blackbirds Sing* (1962). Rodney Hall's trilogy is another example: *Captivity Captive* (1988), *The Second Bridegroom* (1991) and *The Grisly Wife* (1993).

Hidden identities: From person to persona

A practice often used in the colonial period was that of the *nom de plume* which became widespread after Federation. Complex motives were responsible for this burgeoning use of literary pseudonyms. Vance Palmer succumbed to producing potboilers, published under the name of Rann Daly so that there would be no confusion between the texts he wrote to make a living and those he took pleasure in writing. It was the same for Xavier Herbert who wrote stereotypical short stories using the name of Herbert Astor. Arthur Hoey Davis preferred to see the name of Steele Rudd on the cover of his books, while Joseph Furphy wrote *Such is Life* (1903) as Tom Collins in order to blur the distinction between author and narrator. Kenneth MacKenzie hid his identity behind the name Seaforth MacKenzie because of the heretical content of his *Bildungsroman* entitled *The Young Desire It* (1937) that looked at the question of male homosexuality – a rare theme at the time. The twenty-five-year-old character Penworth teaches literature and is rejected by young Charles Fox, who is in love with a girl.

Miles Franklin was renowned for having several *noms de plume*, including those derived from her own name, Stella: An Old Bachelor, Stella Lampe, Sarah Miles, Sarah Mills, SMS, The Glowworm, Vernacular and William Blake. For her pioneer saga she used Brent of Bin Bin and hid her true identity even from her publisher, for certain legitimate reasons. Franklin wanted to surround her novels with mystery to stimulate sales. She blatantly used this strategy to publicise her works without anyone being able to make the connection between her and her writings. Moreover, this pseudonym allowed her to catch out publishing houses that had previously closed their doors to her when she had offered manuscripts under her real name.

In order to be accepted by the Australian reading public, many female novelists hid their gender by using masculine pseudonyms. Marjorie Barnard and Flora Eldershaw co-wrote five novels as M. Barnard Eldershaw – Marjorie being the pen and Flora providing the research. Ethel Florence Lindesay Robertson hid behind the pseudonym of Henry Handel Richardson in her literary trilogy, *The Fortunes of Richard Mahony* (1930).* The life story of her fictional character was inspired to a great extent by her father. Jeannie Gunn borrowed her husband's name when she signed her novel *We of the Never Never* (1908) as Mrs Aeneas Gunn. Two final examples: Doris Kerr wrote as Capel Boake while G.B. Lancaster was none other than Ethel Lyttleton.

Does this mean that Katharine Susannah Prichard, Dymphna Cusack and Florence James would never have been awarded a literary prize without presenting themselves as male novelists? When *Coonardoo* was entered into the competition organised by the *Bulletin* in 1928, Prichard wrote under the name of Jim Ashburton, while James and Cusack entered their co-written book *Come in Spinner* in the *Daily Telegraph* competition as Sydney Wyborne. Some women writers, like Christina Stead, who did not wish to use deceptive strategies in order to gain recognition by the literati, chose expatriation to make a name for themselves elsewhere; in Stead's case, in the United States and in Europe.

The 'cultural cringe' and expatriate writers

At the beginning of the century, many novelists followed the taunting recommendations of the most famous national author, short story writer Henry Lawson, who advocated expatriation or

Low-angle shot of *The Fortunes of Richard Mahony* by Henry Handel Richardson

According to Dorothy Green, this is 'the archetypal novel about white settlement'. In the tradition of Richardson's stories, this trilogy appears under the title of *The Fortunes of Richard Mahony* (1930) – first published in three volumes: *Australia Felix* (1917), *The Way Home* (1925) and *Ultima Thule* (1929) – and is written in an autobiographical vein hovering between realism and romanticism.

Deeply touched by her father's death when she was only nine years old, Richardson immortalised him in this literary saga that covers three generations of Australians. The family chronicle traces the life story of the English protagonist Richard who, inspired by the promise of a better future, sets off on an adventure in the Antipodes after marrying Mary Turnham. When their business affairs do not succeed as well as he had hoped, he decides to renounce his venture and return to his native land (*The Way Home*) where he dedicates himself to medicine. His clientele dwindles but Mahony recovers financial success through a wise investment.

The protagonist tries to start afresh in Victoria. Another departure to Europe forces him to sell everything and to give the money to an investor who disappears without a trace. Richard is once again ruined. In the final volume, he leaves Australia yet again with his wife, who quickly becomes aware of her husband's deteriorating mental state after this last failure. Before long, Richard is placed in an institution. A patient and devoted Mary Mahony takes care of her husband until he breathes his last.

The pages are concerned at first with the gold rush in Ballarat then proceed to Melbourne, a city overtaken by greed, whose prosperity has literally risen from the bowels of the earth. This novelist, a master of characterisation, does not hesitate to structure her characters within a series of contradictions. Mary, altruistic and strengthened by goodness of spirit, is contrasted with the venality motivating diggers in their search for reward on the goldfields.

suicide rather than submitting to the humiliation of the deplorable status of the writer in Australia. Beyond the jest, it is true that those who left to make a name for themselves in Europe or the United States nurtured the hope of more easily obtaining some sort of credence once they returned to their homeland. Lacking recognition, Miles Franklin took notice of this good advice and went to live in Chicago (1906–1915), then London (1915–1932), a period that was broken by twice returning to Australia (1923–1924/1927–1931). Ironically, it was in the Antipodes that she found the inspiration that gave her literary career its second wind.

Like most other countries, Australia suffered the economic repercussions of the 1914–1918 war and the 1930s Great Depression that had relegated cultural activities to the background. Australian literature of the 1920s to the 1950s saw a period of stagnation that hampered creativity and encouraged a number of writers to leave temporarily for short periods like Patrick White, Xavier Herbert and Christopher Koch. Other writers opted for longer stays such as Chester Cobb (who went to England in 1921), Christina Stead, Randolph Stow (who left initially in 1961 but relocated permanently to England in 1966) and Shirley Hazzard who left Australia in 1947 (to go to Hong Kong, New Zealand, Europe), now dividing her time between New York and Capri.

In the first half of the century, Australian novelists were spoilt for choice. They could leave the country or, failing that, evoke in their work the time spent by an 'Aussie' in far-off places. They were free to go offshore to have their literary works published by European or American publishers. At times, they did these three things concurrently. Apart from departure to follow a partner's career as was the case for Christina Stead,* who left her native land in 1928, and Janette Turner Hospital in the 1960s, expatriation was often experienced as a release from provincialism. It was an enriching time for Patrick White and Clive James who felt the need for a patrician education within the colleges of Oxbridge. To be sure, isolation and the 'tyranny of distance' denounced by historian

Panoramic view of Christina Stead

Born in 1902 in Sydney, Christina Stead is a mysterious figure in the history of Australian literature. Even though English companies published her two first books in 1934 (a collection of short stories and a novel, *Seven Poor Men of Sydney*), followed by no fewer than six novels, not one of her works was distributed in Australia before 1965. Although her novels were interesting and praised – the most popular being *The Man Who Loved Children* (1940) and *For Love Alone* (1944) – her lack of recognition is probably explained by her early expatriation. She left the country in 1928 to live in Europe (mainly in London, where she met her husband William Blake), then in the United States and did not return to her hometown until 1974, to spend the last ten years of her life finishing her two last novels, *Miss Herbert (The Suburban Wife)* (1976) and *I'm Dying Laughing* (1986), the latter published posthumously.

Her satirical novels contain central female characters whose ambition is to find a husband so that they can conform to the norm dictated by society. If these women fail to realise their objective, it is because they are disturbed, unreasonable, lesbian or loners. But family happiness is a holy grail difficult to obtain. Stead's stories illustrate this difficulty through the following themes: special friendships, guilty passions, unhappy unions, frustrated desires and solitude. It is obvious that things are not simple for the iconoclastic woman torn between conformity and freedom, between feminism and patriarchy, heterosexuality and homosexuality.

In her monograph, Teresa Petersen puts forward the idea that 'lesbianism as an alternative to heterosexuality is profoundly inherent in Stead's writings.' This can be in either an oblique or an obvious way as in *Dark Places of the Heart* (1966), published a year later with the title *Cotters' England*. The 'rhizomatic' structure (Teresa Petersen) of her novels seems to legitimise the enigmatic and ambiguous character of their content. In 1974, Stead entered the pantheon of under-appreciated authors by being the first recipient of the Patrick White Award.

Geoffrey Blainey greatly influenced native Australians, who legitimately felt that they were on the margins of the metropolitan centre, the cultural pole of reference they coveted. In the first half of the twentieth century, among the expatriates who hoped to broaden their horizons were Helen Simpson, Marcel Aurousseau, Henry Handel Richardson and Miles Franklin. The most recent wave included George Johnston, who settled for a while in 1954 in Greece with his family where he wrote *My Brother Jack*; Barbara Hanrahan (in 1963) and Randolph Stow (in 1966) who went to Great Britain. Thomas Keneally was seduced by the United States and England to take up temporary academic positions and Peter Carey settled in the United States. Some were consoled by noting that culture is exportable; others regretted the brain-drain to other climes more conducive to the practice of their art.

Since Federation, expatriation can be found as a leitmotif in the works of many Australian writers whose central themes were their desire to change latitudes, to experience an alternative way of working and to find recognition elsewhere. For Louise Mack, who had already lived in several European locations (1910–1914), expatriation gave the benefit of 'bifocal vision', to use Bruce Bennett's fine expression. She was therefore able to compare London life with Australian life in her autobiographical epistolary novel *An Australian Girl in London* (1902).

When expatriation was not chosen, publishing became crucial. Though a staunch supporter of a neo-nationalist Australian literature, literary critic and novelist Vance Palmer was quick to advise his writer friends to follow his example and publish their works in London first, to ensure healthy sales in Australia. This attitude gave rise to a cultural feeling of inferiority, the Australian 'cultural cringe', an expression attributed to literary critic A.A. Phillips in his 1950 essay. This phrase captures the propensity Australians have to deprecate themselves and espouse aspects of British culture they hold in high esteem, thereby setting up barriers that prevent them from breaking new ground. Dominated, deprived of initiative and hence of creative imagination, Australia was constrained to use its reproductive imagination to keep trotting out models imposed on it by Mother England. Paradoxically, Vance Palmer was one of the ardent defenders of a neo-nationalist Australian literature.

With very few exceptions (Peter Carey's departure for New York in 1989 being one), the 1980s put an end to the artistic brain-drain as a direct consequence of the Whitlam government's political program that offered several cultural and literary grants, transforming Australia into a land where artistic creativity could develop.

Neo-nationalism or the survival of nationalism

It needs to be acknowledged that wars injected dynamism into Australian society. While a patriotic thrust began with the First World War, the Second World War contributed to an expansion in the book industry. Imports declined and the publishing world turned toward local literary production. It was unquestionably a flicker of hope for national writers who previously had to face competition from foreign writers on their terrain. This paved the way for a consolidation of the pre-war nationalist wave, which endured because of the neo-nationalist trend entrenched in the critical essays of people like A.A. Phillips and Vance Palmer, and in the novels of Katharine Susannah Prichard* and many others. At this time, they all agreed there was a lack of an 'Australian tradition' – a gap that writers filled with bountiful local colour.

A genuine product of the colonial period, the remittance man was an archetypal character who had his hour of glory early in the twentieth century after receiving poor press in the preceding decade. This black sheep experienced exile in the colonies so that his family would avoid the disgrace he had brought upon them. A fallen aristocrat unsuitable for colonial life, he managed to make ends meet with money sent by his parents. Generally, this outcast found some comfort in his wretched existence through alcohol.

Panoramic view of Katharine Susannah Prichard

Born in Levuka (Fiji) in 1883, Katharine Susannah Prichard was educated in Melbourne before attempting freelance journalism in London and returning to Australia in 1916. She was a founding member of the Communist Party of Australia (in 1920) and her involvement impelled her to emphasise political issues to the detriment of the aesthetics of her novels. Mother of three, she was happily married to Hugo Throssell until he committed suicide when overcome by financial difficulties.

There are three categories in her assorted publications. Firstly, there are iconoclastic novels containing risky heretical topics, like the lustful desire of Red Burke (a man of the land) for Deb Colburn in *Working Bullocks* (1926), a subject that evokes the bold topics found in D.H. Lawrence's novels; Hugh Watt's desire for an Aboriginal woman in *Coonardoo: The well in the shadow* (1929) – a book that did not find a publisher in Australia until 1960 – and female eroticism that sets *Intimate Strangers* (1937) ablaze. Then there are the neo-nationalist novels, *The Pioneers* (1915), *Black Opal* (1921) and *Moon of Desire* (1941), written in the romantic tradition and concerned with the wealth that the continent had to offer its settler and Indigenous populations. Finally, there are the politically inspired novels embodied in Prichard's trilogy about the mining industry (especially gold mining) in Western Australia: *The Roaring Nineties* (1946), *Golden Miles* (1948) and *Winged Seeds* (1950). These can be read as a diatribe against corrupt capitalism. Most of Prichard's stories honour an under-represented community and are testimony to her faith in the capacity of the average citizen to achieve success through determination. With the exception of *Windlestraws* (1916) and perhaps *Haxby's Circus: The Lightest, Brightest, Little Show on Earth* (1930), her work emphasises many significant aspects of Australian life.

A novelist, short story writer, poet, playwright and lampoonist, Prichard has more than one string to her bow. Nominated for the Nobel Prize in Literature in 1932, she showcases in the richness of her works the vitality of female writing in the first half of the twentieth century.

The Remittance Man (1907) by Ambrose Pratt remains a classic of the genre devoted to this figure.

Louis Stone also deserves to be acknowledged as having initiated the tradition of larrikinism literature with *Jonah* (1911), avatar of the bushranger novel. Stone's expertise lay in Sydney life, especially larrikin gangs driven to crime because of their poverty-stricken condition. Louis Stone had used participant observation in the streets of the inner suburb of Waterloo to gather raw material for his novel, which he then imbued with melodrama. *Jonah* relates the story of two antithetical characters, leaders of a group of louts, who try to survive in the urban jungle of Sydney. After settling down, the two young men have quite divergent futures: Jonah, who is profoundly unhappy because of his pent up aggression against the world, fails to completely overcome his past despite achieving wealth, whereas Chook, although happy in his marriage to a girl from the larrikin gang, struggles to improve his human condition.

The successful historical novel and war literature

Most bestsellers published from 1910 to 1940 were historical novels and narratives that portrayed the country in fiction with great verisimilitude: *Working Bullocks* (1926) by Katharine Susannah Prichard deals with wood-cutting in Western Australia; Vance Palmer in *The Passage* (1930) depicts the village life of fishermen on the Queensland coast; the Victorian gold rush is explored by Richardson in *The Fortunes of Richard Mahony* (1930); Miles Franklin is interested in the bravery of New South Wales pioneers in *Old Blastus Bandicoot* (1931), while Eleanor Dark traces the settling of the first immigrants in Sydney in *The Timeless Land* (1941), the title of which goes back to the age-old continent that almost outshines the deftly drawn characters. The historicity of these stories serves several purposes. It provides a basis for the establishment of national values; it gives scope to imagine a national destiny other than the official one recorded in history books; and it allows readers to exorcise the traumas of the colonial era.

Novelists of the 1914–1918 Great War aimed at depicting the atrocities of this conflict on a worldwide scale in order to show how absurd and cruel it was. *The Middle Parts of Fortune: Somme and Ancre 1916* (1929) by Frederic Manning is the first Great War novel worthy of the name. It appeared the following year abridged with a new title *Her Privates We*. The book illustrates the engagement of Australian soldiers alongside the British as an expression of support for the imperial centre. Less universal than Manning in his vision, Leonard Mann produced the great classic of the Australian war novel, *Flesh in Armour* (1932). In *Australian Literature: An historical introduction*, John McLaren notes that stories about the First World War have, as a constant theme, a corrupt Garden of Eden. Characters move from a cosy, safe, civilised home environment to the barbarity of battlefields that, at times, become purgatorial in nature and where the individual achieves self-awareness; at other times, such battlefields become a hell exposing the evil morality of a corrupt society.

In *The Penguin New Literary History of Australia*, Robin Gerster emphasises that soldiers in the Australian army had already been involved in numerous earlier conflicts, but that the First World War gave them the opportunity to prove their bravery to the rest of the world. The most surprising event, the debacle of the Anzac landing on the beach of Gallipoli on 25 April 1915, was transformed by the pen of Australian authors into an hour of bravery and triumphant heroism in the face of this ordeal by fire. Writers emphasised the patriotism that motivated the regiments to accomplish a broader mission, which was eventually suicidal. The Anzac heritage can be read in *My Brother Jack* (1964) by George Johnston.

Not all writers exploited the best side of the fighting war figure (the valiant and vigorous volunteer). In *Flesh in Armour* (1932),* Leonard Mann is one of those who use a dominant antihero as narrator. This trend became the norm after 1945, in a period

Close-up of *Flesh in Armour* by Leonard Mann

As with most first novels, *Flesh in Armour*, Leonard Mann's only war novel, contains much of the author's own life experiences, especially in fighting with the Australian Imperial Forces on the frontline in France during the First World War. Frank Jeffreys, teacher and protagonist in *Flesh in Armour*, does not have the makings of a foolhardy heroic fighter – far from it. As a result, he acts as a foil, emphasising the bravery of other soldiers. The inaction and cowardice of his protagonist, which make him the archetypal antihero, perhaps explain why Mann, unable to find a commercial publisher, had to self-publish. In London, Australian Frank Jeffreys falls in love with Mary Hatton. When he finally learns of her love affair with a fellow countryman, he views the situation as desperate and, with his mind unbalanced, he ends his life in a spectacular fashion. Following the example of Frederic Manning's novel *The Middle Parts of Fortune: Somme and Ancre 1916*, Mann's work mainly covers the same geographical landscape.

As with the arduous undertaking of colonisation and the competitiveness of the gold rushes, military conflicts were tests of human endurance and bravery, two qualities that writers emphasised to reveal unknown heroes (in the modern sense of the word). Mann's nationalistic beliefs led him to exalt the Australian spirit. He presents an image of the solid Australian: generous, rebellious, headstrong and ready to serve. *Flesh in Armour* is a steadfast homage to the strength of character, the spirit of engagement and the solidarity of the Diggers, to their intrepidity in combat when their lives were in danger (embodied especially in the character Jim Blount) and pays tribute to those who died on the fields of honour.

While this book in some ways denounces the destructive force enhanced by technological progress, it nevertheless seems to endorse a bellicose ideology by excessively glorifying the Digger. Nevertheless, the novel strongly illustrates the patriotic fervour soldiers demonstrated in fighting for Great Britain.

when the more measured stories did not seek to glorify military endeavour. As a character who refused frenzied heroism, the conscientious objector inspired novelists such as Martin Boyd with *Lucinda Brayford* (1946) and Kylie Tennant who wrote *The Joyful Condemned* (1953). The demystification of war heroism and the 'Digger', as the Australian foot soldier was nicknamed, increased with the writings of such novelists as Martin Boyd, who proclaimed a pacifist position in *When Blackbirds Sing* (1962), Roger McDonald with *1915* (1979) and David Malouf, author of *Fly Away Peter* (1982) – precisely at a time when there were very few survivors of the Great War.

After the Second World War, a pragmatic Australian society with materialistic concerns was rapidly expanding. This was the inspiration for many realistic stories. As a reaction to the far from glorious period of the past, which was marred by the economic crisis, the rise of fascism, dictatorships and the class struggle, a few writers found in socialist realism a definite way to be heard. Their writings emphasise communist ideology by showing the individual being crushed by social forces.

Socialist realism: A tribute to the people

Imported from the Soviet Union, where it originated with Andreï Zhdanov, socialist realism, fashionable in Australia in the 1940s and 1950s, can be defined as a form of neutral expression, without flights of lyricism or value judgments, that attempts to describe ordinary people. As an aesthetic theory that regards art as a form of social conscience, socialist realism transcends the writer's individualism, speaks of the people as a whole and reproduces historical reality. *The Battlers* (1941), Kylie Tennant's third novel, has documentary value and is perhaps one of the most moving examples of this genre in its description of the rejects from the Great War. This was a period emphasising the proletarian novel with titles such as: *Upsurge* (1934) by John Harcourt, *Seven Poor Men of Sydney* (1934) by Christina Stead, *Sugar Heaven* (1936) by

Jean Devanny, *Intimate Strangers* (1937) by Katharine Susannah Prichard, *The Little Company* (1945) by Eleanor Dark, *How Beautiful Are Thy Feet* (1949) by Alan Marshall, and *Power Without Glory* (1950)* by Frank Hardy.

Characteristics common to these works are the profusion of characters that are the playthings of social forces; a plot that tends to be divided into sub-plots; and the presence of utopian ideas in a highly politicised discourse. By examining the proletariat from every angle (strikes, social relationships, work conditions under the impact of the economic crisis, etc.), the advocates of this trend distilled in their writings a populist propaganda. Novels such as *Sugar Heaven* and *Upsurge* competed to be named the most proletarian novel. The militant thrust, which was an integral part of these works, belonged to revolutionary romanticism. This anti-authoritarian literature, which in some way resembled radical literature, set out to overturn the established order by expressing hope for a brighter future.

Populist novelists, like Katharine Susannah Prichard, Jean Devanny, Dorothy Hewett, John Harcourt, Frank Hardy and Judah Waten, went so far in their political commitment as to become members of the Communist Party. Some of these writers banded together in 1944 under the banner of The Realist Writers Group. Others like Vance Palmer, M. Barnard Eldershaw, Leonard Mann, Gavin Casey and Margaret Trist were content to express their militancy in their prose.

Populism promoted a return to a valuing of the common man and to the democratic tradition established by Joseph Furphy. With a few exceptions, like Frank Dalby Davison with *Man-Shy* (1931) (an allegorical story of a heifer which, fighting for autonomy and freedom, tries to avoid being captured by men in the mountains), writers abandoned the hinterland as backdrop to their stories, which they preferred to set in an essentially urban environment. A classic example is Ruth Park with her two early novels, *The Harp in the South* (1948) and *Poor Man's Orange* (1949) that tells

Low-angle shot of *Power Without Glory* by Frank Hardy

Power Without Glory took five years of research and writing before being published and consequently translated into several languages. The novel resulted in Frank Hardy being sued for criminal libel; he was eventually found not guilty. The wealthy Melbourne notable John Wren, on whom the main character was based, initiated the legal proceedings because he did not appreciate the unflattering fictional portrayal. A great many of the characters in the book were inspired from real-life counterparts whose names had been subtly changed, like Frank Ashton representing Labor politician Frank Anstey or Maurice Blackwell being the literary impersonation of State Labor MP Maurice Blackburn.

The title makes no mystery of the author's intentions, for it is an ironic subversion of a well-known classic – the great American Dream success story. *Power Without Glory* covers the period from 1890 to 1950 and relates how John West, a young proletarian born in the fictitious suburb of Carringbush, goes from rags to riches by profitable but fraudulent gambling-related activities. In the years before the Great War, John West experiences a spectacular rise that crowns his self-taught education and entrepreneurial spirit with success. His superficial philanthropy does not prevent readers from discerning his blackened soul when they learn that he is implicated in several murders. The protagonist seeks to corrupt civil servants and the authorities in an attempt to escape the arm of the law. But at the time that he is enjoying ever increasing prosperity, divine justice catches up with him and his personal life crumbles. His wife is unfaithful, his eldest daughter Marjory and the youngest, Mary, both die and his son John, who succumbs to alcohol, commits suicide.

This bulky novel is uncompromising in showing both sides of social success. The Communist Party of Australia, to which Hardy had belonged since 1939, encouraged people to read *Power Without Glory* because this book put the Labor Party on trial while denouncing capitalism as being morally culpable.

of the misfortunes of a poverty-stricken family living in squalid accommodation in Sydney's Surry Hills.

In 1952, a small group of communist writers led by Jack Beasley created the Australian Book Society, with the aim of promoting socialist realism. Under its aegis, Beasley published his manifesto entitled *Socialism and the Novel: A study of Australian literature* (1957) which broadly outlined socialist realism. According to the author, the trend aimed at depicting a society changed by the struggle of the working class to defend socialist values. This is how Beasley explained new fictional archetypes in the novel, such as the farmer up to his neck in debt, the manufacturer anxious about his production, the worker in favour of nationalising businesses, the salaried woman who watches over the household and the brazen greedy capitalist. Socialist realism was presented by Beasley as a form freed from the weight of the past that placed the human condition of ordinary folk at the centre of contemporary society. This humanist impulse also developed a form of literary representation of Aboriginal people that differed from traditional stereotypes.

Representing Aboriginal people

Ignored or marginalised in novels since colonisation, the Aboriginal figure was neglected in Australian literature until the publication of *Coonardoo* (1929) by Katharine Susannah Prichard. Until the 1920s, the depiction of Aboriginal people, when they were not completely integrated into the setting, as in Rosa Praed's novels, presented a double stereotype representing both sides of the same coin. On one side was a pleasant representation of the Other, a cliché of the exotic inherent in the noble savage myth usually associated with primitivism. On the flip side, there were writers who spread an ill-fated image of the Other by linking Aboriginal people with barbarity and villainy. Grant Watson, who explored the theme of solitude in *The Desert Horizon* (1923), gave his informative perspective on Aboriginal people and their values.

Similarly, at the end of the 1930s, poet Rex Ingamells began the Jindyworobaks in Adelaide. The term, a slight bastardisation of 'jindy-worabak' meaning to 'annex' or 'join', was borrowed from James Devaney's glossary in *The Vanished Tribes* (1929). Ingamells developed this philosophy in his manifesto entitled *Conditional Culture* (1938). The most radical of the group thought that only Aboriginal people, strong in their animistic beliefs, were able to produce something culturally authentic, since they had an intimate knowledge of the land. For the Jindyworobaks, it was necessary to put aside Western tradition in order to be inspired by Aboriginal tradition and drink from the one creative source in Australia. This view masked the fact that, until the 1930s, authors (such as Prichard and Watson) with no connection to Indigenous people or their culture, had produced original quality literature. The movement, which gathered together mainly poets under its banner, was misunderstood, discredited and died out in the mid-1950s. The exploitation and appropriation of Aboriginal culture had disturbingly taken on too many colonialist undertones.

The Timeless Land, Eleanor Dark's novel of 1941, devoid of stereotypes, had already revealed a more sensitive attitude towards the Aboriginal condition. Prichard's *Coonardoo*, Mary Durack's *Keep Him My Country* (1950) and some of Vance Palmer's stories such as *The Man Hamilton* (1928) and *Men are Human* (1930) are iconoclastic in that they show an interest in Aboriginal culture and deal with the union between a white man and an Aboriginal woman. In these stories, the Aboriginal woman, as the prey of man's desire, guarantees the connection between man and the land. If at times she is seen by some readers as 'the noble savage', she is no less a complex person. This is a long way from the racist ideology of the colonial era and the classical representations of cardboard Aboriginal characters. The poignant story of *Coonardoo* highlights deeply ingrained prejudices by depicting Hugh Watt, a white man, torn between his love for the Aboriginal woman of the title and the prying eyes of European society. Ensnared by guilt, Hugh cannot accept her and even goes so far as to banish the Aboriginal woman for something she did not do. Coonardoo falls seriously ill and dies in exile. Xavier Herbert goes further with *Capricornia* (1938)* in which a mixed union results in the birth of a mixed-blood child.

The Aboriginal woman is later transformed into a sturdy character in the work of Nene Gare. In *The Fringe Dwellers* (1961), Gare tells of the failure of an Aboriginal family to integrate into an Australian suburb. Despite efforts made by young Trilby – a strong-minded astute woman who wishes to climb the social ladder whatever it costs by proving that Aboriginal people are just as capable as others – the Comeaway family, overcome by social problems, have to leave their low-level accommodation and return to Nigger Hill in the insalubrious Aboriginal camp, living on the fringe of white society; hence the title of Gare's novel.

The figure of the mixed-blood Aboriginal rose to fame in Australian literature thanks to Napoleon Bonaparte, the top-class sleuth who appears in twenty-nine of thirty-two novels by Arthur Upfield, originator of the ethnological crime novel that casts a humanistic eye on the Aboriginal condition. Upfield's literary genius was restricted unfortunately to his depiction of Bony, the nickname given to the key character in his detective stories, who belongs to the tradition of intuitive Aboriginal trackers. The writer traces the life of his star detective from his birth in *Wings Above the Diamantina* (1936). As a bridge joining two cultures, Bony – an intuitive, dark-skinned man as affable as he is seductive – has to find his place in a society scornful of the value of mixed blood. Father of three children from his marriage to a part-Aboriginal woman, Napoleon Bonaparte became Upfield's favourite inspector from the time of his first novel *The Barrakee Mystery* (1929), contributing greatly to the fame of his English-born creator. The novel most relevant to the current study is unquestionably *An Author Bites the Dust* (1948), in which Upfield attacks the Australian literati who, at the time, still considered crime fiction as an offshoot of an

Low-angle shot of *Capricornia* by Xavier Herbert

The publication of *Capricornia* in 1938 was beset with difficulties. Initially called *Black Velvet,* the novel, which explored the subject of interracial sexuality, contained material that would have given the boldest of publishers cold feet about accepting the manuscript. After the first draft was rejected by a number of publishing houses at the start of the 1930s, Xavier Herbert rewrote the narrative producing a hefty tome which he had to halve in 1933 on the advice of publisher P.R. Stephensen, who went bankrupt before the book could be published. Angus & Robertson ended up accepting the final draft of the manuscript, which had already been submitted to them twice before.

Covering half a century of history (1880–1930), *Capricornia* is a dense and copious novel swarming with Dickensian characters. The Shillingsworth family are at the centre of the book when they arrive at the beginning of the twentieth century in Capricornia, an imaginary region in the Northern Territory. Mark, one of the Shillingsworth brothers, has a relationship with a young Aboriginal woman and fathers a mixed-blood son who later takes the name of Norman Shillingsworth. Implicated in a sordid affair, Mark abandons his son, who later finds him after discovering his filial connection. The novel concludes with young Norman's initiatory journey to find his Aboriginal roots. The Shillingsworth story is carried on in Herbert's *magnum opus* of 1975, *Poor Fellow My Country*, which won that year's Miles Franklin.

When all is said and done, *Capricornia* is a strongly political work that denounces, through a wry sense of humour, the iniquitous cruel treatment meted out to Aboriginal people, victims of xenophobia. Nevertheless, with the topos of geographic emptiness being inescapable for a country that is to a large extent desert, one is tempted to suggest that wordy authors like Xavier Herbert try, no matter what, to fill the gap with a myriad of objects and names.

To commemorate the jubilee of the first publication of *Capricornia*, the playwright Louis Nowra adapted the novel for the stage.

inferior literature. In *An Author Bites the Dust*, Bony investigates the supposed crime of famous writer Mervyn Blake. Apart from the detective plot, the book's interest lies in its denunciation of the Australian literati, which was made up of cliques divided between authors of great literature and potboiler enthusiasts dealing with publishers ready to sacrifice literary genius for excessive economic profits.

CHAPTER 4

Exploited and Manipulated Reality (1951–1965)

After the First World War, literature experienced a period of free expression in terms of the use of words and ideas. Writers explored new genres and trends (the romance, the *avant-garde*) and developed some themes that had been anecdotally treated up until then: urbanism and suburbanism, for example. In order to shake off the cultural complex that constrained artistic creation, Australian writers rejected the models imposed on them and gave free vent to their prolific imaginations.

Second World War novels

In contrast to the delayed arrival of Great War novels, readers did not have to wait a decade after the conflict ended before writers took up the Second World War with the necessary distance needed to analyse and treat it. As for publishers, they had noted from the first battle that war-impassioned readers made this genre a financial certainty. Moreover, novels had been in short supply in Australia – a direct consequence of the rationing that had hit England severely at the time. Because of a combination of these factors, the Second World War had not even ended before some novelists like Glassop and Aldridge were already writing about it. Lawson Glassop dedicated a historic diptych to it: *We Were the*

Rats (1944) and *The Rats in New Guinea* (1963). James Aldridge, whose novels deal with the war in Europe, published *The Sea Eagle* in 1944. It tells of the support given by Resistance groups in organising the escape of Australian soldiers abandoned on Crete behind enemy lines.

In a variant in which the Pacific became the theatre of war in the jungles of New Guinea and the Solomon Islands, military panache is remembered, especially in *The Climate of Change* (1954) by Jon Cleary, who caught readers' imaginations and contributed to the popularisation of war literature. Reminiscent of the evil forest in medieval symbolism, the jungle was a stressful, treacherous and deadly place that fuelled fear of the Yellow Peril – a hideout for despicable human acts. In the novel *The Last Blue Sea* (1959) by David Forrest, the flesh-eating jungle of New Guinea held a central dominant place. To this should be added T.A.G. Hungerford's novel *The Ridge and the River* (1952), not to forget the aforementioned *The Rats in New Guinea* and Eric Lambert's *The Veterans* (1954) – the eagerly awaited sequel of his very famous *The Twenty Thousand Thieves* (1951). In this first volume, Lambert evokes the gallantry with which the Australian soldiers of the 9th Division fought on the Middle Eastern front at Tobruk and El Alamein, a viewpoint that contrasted with that of British authors, who generally ignored the presence of Australian soldiers.

While these titles tend to suggest that war could be experienced only in Europe and Asia, there was also a batch of novels that treated conflict on Australian soil and looked into its repercussions. Among them are Kenneth McKenzie's *Dead Men Rising* (1951), co-authors Dymphna Cusack and Florence James's *Come in Spinner* (1951) and the work of Xavier Herbert. The latter joined this group with his wide-ranging second novel *Soldiers' Women* (1961) which explores the social and sexual behaviour of women faced with the presence of Americans in the streets of Sydney. The novel is mainly concerned with a matriarchy led by Esmeralda La Plante, in which women's power to change is measured in terms of their assets and attire.

It is generally recognised that the frontline infantry was the mainstay of the Great War effort. The Second World War was to emphasise aerial combat – seen in, for example, *No Moon Tonight* (1956) by Don Charlwood – and naval manoeuvres, as shown in a classic of the genre, *Gimme the Boats* (1953) by James Edmond Macdonnell, as well as Ronald McKie's *Proud Echo* (1953). More sensitive topics, such as the Holocaust and the sadly infamous concentration camps, are not evoked until later in 1982 with great humanity by the elegant style of Thomas Keneally.

Some authors tackled prisoner-of-war narratives. This was the case for Randolph Stow, who touched on POW fiction with *The Merry-Go-Round in the Sea* (1965)* and Russell Braddon, who wrote *The Naked Island* (1952), a fictionalised account of his own experiences under the yoke of the Japanese army. *A Town Like Alice* (1950) is the best-known work by the great romance novelist Nevil Shute. It shows certain aspects of Australian life through the experiences of a young English woman Jean Paget who is held prisoner by the Japanese for a month and a half. Strangely enough, conflicts subsequent to the Second World War (in Korea, Vietnam and Iraq) have inspired Australian authors less.

Paraliterature or the rise of pulp fiction

Traditionally ignored by academia, paraliterature nevertheless saw a rapid growth in its readership in the 1950s. Australian pulp fiction originated from the 1939 government embargo on American pulp magazines and flooded the local market from 1949 for over a decade. In this ephemeral industry, publishing houses had scarcely made a name for themselves before they disappeared without warning, while authors were ceaselessly hired and fired. This went largely unnoticed since they signed their works with a generic pseudonym and thus took on a status similar to that of a ghost writer. In the words of Toni Johnson-Woods: 'This was the age of formula fiction and not the celebrity author'.

These slim paperbacks (fewer than a hundred pages) came in

Close-up of *The Merry-Go-Round in the Sea* by Randolph Stow

The Merry-Go-Round in the Sea is Randolph Stow's fourth novel and probably his most accomplished. It is difficult not to allude to the similarities between this novel and *The Boys in the Island* (1958) by Christopher Koch. Both of them focus on growing up and are strongly autobiographical. Pursued by loneliness, a young male central character (Rob Coram for Stow and Francis Cullen for Koch) moves from innocence to experience, changing completely after an eye-opening reality check forces him to swallow the bitter pill of disillusion. If we overlook the differences in style between Koch and Stow (the latter is more prosaic in his approach), these two novels are very similar except that the family, omnipresent in *The Merry-Go-Round in the Sea,* is almost non-existent in Koch's work.

The 'merry-go-round in the sea' that frames and punctuates Stow's narrative is a shipwreck that symbolises fullness and oneness. It also represents a microcosm to which Rob wishes he belonged. The two-part coming-of-age novel is structured around young Rob's cousin, Rick Maplestead, who is fifteen years older. This attractive *doppelgänger* is captured by the Japanese at a time when the silent threat of war and its potential dire consequences hover over Australia.

In the second part, Rick is a returned, maladjusted prisoner-of-war with a far from glorious past. He is unable to love Jane Wexford and cannot fit into an Australian society he judges to be entirely boring. As a misfit, Rick rejects the determinism that undermines him by exclaiming that he no more wants a family than a country. Disillusioned, he leaves to spend the rest of his life in England, just as the author did in 1966. Cousin Rob also has a sudden self-revelation: he realises his father loves him when the latter saves Rob from drowning, and comes to accept the fact that his 'merry-go-round in the sea' was just a childhood illusion.

a variety of different genres, from the western to crime fiction, romance and science fantasy. The western was similar to the colonial novel, with its chauvinist world of colonisers, bushrangers and gold-diggers. It was soon supplanted by science fantasy that aimed to quell anxieties caused by technological progress, the use of nuclear power and an amoral exploitation of science. This genre was immediately followed by romance fiction that gave new roles to women. These novels were often serialised in highly popular women's magazines. Crime novels thrived as well, using local settings and humour-packed detective plots.

The majority of these novels, with their strongly violent and unpredictable plots, were, alas, very poor stylistically. To compensate for this lack of depth, they concentrated on marketing. The front cover had to be attractive, generally with striking colours, a catchy title and an erotic vamp to seduce the reader. As Toni Johnson-Woods put it, 'the lurid lasses, enticing titles and feverish blurbs are the hallmarks of pulp fiction'. These covers were an invitation to sexual desire and every now and then they came up against Australian censorship. However, mass production was such that it offered readers plenty of choice.

In the 1960s, literary output was divided into two categories: highbrow and lowbrow fiction, even though some authors like Thomas Keneally were able to produce both. In contrast to the flimsiness of paraliterary fiction, the content of the Australian novel, under the influence of some very politically engaged authors, was about to undergo an unprecedented politicisation.

The Realist Writers Group and the politicisation of the novel

After 1945, intellectual debate in Australia centred on political dissension between the nationalist left-wing radicals and the right-wing conservatives. Even though novels that were more or less political in content had been published since the colonial period, the postwar era saw the beginnings of the politicisation of the novel. In *Writing in Hope and Fear: Literature as politics in postwar Australia*, John McLaren shows how the novel morphed into a textual space for political expression, writing within which was mainly motivated by both fear of and hope for a long-awaited drastic change. Logically, the renewal brought about by the Whitlam Government would dispel such speculations.

The Realist Writers Group (1944–1964) was a collective of authors of socialist and communist leanings spread throughout Australia who pursued political commitments that had begun in the 1940s. Though following the lines of realism as practised by the Bohemians of the *Bulletin*, they were concerned more with the future of the worker. The first small group of these proletarian literary organisations was established in Melbourne in 1944. Among its main members were the novelists David Martin, Walter Kaufmann, Ralph de Boissière, Frank Hardy, Katharine Susannah Prichard, Eric Lambert, poet Laurence Collinson (who also wrote a novel in 1973), poet John Manifold, and novelist and short story writer John Morrison, to mention a few. Some of the titles were *Port of Call* (1950) by John Morrison; *Crossroads* (1961) – one of the two novels by Walter Kaufmann where the action takes place in Australia; and Ralph de Boissière's *No Saddles for Kangaroos* (1964) which evokes the strength of union action in saving a car manufacturing firm.

The Realist Writers Group, who intended to be the architects of a literary renaissance, published their philosophy in an anonymous article entitled 'The Writer and the People' which appeared in 1952 in the first edition of *The Realist Writer*. Its main dogma was that the realist writer shared the people's concerns. The text became the pretext for militancy and the aim of the writer was to represent people in everyday life while ignoring the aesthetic dimension of the fictional form. Narratives had to be written in plain language without embellishment – that is, devoid of all artifice.

These Realist Writers distilled their prose in *The Realist Writer* (1952–1954), a paper published under the leadership of Bill Wannan, first in Melbourne, then in Sydney. In 1954, *The Realist*

Writer was absorbed by a new publication of populist sensibility entitled *Overland*, under the direction of the communist Stephen Murray-Smith. This Marxist literary journal was meant to oppose the right with a very sturdy nationalist motto borrowed from Joseph Furphy: 'Temper democratic, bias Australian'. A majority of writers affiliated with the Communist Party of Australia (like Katharine Susannah Prichard, Eric Lambert, Judah Waten, Frank Hardy and John Morrison) already collaborated with the *Communist Review* (1934–1966). This magazine allowed them to present their populist aims even though it was published irregularly due to censorship in the early 1940s. One of these committed authors, Judah Waten, wrote seven novels drawing on his Russian background and his Jewish culture.

This new movement of realist writers died out in the early 1960s. At the start of the 1950s with the cold war in the background, it had already shown signs of weakening and of some dissension between docile and slavishly obedient authors who carried out the dogmas to the letter (like Frank Hardy, de Boissière and Lambert) and those who started dreaming of artistic freedom and considered the organisation too ossifying (such as Manifold, Martin and Morrison). In addition, there were disputes and infighting; the group disintegrated and dispersed geographically after Lambert, Hardy and Murray-Smith disagreed. Perhaps modernism, their sworn enemy, could have reconciled them.

Modernism or realism rejected

In the postwar years, realism, worn threadbare, gave way to literary modernism. This loose term, which would not be applied fully to Australian writing until the 1960s, was defined as using new methods of expression to reflect changes in the modern era by creating an alternative to literary orthodoxy. In short, modernist literature essentially generated introspective writings of a dream-like quality with an acute awareness of the limited potential of language. From this we get the interior monologue and stream of consciousness, popularised by James Joyce. Characters have a propensity to be alienated and evolve within a symbolically charged environment that permeates different layers of the narrative. European modernism left its mark more on Australia's art than on its literature. It had begun to influence the novel in the 1920s with Chester Cobb, the first writer to use stream of consciousness in his novels *Mr Moffat* (1925) and *Days of Disillusion* (1926). Other isolated attempts were made, such as those of the poet Max Harris who, with *The Vegetative Eye* (1943), tried to write an experimental novel structured in such a way as to reflect the internal world through which reality is perceived. This book was overly ambitious and unfortunately did not capture readers' imagination.

Weary of the realist tradition, Patrick White,* who shared some stylistic similarities with Virginia Woolf and James Joyce, followed a new artistic path with his first novel *Happy Valley* (1939), taking up the stream-of-consciousness style Cobb had experimented with earlier. For Patrick White, as for his contemporaries Koch and Stow, the geographic quest was an external metaphor for the internal spiritual quest. Such mapping enabled Australian authors to explore the inner workings of the psyche in order for reality to be revealed through the mind. White's remarkable novel *The Tree of Man* (1955) is a modern version of the traditional pioneer saga and symbolises the ephemeral nature of man's achievement, which fails to resist both the ravages of time and the destructive forces in the universe. In his essay 'The Prodigal Son', first published in *Australian Letters*, the author revolts, not without mockery, against the conventional world and affirms that he tried to prove that the 'Australian novel is not necessarily the dreary, dun-coloured offspring of journalistic realism'. With White, the narrative discloses mythical and symbolic dimensions, as individuals resolve to accept their weaknesses and the social changes they have to face.

Patrick White gave a boost to modernism with novels whose

Panoramic view of Patrick White

Although born in 1912 in London, where he lived for six months before his parents went back to New South Wales, Patrick White is deeply Australian. The first Australian writer to be awarded the Miles Franklin Award and also the Nobel Prize for Literature, White had difficulty at first in gaining the recognition his work deserved. After achieving wide acclaim in the United States and in Europe – a popularity he would never equal in the Antipodes – he came to the disappointing realisation that no one is a prophet in their own country.

His first novels show his increasing taste for the universal. While the regional plot of *Happy Valley* (1939) remained within New South Wales, the characters in *The Living and the Dead* (1941) evolve in a predominantly English world. More cosmopolitan in nature, *The Aunt's Story* (1948) depicts Theodore Goodman's life in many parts of the world.

Some would divide White's twelve novels into three periods:

- The three above-mentioned early novels, that draw from the author's childhood memories to create literary motifs.
- Novels governed by epic heroes' exploration of unknown land (*The Tree of Man*, 1955 and *Voss*, 1957) or visionaries who give us their evocations (*Riders in the Chariot*, 1961, *The Solid Mandala*, 1966 and *The Vivisector*, 1970).
- Novels dominated by complex characters, if not divided souls, that experience a degree of self-revelation (*The Eye of the Storm*, 1973, *A Fringe of Leaves*, 1976, *The Twyborn Affair*, 1979 and *Memoirs of Many in One*, 1984).

The Hanging Garden, a final novel of which White only completed a third, was released for the centenary of the author's birth.

White can be defined as an elite aesthetic perfectionist, an uncompromising man – or rather a man flayed alive, recognised as having the gift of a caustic style and a habit of making provocative statements. Like Xavier Herbert, though reclusive, he did not hesitate to speak out in the defence of his beliefs. Hostile to nuclear energy and the exploitation of uranium, White fought for ecology and the Labor Party. He openly supported the Whitlam Government and republicanism.

plots were not confined to Australia. For example, *The Living and the Dead* (1941), which he wrote when staying in the United States, takes place in England. White made amends with *Voss* (1957; adapted later as an opera with libretto by David Malouf), unquestionably his most popular work with Australians. This novel was inspired by a historic event: the disappearance of the explorer Ludwig Leichhardt who set out on an expedition in March 1848 to cross the continent from east to west. He ended up vanishing without trace. In almost lyrical style, White retraces the physical voyage that is both interior and symbolic. This introspective search culminates in the death of the eponymous character when he meets his inescapable destiny. While the Australian soil rapidly absorbs the German traveller's blood, the character is transformed into a sacrificial, even Christ-like, figure. Religious symbolism runs throughout White's work and his writing could be said to be 'noble' in its refinement and formality. The author touched a chord that resonated with his fellow citizens by exploiting this journey into Australia's heartland deeply embedded in the Australian psyche. Because of the geographic vacuity that White called 'the Great Australian Emptiness', Australia is defined in *Voss* as a perimeter that encircles a void. Ross Gibson gives a fine analysis of *Voss* in his work *The Diminishing Paradise*.

In 1957, White became the first recipient of the Miles Franklin Award* for his novel *Voss*. The need for such a prize probably came from the fact that, while she was alive, Stella Franklin was never able to live to write, since she needed to write to live. Over time, the prize has gained in prestige and financial reward to become the most generous and the most sought-after Australian prize for fiction. It is now worth $60,000, having more than doubled in value since 1991.

The 1950s also saw a stronger, more liberal trend that opposed the inward-looking attitude brought about by neo-nationalism. This was an *avant-garde* era and some non-Aboriginal novelists, who blended European heritage and Aboriginal culture, proved

Low-angle shot of the Miles Franklin Award

In line with the wishes of Stella Franklin, who bequeathed almost all of her estate estimated at £8,996 to establish this literary prize, the Miles Franklin Award must give preference to a published work 'of the highest literary merit and which must present Australian Life in any of its phases'. Founded in 1957, the award has ever since crowned 58 novels with glory and increased their sales.

As is the case with any respected prize, the Miles Franklin has had its share of controversies. In 1994, the jurors unleashed a debate by excluding Frank Moorhouse's novel *Grand Days* (1993) from the competition, claiming that its Australian content was practically insignificant. The story traces the career of a young Australian woman who, after the Great War, works for the United Nations in Geneva. In 1995, the committee tried to make amends by celebrating *The Hand That Signed the Paper* by Helen Demidenko, but it later transpired that the author was a Ukrainian-impersonating plagiarist. After this scandal, the jury decided to play it safe in 1996 with *Highways to a War* by Christopher Koch. Pocketing the prize money, Koch started another controversy when he revealed his uncharitable thoughts about academia.

Today, some people think it is high time the overly restrictive selection criteria of this award should be revised in order to take into account novels whose characters, settings, themes and plots are located outside Australia. The list of recipients of the Miles Franklin is also widely criticised for comprising chiefly middle-aged novelists, few of whom are women (approximately one third of all prize-winners), let alone Aboriginal (Kim Scott and Alexis Wright being the exceptions). There is a sneaking suspicion that the judging panel might almost be guilty of ageism, sexism and racism. Despite the criticism, this national and nationalistic prize is still regarded as a reliable benchmark for identifying great Australian novels. The winner in 2010, Peter Temple's *Truth*, indicated that popular genres like crime novels are now taken seriously.

And the winner of the 2015 Miles Franklin is ... Sofie Laguna for *The Eye of the Sheep*!

the Jindyworobaks' belief that an author could evoke a culture that was not their own in fiction without necessarily showing prejudice. This was the case for the prolific and popular author Arthur Upfield, with his series featuring Napoleon 'Bony' Bonaparte. Also in this tradition of synchronising Indigenous and non-Indigenous cultures stands Randolph Stow, especially with his novels *To the Islands* (1958) and *Tourmaline* (1963). *To the Islands* tells of the last days of an Anglican missionary called Stephen Heriot. Following the advice of Justin, an Aboriginal man with animistic or totemic beliefs, he is able to find peace by reconciling himself to the environment. The philosophical novel *Tourmaline* presents a water diviner named Michael Random who turns into a guru of sorts in the town of Tourmaline. This prophet from the desert hopes to inject renewed spiritual grace into his new church, which is essentially a synthesis of Christian and Aboriginal beliefs.

Stow published most of his novels before 1965; these included *To the Islands* (1958), *Tourmaline* (1963) and *The Merry-Go-Round in the Sea* (1965), all lyrical works that have some affinity with the writings of Patrick White. His first two novels, *A Haunted Land* (1956) and *The Bystander* (1957), were realist works that did not have the impact of the ones that followed. *To the Islands* was the first to introduce a poetic quality which matured with the publication of *The Merry-Go-Round in the Sea*, a more balanced work. *To the Islands* reads like a religious allegory recounting the last days of Heriot, a bitter missionary based in Western Australia who experiences a serious existential and religious crisis.

A contemporary of Stow, Christopher Koch constructed his first book *The Boys in the Island* (1958) as a lyrical novel that sits somewhere between a *Bildungsroman* and an *autofiction* (a term coined by Serge Doubrovsky to describe fictionalised autobiography). This novel is about growing up and the search for identity, which sheds light on the existential question of origins. Koch is an author concerned with both content and form. Using Flaubert's *gueuloir* test (reading the text out loud), Koch worked and reworked his prose until he was satisfied with its euphony. *The Boys in the Island*, a strongly autobiographical novel, tells of Francis Cullen's childhood from the age of four to maturity. After going through the main stages of adolescence with a series of first experiences (first love, kiss, glass of alcohol, flirt, sexual encounter, etc.), the young Tasmanian is involved in a car accident – a reality check tinged with bitterness and nostalgia for a golden age that he finally renounces. At the end of his adventure, Francis gains maturity after a self-revelation that has him mourning his wild dreams. *The Boys in the Island* marked the beginning of Koch's archetypal protagonist, who is constantly in expectation of an event that will upset his habits; of a revelation about life that will transcend the ordinary. Overcome by ennui and solitude, Francis Cullen colours his world with bovarism to protect his illusions. His quest for alterity translates into a search for a physical or imaginary place. In this novel, the quest is essentially imaginary even if it becomes substantive with the discovery of the Australian continent, a true *terra incognita* for the young protagonist. Francis Cullen is looking for a mysterious country called 'Otherland', the author's neologism, which the reader has difficulty placing geographically.

The Boys in the Island, a narrative in which contemplation is greater than action, reveals the lyrical tendency of a novelist who had already tried his hand at poetry earlier in his writing career. This *Bildungsroman*, which Koch started in 1954, can be seen as a poetic novel since the author uses poetic conventions to achieve lyrical effects. Similes, metaphors and other stylistic devices are abundant on every page, while descriptions sometimes border on hypotyposis or take on a zoomorphic or anthropomorphic character. With small strokes, these elements contribute to the effect of an impressionist painting. The flights of poetic lyricism and the seeming need to escape in quasi-dreamlike prose represent an attitude of rejection by one faced with the closed horizons of Australia, a country on the verge of an urbanisation epitomised by sprawling outer suburbs.

The emergence of a 'suburban nation'

In *The Penguin New Literary History of Australia*, Brian Kiernan correctly wrote that, with a few exceptions, the rural environment prevailed in the Australian novel up until 1945. The bush dominated stories so much that it engendered an ossifying stereotypy writers were duty-bound to abandon. After 1945, Australian literary works evoked urban themes that mirrored the country's economic rise. Some stories gave more than their due to the growing expansion of the outer suburbs, symbol of 1950s and 1960s modernity. It can even be said that the increasing industrialisation in Australia engineered the rise of a 'suburban nation', a term used by Brian Kiernan.

For most novelists of this period – Gavin Casey, George Johnston, Christopher Koch, Randolph Stow and Patrick White – the suburb was synonymous with a *tedium vitae* it was necessary to escape from at all cost. The grievances of the characters who are its victims are many: enclosure, halfheartedness, ugliness, boredom, mediocrity and conformity. Among these authors, we find Gavin Casey who gives an analysis in *Amid the Plenty* (1962) of the suburbs in the 1950s with its everyday happenings in the lives of the Mayhew family. *My Brother Jack* (1964),* the first novel of George Johnston's trilogy, also scrutinises a suburb that has nothing to offer.

For some critics like A.L. McCann, what defines Patrick White's novels is the support of an anti-suburban tradition that rejects the comforts of an Australian society considered too materialistic. According to them, White chose to depict the desert or the bush (explored in *Voss*) rather than the suburb. But these arguments tend to make us forget that White dedicated no less than two novels and several short stories and plays to the suburbs: *Riders in the Chariot* (1961) – a book in which White created an imaginary Sydney suburb called Sarsaparilla, modelled on Castle Hill, where the author had lived for a while – *The Solid Mandala* (1966) and 'The Night the Prowler' (1978). Sarsaparilla is the archetypal

Close-up of *My Brother Jack* by George Johnston

Honoured by the jurors of the Miles Franklin Award, *My Brother Jack* is the first novel in an autobiographical trilogy completed by *Clean Straw for Nothing* (1969) and *A Cartload of Clay* (1971), an unfinished work published posthumously. Set in Melbourne in the interwar period and told through a restorative *ab ovo* narrative, *My Brother Jack* opposes the destinies of the two Meredith brothers who grow up in a family of four children (Jean the eldest, Jack, David and Marjorie, the youngest) under the iron rule of the father.

Jack, a young, hedonistic and extroverted athlete and a bit of a rogue, is the embodiment of the Australian spirit with his virile presence. He mentors David, the introverted and slightly unassuming narrator who endures life and the taunts of his elder brother and his father. After a few successfully published freelance articles, David quickly takes refuge in a career as a journalist for the *Morning Post* and then publishes a few works. David's unhappy union with Helen Midgely grounds him to a straight-as-a-die existence in a dreary suburb. In contrast, Jack fares well from life and is happily married to Sheila Delaney, of the same age, whom he met at Wimmera while on a bush adventure. When the Second World War breaks out, Jack signs up but, by a stroke of cruel irony, an accident prevents him from proving his worth on the field of battle, while his less valiant younger brother closely follows the action as a war correspondent. David, who becomes infatuated with Cressida Morley, uses this opportunity to flee the suburb and his now very shaky marriage.

In 1965, the book was adapted into a television series by Charmian Clift, the author's second wife. The current popularity of *My Brother Jack* is explained by its documentary value: it evokes, with detailed descriptions of suburban life, the horrific consequences of the Great War and the Depression. The Meredith trilogy, which eclipsed his earlier more commercial works, is considered to be the peak of George Johnston's literary career.

suburb, a living space that combines ugliness, mediocrity and consumerism. In *Riders in the Chariot*, White's representation of life in a kitschy suburb echoes the jocular tone used by comedian and writer Barry Humphries who created in 1955 the archetypal suburban housewife Dame Edna Everage. As her name suggests, she is the embodiment of mediocrity raised to its peak (that of a Dame endorsed by the British honours system). White's novel combines the visions of a chariot of fire held by four 'illuminates': Mary Hare, Ruth Godbold, Alf Dubbo and Mordecai Himmelfarb. The author takes up the theme of the artistic endeavour of painting, which would become central in his eighth novel *The Vivisector* (1970). *The Solid Mandala* (1966), informed by Jungian psychology and set firmly in a resolutely suburban Australia with Sarsaparilla reappearing, makes use once more of the vision theme: in this case, that of Arthur and Waldo Brown, fraternal twins whose personalities are presented as poles apart, thus epitomising conflicting parts of human nature. In contrast, 'The Night the Prowler' is a short story that is a social critique of the role of a conventional, refined society comfortably settled into the humdrum routine of daily life. It tells of the unhappiness of Felicity Bannister, a girl from the suburb of Sarsaparilla who claims she has been raped by a prowler. Overcome by grief, she breaks her engagement to John Galbraith, a promising young diplomat, while her parents Humphrey and Doris do their best to save face.

For Koch and Stow, the suburb is a deathbed it is wiser to flee. With *Across the Sea Wall* (1965), Koch gives a tacit criticism of suburban spleen which weakens the people living there and bogs them down. At twenty-three years of age, the main character Robert O'Brien is imprisoned in the daily routine of a quiet suburb. He is tired of his secure public service job and of his regular-as-clockwork life as a married man. He harbours illusions and dreams of another life. This urges him to undertake a Socratic quest with his best friend James Baden.

More recently, Steven Carroll published a trilogy about a

Melbourne suburb – *The Art of the Engine Driver* (2001), *The Gift of Speed* (2004) and *The Time We Have Taken* (2007). This last volume, winner of the 2008 Miles Franklin, alludes directly to *My Brother Jack*. If the suburb has nothing to offer other than boredom, it would seem that the city, more conducive to distractions, has more to offer at its core, as demonstrated in stories written in the closing years of the twentieth century.

CHAPTER 5

Literature of Minorities in a Cosmopolitan Era (1966–1980)

In an article published in the only edition of the journal *Australian Mercury* (1935) entitled 'The Foundations of Culture in Australia: An essay towards national self-respect', Percy Reginald Stephensen declared: 'Art and literature are nationally created, but become internationally appreciated'. With this in mind, it is not an exaggeration to claim that the novel has dominated Australian twentieth-century literature since the 1970s by reaping an impressive harvest of international literary prizes: the Nobel Prize for Patrick White; the Booker Prize for Peter Carey, Thomas Keneally* and Richard Flanagan; Le Prix du Meilleur Livre Étranger for Peter Carey; the Prix Femina Étranger, the Impac Dublin Literary Award and the Neustadt International Prize for Literature for David Malouf; the Orange Prize for Kate Grenville; the Hawthornden Prize for M.J. Hyland; not to mention the Commonwealth Writers' Prize for Alex Miller, David Malouf, Peter Carey (twice!), Murray Bail, Richard Flanagan, Kate Grenville, and Christos Tsiolkas, and most recently Le Prix Médicis Étranger for German-born Australian expatriate Lily Brett.

In a context that was propitious to social advances, cultural groups (Aboriginal people, women, homosexuals and various under-represented ethnic minorities) attempted to make the

Panoramic View of Thomas Keneally

Thomas Keneally was born in 1935 in Sydney where he spent some of his childhood. Exactly like Gerald Murnane who was also guided by his Catholic faith, Keneally studied theology for a time before renouncing priesthood and dedicating himself to teaching and writing. This may be one of the reasons why his writings are haunted by the ethics of good and evil.

Keneally's *The Place at Whitton* (1964) was the first of a long string of novels that were somewhat uneven in quality. His most popular novels are: *Bring Larks and Heroes* (1967) and *Three Cheers for the Paraclete* (1968) – both awarded the Miles Franklin; *The Survivor* (1969), *The Chant of Jimmy Blacksmith* (1972), *Gossip from the Forest* (1975), *A Family Madness* (1985) and *The Playmaker* (1987). In the meantime, the author acquired an international reputation with his poignant story of the survivors of the Holocaust in *Schindler's Ark* (1982), later renamed *Schindler's List*. It traces the exceptional actions of an ordinary man faced with the horrors of the Second World War. Oskar Schindler's list saved more than a thousand Jews from the death camps. Glorified by the prestigious Booker Prize, this 'faction' helped Keneally obtain the illustrious Australian distinction, the Order of Australia (AO), for services to literature.

Because of his numerous travels abroad and time spent as an expatriate (mainly in English and American universities), Keneally is considered a universalist who speaks unpretentiously to the general reader. Essentially, he is passionate about history, war and violence, human tragedy, religious fervour, Irish heritage and the frailty of the human condition. According to Peter Pierce, Keneally cultivates the art of melodrama in line with other novelists such as Marcus Clarke, Christina Stead, Patrick White, Kate Grenville and the like.

In the 1990s, the novelist, acknowledging his Irish origins, stood up for the Australian republican movement by publishing many articles and reflective works on the subject, including *Our Republic* (1993) and *The Great Shame* (1998).

novel a place within which their militancy could flourish, to the detriment of simplistic notions of nationalistic unity.

In the 1970s, literature was at its peak. Publishing opportunities multiplied and remained constant, despite being challenged by the renaissance of the Australian cinema which, after all, brought several literary works to the screen. This association of the literary world with the entertainment industry was not without its consequences; the writer was forced to become a public personality, even a celebrity. The keywords for gaining media recognition were visibility and ubiquity. The promotion of literary events such as the growing number of festivals, signing sessions and literary lunches with the literary guest star, was part and parcel of this overexposure of the writer in the media.

The 1970s was the Grant Generation: some authors were able to take distinct advantage of the financial aid granted by the Australian Council's Literature Board established by Prime Minister Gough Whitlam (1972–1975). Among the many writers who benefited from this were Robert Drewe, Rodney Hall and Frank Moorhouse, but only David Malouf, Peter Carey and Helen Garner were able to enhance their literary careers significantly.

When he received the Nobel Prize in 1973, the year *The Eye of the Storm* was published, Patrick White became living proof of the reputation Australian literature had established worldwide. But no man is a prophet in his own country and his case demonstrates how difficult it is to obtain recognition from one's peers in a country that sometimes seems to encourage averageness. So Australian writers had to aspire to international recognition, without which they were not given a place of honour at home. Moreover, the writer's profile had changed, and the norm was now to be an informed and erudite university-educated person, such as Thea Astley, Peter Carey, Beverley Farmer, Helen Garner, Christopher Koch, Randolph Stow, Barbara Hanrahan and many others.

What the diverse novels of this period have in common is their heterogeneous nature, which results from the experimental mode, the subversion or confusion of genres, an interest in new forms of expression and the questioning of the commonly held definition of Australian identity. This crisis urged authors to examine their place in society and in the world at large. In this phase of development, Australian literature established close links with trends in foreign literatures in order to acquire a multicultural dimension.

The birth of the Aboriginal novel

The birth of the Aboriginal novel started well after the rise of Indigenous poetry and just after the rise of drama, with works from playwrights such as Jack Davis and Kevin Gilbert, Robert Merritt and Richard Walley. It was in the 1960s that a strongly developing Aboriginal literature made its mark by expressing its own legitimate concerns. While Australian literature in general still showed strong connections with Great Britain, Aboriginal authors were cultivating what Jean-Marc Moura called 'an aesthetic sense of resistance' by emphasising the concept of Aboriginality. Colin Johnson* has called Aboriginal literature 'a literature of the Fourth World, that is, of the Indigenous minorities submerged in a surrounding majority and governed by them'.

Since it is an oral culture, Aboriginal tradition is closer to poetry and song than to the novel. Consequently, literary expression used by Aboriginal novelists is in both a form (the novel or the act of writing) and a language (English) foreign to their traditional culture. According to Colin Johnson, 'Aboriginal writing is a white form in that it is mostly written in English, and too often a polished English which is divorced from the community itself'. This has brought about a reverse movement, a symptom of Aboriginal acculturation that has resulted in detachment from their tradition and heritage. Aboriginal writers opposed Western linear time in their works with the omnipresent notion of circular time. Nevertheless, historicity or chronological time, a Western notion that supplanted Aboriginal mythic time, paradoxically

Low-angle shot of Colin Johnson

Born in 1938 in Narogin, East Cubelling in Western Australia, Colin Johnson spent the last part of his adolescence serving two prison sentences for acts of delinquency – this experience was the inspiration for the play *The Delinks* (1959) and contributed to his setting up a repression/expression discourse. Popularly thought of as the spearhead of Aboriginal writers, Johnson is a politically engaged author who denounces the appropriation of Australia by non-Indigenous people. Accustomed to changing his identity, Johnson used three different names in the space of a few years. At first, he called himself Mudrooroo Narogin, as he was born near this Western Australian region; then he was Mudrooroo Nyoongah, referring directly to the people he identified with. Finally he chose Mudrooroo, since Aboriginal people addressed one another by their first name; the family name being used to identify bloodline. He began as a bohemian freethinker before being involved with Buddhist monks and reinventing himself as the Reverend S.A. Jivaka.

In 1965, he published his first novel *Wildcat Falling* before travelling throughout Asia and India, where he studied Buddhism for three years. On his return to Melbourne, he continued with a second novel *Long Live Sandawara* (1979) before writing *Doctor Wooreddy's Prescription for Enduring the Ending of the World* (1983), which was the novel most favoured by academics. Like his more poetic work *The Master of the Ghost Dreaming* (1991), *Doctor Wooreddy's Prescription* is a truly postcolonial work fighting the negative effects of colonisation by challenging non-Indigenous Australia's official version of contact history. He published several poems between these two books and then published another novel *Doin Wildcat* (1988). He completed his Wildcat trilogy with *Wildcat Screaming* (1992) before starting the series 'Master of the Ghost Dreaming' with *The Kwinkan* (1995) and *The Undying* (1998). Wearing his theoretical hat, he published several critical essays about Aboriginal literature, including *Writing From the Fringe* (1990), *Us Mob* (1995) and *Indigenous Literature of Australia* (1997).

Politically engaged in different movements for the defence and protection of Aboriginal communities and their land rights, Mudrooroo taught his adopted culture in many Australian universities over an extended period.

plays a prominent role in Aboriginal protests related to land rights.

While *Native Legends* (1929) made David Unaipon the first Aboriginal person to record their myths (and therefore the first Aboriginal writer), Colin Johnson,alias Mudrooroo, was incorrectly hailed as the 'first Aboriginal novelist' – incorrectly, as it was later revealed that he had usurped an Aboriginal identity. In 1996, Victoria Laurie disclosed the writer's secret. Contrary to expectation, his father, Thomas Creighton Patrick Johnson, was an Afro-American and his mother Elizabeth Johnson (née Barron) was of Irish descent. It is no surprise, then, to learn that the novelist had very limited knowledge of Aboriginal languages. This controversy caused no end of trouble for the literary community for it had regarded Johnson as the standard-bearer of the Aboriginal cause. So Colin Johnson's *Wildcat Falling* (1965) was not the first Aboriginal novel published.

As a result of this scandal, it was considered necessary to redefine who the first Aboriginal novelist was. This privilege was given to Monica Clare with the publication of a small book of fewer than one hundred pages in length entitled *Karobran: The story of an Aboriginal girl* (1978). This novel tells of the narrator's childhood growing up in a one-parent family on a sheep station in New South Wales. Evoking the dramatic experience of the 'Stolen Generation' as lived by young Clare, the novel explains her subsequent political militancy as she seeks to improve the condition of Aboriginal people. The Aboriginal title, which means 'unity', strongly evokes Clare's desire to bring her people together.

The Australasian genre

From the 1970s, Australia turned towards Asia and the Pacific region and this gave birth to the Australasian genre with Christopher Koch* as one of its forerunners. With the implementation of the White Australia Policy in 1901 and its Immigration Restriction Act, coloured people, especially Asians, were ill-accepted and faced open hostility if they wanted to settle on

Panoramic view of Christopher Koch

Christopher John Koch was born in 1932 in Hobart, Tasmania, to an Anglican mother and a Catholic father. His Anglo-Irish and Germanic background strongly influenced the themes, actions and narratives in his novels. His typical protagonist is a Westerner trying to find, by every means possible, an 'otherworld' that is sublimated, imagined or idealised.

The Boys in the Island (1958) is, in the tradition of first novels, a story of discovery. *Across the Sea Wall* (1965) marks the start of an enduring interest in Asia, noticeable in *The Year of Living Dangerously* (1978). This third book tells the story of Guy Hamilton, an Australian journalist sent to Jakarta to write about the Indonesian political crisis taking place at the beginning of the 1960s. This novel was ineligible for the Miles Franklin since its content was not sufficiently Australian. With *The Doubleman* (1985), Koch explores the multiple possibilities of the imagination, but he reverts to the historical novel with *Highways to a War* (1995). Michael Langford, a big-hearted quixotic journalist, travels through Asia in search of scoops, often risking his life. The companion novel *Out of Ireland* (1999) has another idealist as its hero, Robert Devereux, who is sentenced to exile for sedition. He is expelled from Ireland to carry out his punishment first in the Bermudas and then in Van Diemen's Land (Tasmania). Obsessively concerned with the imperceptible, Koch feels that our minds and lives can only be expanded by embracing the invisible. Hence his exploration of the nature of secrecy and spying in *The Memory Room* (2007). With his farewell novel, *Lost Voices* (2012), Koch is on his home territory, grounding his narrative in the Hobart of the 1950s where the proximity of the convict days becomes a haunting past.

Koch received a number of prizes for his novels, which are infused with a conservative ideology. Although he was largely ignored by academic critics as a result of his egoistical personality and strong opposition to university orthodoxy, tributes flowed when he died in his home town in 2013.

Australian soil. Multiculturalism, which had originated in 1966 then intensified in 1973 under Prime Minister Gough Whitlam, sounded the death knell to this racist government policy, which was scrapped officially in 1978. Since then, there has been what some call 'the Asianisation' of Australia with a fad for Eastern culture and a burgeoning of Australian travel stories in which the main action takes place in Asia. Christopher Koch paved the way for his contemporaries with the publication of *Across the Sea Wall* and *The Year of Living Dangerously*. Some fifteen years later, *Highways to a War* strengthened this attitude. From then on, Asia was popular in the Antipodes and became a source of inspiration for many intellectuals, of whom Nicholas Jose is perhaps the most prominent.

Until the first half of the twentieth century, Asia had been neglected in Australian literature. It either had a passing mention in travel stories or was relegated to illustrations and settings in other genres. When it did appear in a minor way, Asia was absorbed, along the lines of the classical Orientalist cliché, into the female stereotype of seductress (an exotic Asia, seducing tourists) or into a destroyer (hell in the jungle for Western soldiers). This was later skilfully taken up by Koch in *The Year of Living Dangerously* (1978) and *Highways to a War* (1995) in which Indonesia and Cambodia represent much more than settings. In *Across the Sea Wall* (1965), twenty-three-year-old Robert O'Brien decides to travel by boat to England with his best friend James Baden. On the way, they stop off in Colombo and travel across India with the help of a native guide. After a few setbacks, Robert returns home. Koch's originality is to show with this book that Asia really has more to offer than being just a transit place for young Australians heading off to Europe. In providing an exotic atmosphere and a situation suitable for introspection, it tends to reveal the strengths and weaknesses in those who take the trouble to spend time there.

Asia is Koch's preferred locale, as shown in his third novel *The Year of Living Dangerously*. This is a literary jewel that brought the author international fame and success by introducing the character of the journalist as a privileged observer of a foreign society. Indonesia, more than just an exotic setting, becomes for the protagonist Guy Hamilton the stage for multiple political manipulations, intrigues and power games that reach their fever pitch in a bloodbath during the Indonesian communist insurrection of 1965 and the subsequent fall of President Sukarno. The popular and critical success of the novel was such that it was adapted for the screen by Peter Weir (1982) and for the theatre by Andrew Ross (1999) – evidence of its universal scope.

Koch influenced his contemporaries, such as Robert Drewe who published *A Cry in the Jungle Bar* (1978, location: Manila), followed soon after by Blanche D'Alpuget who wrote *Monkeys in the Dark* (1980, location: Indonesia) and *Turtle Beach* (1981, location: Malaysia); Ian Moffitt with *The Retreat of Radiance* (1982, location: China); Janette Turner Hospital followed suit with *The Ivory Swing* (1982, location: India); then it was Margaret Jones' turn with *The Smiling Buddha* (1985, location: Khamla, an imaginary country in South-East Asia) and Rod Jones with *Julia Paradise* (1986, location: Shanghai); not forgetting R.F. Brissenden who wrote *Poor Boy* (1987, location: Thailand). In 1995 with *Highways to a War*, Koch explored Asia further with the wanderings of Michael Langford, an Australian journalist in Singapore, Thailand and Cambodia. After Langford's disappearance in April 1976 in a Khmer Rouge-infested Cambodia, his childhood friend Raymond Barton tries to reconstruct and record his life. Most of these Australian-born writers drew from their experiences as journalists to form their white protagonists' characters as observers and commentators. Their initiation journey in Asia, often motivated by professional imperatives, rapidly takes on the appearance of a spiritual quest set against an exotic background. *The Memory Room* (2007), set in part in China, confirms Koch's return to the Australasian genre with espionage as a backdrop. It interweaves the destinies of journalist Erika Lange and Vincent Austin, who works for the secret service.

As Robin Gerster observes in *Hotel Asia: An anthology of Australians travelling in the 'East'*, travel stories published from the end of the 1970s onwards follow an archetypal pattern that can be summarised as follows: after the first scene at the airport and once in Asia, the characters are taken aback by a heightened awareness of their senses (especially sight and smell). They are confronted with poverty, insecurity and poor hygiene, the cause of serious infections. The characters are victims of erroneous perceptions that are corrected throughout their initiation. It is commonplace in this genre to have a journalist as the protagonist seeking to elucidate the mysteries of Asia, but ending up being part of a small group of expatriates. These Westerners sustain stereotypes such as the submissive exotic woman, or Asia as a dissolute and libertine paradise, a quasi-official refuge for sexual deviants. In literature, the East becomes a space at once exotic and erotic, where the sky is the limit. As a result of a phallocentric view of the world that addresses the fantasies of patriarchal societies, the representation of Asia – a place for all obsessions and perversions – is a large domain of females waiting, and wanting, to be dominated by hyperactive, virile Western men (the men in *The Year of Living Dangerously* are described as 'sex-starved').

In her study *The Yellow Lady: Australian impressions of Asia*, Alison Broinowski lists the clichés in Australian stories set in Asia. First of all, there is culture shock on arrival, descriptions of odours, crowds and colours; then there is a guide and a quest inland and/or the climbing up of a mountain followed by the hero's self-revelation; a brief affair with an exotic woman, and, finally, the return home. Faithful to his dichotomies, Koch gives the reader a double representation of Asia, a continent that evokes in the Australian imagination both fascination and repulsion. One of the faces of Asia – the mask of illusion, as it were – is a creature of seduction taken straight from the Western romantic vision. Adorned with resplendent flowers of an exotic nature stirring up the curiosity of tourists, the feminisation of Asia presented as an allegory of the *femme fatale* is not lost on the perceptive reader. To incite the most libertine fantasies, Asia, even if at first it is impenetrable, inaccessible and appears mysterious to the foreigner, ends up being exhibited and inviting concupiscence. The other face of Asia is one of an aggressive gargantuan monster that swallows or mutilates (semi-)Westerners who dare to defy her. In this context, climate becomes a fearsome weapon. The scorching heat fuels this overwhelming power which, while it does not completely overcome the foreigners, drives them into insanity.

In the last half-century Asia and Australia have moved closer. Australia has a substantial population of Asian background, and many aspects of Asian life have become familiar. Fiction has reflected those changes, with new voices and new literary approaches characterising Asian and Pacific Australian fiction.*

Literary multiculturalism

While Australia is now defined as a nation of migrants, the typical Australian protagonist in novels up until 1965 was confined to the ethnospecific values that were in current use until 1945, when 90 percent of pre-Second World War immigrants were British. Until then, any individual who mastered the English language, willingly espoused British traditions and had an ancestor from the British Isles, was the epitome of the average Australian. Multiculturalism put an end to this Anglomorphism.

In the multicultural era, immigrant writers wanted to share their vision of the human condition. While each work has its own specificity, there are, nevertheless, a number of common themes embodied in this 'literary multiculturalism', to use Xavier Pons's phrase. They are: experiences of dislocation, the journey, culture shock, the difficulties of integration, the mastery of a new language to understand the adopted culture and so on. The importance of language is a key concern of the Romanian-Greek Antigone Kefalá in her writings, two stories grouped together in *First Journey* (1975) and *The Island* (published much later in 1984).

Low-angle shot of Asian and Pacific Australian fiction

The Pacific war brought Australians into direct contact with the Asian and Pacific countries in Australia's region, and from this experience some informed fictional accounts emerged. George Johnston's *The Far Road* (1962), which focuses on two correspondents covering the Sino-Japanese war in 1944, is among the best. The 1960s saw a new generation of Australians travel in Asia and the relaxation of migration controls saw Asian migration to Australia, in large numbers from Indochina in the 1970s and from China in the 1980s and 90s. Novels of cross-cultural experience have developed, written from the inside, with a stress on social change and conflict, individual identity and the problems of moving through different worlds. Examples include the Vietnam war novel *My Name is Tian* (1968) by Korean-born Don'o Kim, the Vogel-winning *Birds of Passage* (1983) by Brian Castro, in which a modern Chinese-Australian revisits the racist treatment of his ancestors in Australia's past, and *Visitants* (1979), Randolph Stow's harrowing multi-vocal drama of a patrol officer's death in Papua New Guinea. In *The Hamilton Case* (2003) and the Miles Franklin winning *Questions of Travel* (2012), Michelle de Kretser adapts material from her native Sri Lanka into a complex interplay of narrative viewpoints. Nicholas Jose moves between past and present in relation to China in *Avenue of Eternal Peace* (1989) and *The Red Thread* (2000), as does Ouyang Yu in *The Eastern Slope Chronicle* (2002). Yu's work moves critically between Australia and China. Migration (from Singapore) is a theme for Hsu-ming Teo in *Love and Vertigo* (1999). Indian-born Aravind Adiga, partly educated in Australia, won the Booker Prize with *The White Tiger* (2008), controversial for its sharp social critique. Merlinda Bobis's *The Solemn Lantern Maker* (2008) depicts political corruption in the Philippines with an insider's knowledge. *The World Waiting to be Made* (2000) by Perth-based Simone Lazaroo opens up the possibility of new, hybrid personal identities and relationships. The multiple viewpoint that characterises much Asian and Pacific Australian fiction is apparent in story cycles too, the most celebrated of which is *The Boat* (2008) by Nam Le.

In these works, Kefalá portrays an alienated young European in search of answers to existential questions.

Among the immigrant novelists, there is the Russian-born Judah Waten who is still famous for *Alien Son* (1952), 'a kind of novel without architecture' that evokes his childhood memories. While it is true that he tried his hand at the novel in the 1950s, he wrote most of his literary works after 1965. His most multicultural novel is *So Far No Further* (1971) which deals with Jewish and Italian immigration. The Austrian-Italian Pino Bosi should also be mentioned. His arrival in Australia in 1951 was the inspiration for *Australia Cane* (1971), published in his native tongue and dealing with Italian immigration to Australia in the 1950s. A similar case is that of Walter Adamson, whose novel was originally published in German in 1974 and then translated into English as *The Institution* (1976). Manfred Jurgensen is also the author of a novel in German *Wehrersatz* (1978), published in English in the 1980s. The Yugoslav anthropologist Sreten Bozic, who signed his books with the Aboriginal name of B. Wongar, evokes in *The Trackers* (1978) the surrealistic experience of an Asian who wakes up one day in the skin of a black man, thus bringing an external view to European culture in Australia. To these can be added Korean Don'o Kim, author of novels about Asian culture, like *My Name is Tian* (1968) and *Password* (1974) and Malaysian born Beth Yahp who arrived in Australia in 1984 and wrote her way to fame with her award-winning story *The Crocodile Fury* (1992). Largely set in Malaysia, these tales that the author recalled from her grandmother and then fictionalised met international success when translated into many languages.

The new generation of novelists today has a considerable number of writers of non-Anglo-Celtic background. A few names to note are: Sophie Masson, who is French; Ania Walwicz, Polish; Bangladeshi writer Adib Khan and the Austrian Renate Yates who specialises in social satire. Others born in Australia between two cultures, like David Malouf with his Lebanese ancestry,

Morris Lurie whose family is Polish, Angelo Loukakis with Greek ancestry and Christopher Cyrill who evokes his Indian culture in his first book *The Ganges and its Tributaries* (1993), willingly draw the ethnic inspiration of their novels from their individual cultural heritage. Immigration and hybrid identity remain at the heart of authors' concerns in the postmodern era, as in the case of Portugese/Chinese/English Brian Castro with *Birds of Passage* (1983) and of Eva Sallis, whose novels *Hiam* (1998), *The City of Sealions* (2002), *Mahjar* (2003) and *The Marsh Birds* (2005) pay tribute to her adoptive Arab Islamic culture.

This literary multiculturalism, which colours the pages of Australian literature with exoticism and injects new blood into the British culture, paved the way for a redefinition of the Australian identity. It is the general view that these mixed and woven texts from a cosmopolitan tradition have contributed to the breaking up of the monolithic Anglo-Celtic identity, by creating a mosaic of individual writings. It has to be said, to qualify such praise of the diverse, that the ontological concerns and humanism shared by these novelists have contributed somewhat to smoothing out differences.

Feminisation of the novel: Heart matters

In the 1970s, women's writing was flourishing and prosperous. During the 1970s to the 1980s, the years of the Women's Liberation Movement in Australia, about ten independent feminist publishing houses appeared. As a consequence, the writing profession was fast becoming feminised. Thea Astley, Elizabeth Harrower, Jessica Anderson, Barbara Hanrahan, Shirley Hazzard, Helen Garner and Beverley Farmer are the great names of this prolific period. On the whole, women writers confined themselves to specific themes: relationships between couples, female identity, the family, the trauma of growing up, for example. Some cast a caustic eye on society, although tempered with a sentimental tone. Others, like Kerryn Higgs who signed *All That False Instruction* (1975) as

Elizabeth Riley, were considered staunch proponents of feminism.

In *Monkey Grip* (1977), Helen Garner saw female emancipation as a woman's right to use her body and enjoy her sexuality as she wished, even though the bohemian lifestyle of the female protagonist Nora has very little in common with that of the average woman. Unlike Garner, Thea Astley,* the doyenne of women writers of this period, painstakingly represented sexuality in her writings. According to her, performance is less important than the impulses of the heart. Astley was an exception since, strictly speaking, she did not play a part in the feminisation of the novel. In fact, it is difficult to place her with feminist writers as she never used a female protagonist, even though she often denounced domination, brutality and cruelty in a corrupt world governed by men. Astley deliberately made her narrative voice neutral so it would be taken as masculine.

Astley had already written four novels before Elizabeth Harrower published *The Watch Tower* (1966) in a satirical style. In this work, Harrower uses the classical image of marriage as a prison. Even at work, under the yoke of her demanding employer, Clare cannot escape male domination. In Harrower's work, the characters' psychology is as finely honed as in the writings of Christina Stead. Penelope Rowe is also interested in marital union, especially the impact that children can have on it, as depicted in *Dances for the Ducks* (1976). The institution of marriage is also one of Jessica Anderson's preoccupations – in particular in *Tirra Lirra by the River* (1978), a novel in which heroine Nora Porteous flees from an oppressive marriage, leaving Australia to live in London. Anderson continues her social satire with *The Impersonators* (1980). The reading of a patriarch's will is the catalyst for a plot that reveals the true nature of the characters, as human relationships are brought under close scrutiny. Another woman writer who criticised society is Barbara Hanrahan, who published ten novels between 1970 and 1980, with another published posthumously, *Good Night, Mr Moon* (1992). Her novels are rich in contrasting

Panoramic view of Thea Astley

Born in Brisbane in 1925, Thea Astley, who dreamed of being able to earn her living by writing, had to reconcile publishing novels with teaching until her retirement in 1980. In Australian literary history, she is the embodiment of a disconcerting paradox.

A prolific writer, she churned out her fictional works and gained generous critical success very early. (She is the only person to be awarded the Miles Franklin four times, with *The Well Dressed Explorer, The Slow Natives, The Acolyte* and *Drylands*.) But she was slow in becoming the subject of an academic study. Perhaps this is why she built her reputation outside Australia, notably in the United States.

Astley's works are heavily influenced by a feminist bent, whether it is with a cultivated protagonist, Elsie Ford, who deceives her uncouth lover in *Girl With a Monkey* (1958), or by denouncing situations in which vulnerable women are destroyed by men. For example, Robert Moller's seriously ill wife is openly subjected to adultery in *A Descant for Gossips* (1960). In *A Kindness Cup* (1974), a fleeing pregnant Aboriginal girl is pursued by a group of white men who force her to suicide by throwing herself into the void. Another example is *An Item From the Late News* (1982) in which men are portrayed as violent sadists, bestial and destructive.

In the 1980s, Astley started opting for female narrators to relate her stories, as seen in *An Item From the Late News, Reaching Tin River* (1990) and *Coda* (1994). Irony and social satire are present in all her eclectic works. *The Well Dressed Explorer* (1962) and *The Acolyte* (1972) are criticisms of two egotistical monsters: musician Holberg and Casanova George Brewster. *Beachmasters* (1985) is political fiction based on the insurrection by Jimmy Stevens in Vanuatu, which becomes the insurrection by Tommy Narota in Kristi. *It's Raining in Mango* (1987) is a historical novel that evokes the despoliation of the Aboriginal population. Her last novel *Drylands* was published in 1999.

themes and often open with a scene of orderly life that serves only as a façade for a corrupt world, as shown in her most famous novels *The Peach Groves* (1979) and *The Frangipani Gardens* (1980).

For Shirley Hazzard, the novel is an affair of the heart, of its vicissitudes and complexities throughout the world but rarely in Australia. Only a portion of her most remarkable novel of the period, *The Transit of Venus* (1980), takes place in Sydney. The events in *The Evening of the Holiday* (1966) and *The Bay of Noon* (1970) take place in Italy while her second book *People in Glass Houses* (1967) takes the reader to New York. In contrast to Hazzard, whose works are concerned thematically with female identity, Beverley Farmer treats the subject stylistically. According to Xavier Pons, Farmer demonstrated 'écriture féminine' by 'dramatising the self' in her first novel *Alone* (1980). Her writings are filled with emotions and testify to a fascination with water imagery, the female element *par excellence*. The feminist enterprise is carried on into the 1980s by novelists such as Elizabeth Jolley and Olga Masters with her two novels *Loving Daughters* (1982) and *Amy's Children* (1987).

Sex in text: The return of the repressed

In the 1970s, the loosening of the censorship laws allowed authors to be more daring if they wanted to broach the theme of sexuality. From then on, a libertine storm swept through the literary panorama opening up new perspectives; erotic literature expanded and some writers concerned with realism included explicit scenes of sexual relationships in their novels.

This relaxing of mores was used by authors such as Frank Moorhouse and Michael Wilding who wrote erotic stories for commercial gain and to assert their own sexuality. At the end of the 1960s, these authors, along with a few others, made up the 'Balmain group' taking up the name of the Sydney suburb. Michael Wilding accounts for an alternative lifestyle in his first novel *Living Together* (1974), while at the same time exploring in literature the full gamut of sexual practices.

It is difficult to consider Frank Moorhouse's narratives before 1993 as novels since the author repudiates the genre. Some of his collections of prose – *Futility and Other Animals* (1969), *The Americans, Baby* (1972) and *The Electrical Experience* (1974) – were subtitled 'discontinuous narratives', a concept taken from *The Salzburg Tales* (1934) by Christina Stead that linked the stories of various independent characters. For Moorhouse, individuals suffer mainly from isolation that they try unsuccessfully to temper with an intimate heterosexual or homosexual relationship.

The minority homosexual groups had to wait until the 1970s to have a voice in literature. Among the female authors who evoked lesbian relationships in their writing are Elizabeth Riley with *All That False Instruction* (1975); Elizabeth Jolley with *Palomino* (1980), the story of a love affair between sixty-year-old Laura and young Andrea, victim of an incestuous relationship with her brother; and Beverley Farmer, whose short novel *Alone* (1980) deals with relationships that are more sensual than sexual. It is interesting to note that *All That False Instruction: A Novel of Lesbian Love* was reedited in 2001 under the author's real name, Kerryn Higgs, and published in a different format. Higgs then set the action back in its initial context of Melbourne. The precautions of anonymity were taken in 1975 so that Higgs would not have to oppose her family in dispute proceedings, as they considered the subject highly sensitive. Male homosexual desire was also the subject of some novels of this period. *The Flesheaters* (1972), David Ireland's most daring work, partakes of this trend with its strong themes of cannibalism, sadism, perversion and transgression – themes that were later taken up by Christos Tsiolkas in his individual style in *Dead Europe* (2005). In this novel, the realistic narrative frays, allowing the fantastic to elaborate on reality by introducing the themes of vampirism and superstition.

Sexual ambiguity was a definite characteristic of the period, especially in the works of Patrick White and David Ireland.* By adopting an epicene first name for the narrator Lee Mallory,

Panoramic view of David Ireland

Born in 1927 in a Sydney suburb, David Ireland was the second Australian author to be awarded the Miles Franklin on three occasions. His complex modernist-style narratives disturb readers preferring classically structured stories. Narrators are self-effacing; a stream of characters makes it difficult for readers to identify with the hero (if there is one); the story refuses to be linear and the plot is subdivided. According to Ken Gelder, Ireland is a specialist of the 'atomic novel', fragmentary in nature, that goes against the conventions of the genre. It is unwise to place one's confidence in the narratives of this writer, whose imagination sets out to disconcert the reader. An admirer of novelist Machado de Assis, Ireland experimented with the novel genre throughout his life.

Included in his works are regional stories that take place in Sydney or in New South Wales: *The Unknown Industrial Prisoner* (1971), *The Glass Canoe* (1976), *The City of Women* (1981) and *The Chosen* (1997). He also makes attempts at transmutation when he places himself in the skin of a woman, Alethea Hunt, in *A Woman of the Future* (1979), then of a dog in *Archimedes and the Seagle* (1984). *The Chantic Bird* (1968) and *The Flesheaters* (1972) evoke gloomy predatory universes; then there are more conventional novels like *Burn* (1974), which focuses on the Aboriginal community, and the autobiographically inspired *Bloodfather* (1987).

Helen Daniel asserts that Ireland's novels 'are built on a battle of structures, between the urge to order and the disorder of reality which refuses to be contained in the tidy structures we erect around it'. It is true that the author enjoys upsetting society's conventions in order to question the contemporary world in an incisive and uncompromising way. As a result, the heretical content of *A Woman of the Future*, *The Flesheaters* and *The Glass Canoe* came up against puritanical Australian censorship.

While certain critics have noted a certain quality of pessimism or nihilism in Ireland's dystopias, the tone of *The Glass Canoe* is enlightened by humorous eloquence.

Ireland suggests androgyny and bisexuality in *The Flesheaters* (1972). White, in his later works, displays less restraint in evoking alternate forms of eroticism traditionally overshadowed by heterosexuality. *The Twyborn Affair* (1979), his most audacious novel, unambiguously evokes homosexuality and transvestism. The reader follows the evolution of a polymorphous protagonist with multiple identities. In the first part, Eudoxia is presented as the catamite of the sixty-year-old Greek Angelos Vatatzes. In the second part, Eudoxia becomes the bisexual Eddie Twyborn, a jackaroo on a farm who seduces the owner's wife Marcia Lushington and the manager Don Prowse, before taking the form of Eadith Trist, madam of a London brothel. The sexuality of this protean figure, though briefly evoked, is yet described in detail because, to take up David Coad's argument, far from seeking to provoke readers, sexuality is rather indicative of the protagonist's psychology and Oedipus complex. To some extent, *The Twyborn Affair* partakes of the representation of traditionally invisible alternative models of sexuality in literature and which, according to Robert Dessaix, have been given topicality in the 1980s and 1990s due to a loosening of sexual repression. In the 1970s, Australian society gradually came to an acceptance of same-sex desire: homosexuality has been decriminalised throughout the various states in fits and starts from 1975 till 1997, starting in South Australia and ending with Tasmania. The themes of homosexuality and transvestism which White tackled earlier in his fiction are now taking centre stage and fused with identity concerns, even though the author did not intend his novel to be a piece of queer activism. Judging from David Marr's official biography, the discreet White has never been interested in queer activism and never got involved in the Gay Rights Movement.

Finally, for some novelists like Gerald Murnane, characters are governed by their desire and sexual drives. In *Tamarisk Row* (1974), adolescent Clement Killeaton explores his budding sexuality, a theme taken up again in *A Lifetime on Clouds* (1976), which depicts the emotions and sexual fantasies of Adrian Sherd, a young man from Melbourne, scarcely older than Clement, with an obviously strong interest in masturbation. Inhibited by an overly strict Catholic education, Adrian takes refuge in a fantasy world (a lustful America, union with Denise McNamara and priesthood) to assuage the force of his sexual drive. Helen Garner's *Monkey Grip* (1977) contains several more explicit passages about heterosexual relationships. A precursor of what is called 'grunge' fiction, Garner's debut novel neatly separates sexuality and love, according to Ken Gelder. At the end of her search for love, the protagonist Nora is demoralised and depersonalised, admitting that she sees her 'body as an object, and an unsatisfactory one at that'. Garner's audacity lies also in her choice of crude words that would most certainly shock some readers. *Puberty Blues* (1979), co-authored by Gabrielle Carey and Kathy Lette, transposes the grunge spirit, with its consumption of illicit substances and random sexual encounters, to the surfing beach culture usually depicted as an essentially male-oriented institution. This feminist novel is a classic account of adolescent sexual emancipation. In *Puberty Blues*, Debbie and Sue mix with a group of adolescent boys they revere as the kings of the glide of Greenhill Beach until they decide, much to the boys' displeasure, to break the male monopoly by trying to surf.

This generation of writers allowed the following generation to evoke sexuality freely without fearing censorship nor offending the reader's sensitivity. Erotic and grunge fiction capitalised on the libertarian trend by giving more than its due to the sex act through pornographic descriptions. This is how some female writers, like Nikki Gemmell who published *The Bride Stripped Bare* (2003) anonymously and Peta Spear, author of *Libertine* (1999), spiced up their romances.

Shortlisted for the Miles Franklin Award and written in a fluid and elegant style, Rod Jones's *Nightpictures* (1997) shares some striking similarities with the author's internationally successful debut novel *Julia Paradise*: a mental patient involved with a professional of the mind, incestuous desires, psychoanalytic culture, a clever twist and deceitful appearances. *Nightpictures* tells the story of Dieppe, a dark female character, who is having a bizarre non-committal affair with an Australian expat nicknamed Sailor, teaching at the Oxford School in Venice. Male sexuality, largely depicted as imperious, animalistic and performance-driven, is meant to address Dieppe's incestuous fantasies until narrator-cum-protagonist Sailor makes a terrible mistake. He cements the division of love and sex with emotional attachment and falls head over heels in love with his enigmatic and arousing sex friend. By mingling the erotic and the Gothic in *Libertine* (1999), Spear tells the wartime story of a manipulative prostitute who has a regular 'fuck-buddy', known as The General, and a lover named Sol. Unlike its representation in *Nightpictures*, sex does not purport to be an end in itself in *Libertine*. In the eyes of Peta Spear, sex – when not a commercial transaction – epitomises the intensity of life and becomes a means to indulge in an emotional embrace.

At the beginning of the 1990s, queer studies were still not as popular in Australia as in the United States. Queer studies explore relationships that are not sufficiently widespread to be integrated into the norm: homosexual, bisexual and transgender. These studies, a direct result of the gay liberation movement, emphasise the flexible, fluctuating character of human identity. Aesthetic representations in relation to queer theory seek to shake prejudices about identity, sexuality and power relationships. The Australian novel became impregnated with this ideology as it entered the postmodern era.

CHAPTER 6

Postmodernism and New Tendencies (1981 onwards)

Poetry, which had been extremely popular in the 1960s and 1970s, was replaced at the start of the 1980s by the novel as the dominant literary form. Faithful to the postcolonial trend, novelists on the margin of the European literary tradition constructed their works according to a new set of values: fictional characters faced ontological uncertainty; literary categories blended, sometimes to the point of confusion, to produce hybrid stories which elude classification; commonly accepted historical allusions were contested and the 'hero' was supplanted by a central character with modest ambitions and almost non-existent charisma.

The Australian novel was renewed by a generation of new novelists like Brian Castro, Luke Davies, Richard Flanagan, Janette Turner Hospital, Antoni Jach, Julia Leigh, Andrew McGahan, Anthony Macris, Alex Miller, Eva Sallis (a.k.a. Eva Hornung), Mandy Sayer, Christos Tsiolkas, Tim Winton and Alexis Wright, as well as long-established authors who competed with creative originality, such as Murray Bail, Peter Carey, David Ireland, Christopher Koch, David Malouf, Frank Moorhouse, Gerald Murnane and Michael Wilding. This new generation of writers attempted to produce novels while at university. They either published their manuscript written as part of the requirements of a Creative Writing program – as was the case for Tim Winton with his first book *An Open Swimmer* (1982) and Philip Salom with his second novel entitled *Toccata and Rain* (2004) – or they would teach creative writing at university like Carmel Bird, Brian Castro, Janette Turner Hospital, Antoni Jach, Nicholas Jose, Sallie Muirden, Sue Woolfe, and many more.

The adventure of the novel and flourishing imaginations

Some novelists who made a name for themselves in the 1970s confirmed their imaginative capacities for renewal by revisiting the conventional aspects of the novel to come up with original stories. The four storytellers often grouped together for their strong interest in the mind and its capacity for creative representation are Gerald Murnane, Peter Carey, David Ireland and, pre-eminent among them, Christopher Koch. His concept of 'Otherland', a secret alterity to discover, elaborated in *The Boys in the Island* (1958) returns in *The Doubleman* (1985) in the form of 'Otherworld'. With this fourth novel, Koch comes back to his native land to retrace events following the stages in the life of his main character Richard Miller, from early adolescence to maturity. The novel, which reads like a modern fairy tale, reveals the exponential possibilities of the creative imagination to flee from reality. Struck down with poliomyelitis as a child, young Miller develops a fertile imagination in hospital and throughout his convalescence, which helps him compensate for his impaired mobility.

Common to Gerald Murnane* and Christopher Koch's fantasy-packed worlds is the male protagonist's ability to withdraw into his imagination in order to experience soothing pleasure. For the main characters, the less than satisfying reality vies with an enticing otherness whose charms and strength lie in the unprovable and, therefore, irrefutable nature of its existence. *The Plains* (1982) is the closest a utopian novel can get to Thomas More's *Utopia*: emphasis is on the collective and not the individual, which explains why the

Panoramic view of Gerald Murnane

Born in 1939 in Melbourne, Gerald Murnane has written short stories, essays and seven novels: *Tamarisk Row* (1974) and *A Lifetime of Clouds* 1976) are semi-autobiographical *Bildungsromane* while *The Plains* (1982) and *Inland* (1988) are two metafictional pieces that explore the role of the artist and creation. A great stylist and master of the minimalistic use of words, Murnane is interested in the power of language, in representations of reality, exploration of the conscience and the search for a hidden truth lodged in dreams, memory and meditation. The essentially contemplative nature of his works is derived from this. Influenced by Marcel Proust, Thomas Hardy, Emily Brontë and James Joyce, Murnane wrote novels that are true static odysseys of the conscience with almost no action.

According to critic Imre Salusinszky, Murnane produces monomaniacal writing and 'has the courage of his own obsessions' which he pursues in his novels. His preferred subjects include: exile, the nature of reality, the interweaving of the real with the imaginary, the contiguity of interior and exterior dimensions, the questioning of the reality of our sensitive world, the connection between perception and description, and the conditioning of male sexuality, among others. In her book entitled *Liars: Australian new novelists*, Helen Daniel places Murnane among the writers she has identified as 'liars'. The others are Frank Moorhouse, Peter Mathers, Nicholas Hasluck, Murray Bail, Peter Carey, Elizabeth Jolley, David Foster and David Ireland. As well as the theme of mendacity and their interest in deceiving, what these writers have in common is an aesthetic of fragmentation and heterogeneity where the stories are perceived mainly as literary constructions opening up new vistas on reality.

Murnane, who stopped writing in the 1990s, recently started publishing metafictional novels again. *Barley Patch* (2009), *A History of Books* (2012) and *A Million Windows* (2014) are illustrative of the accretion technique he uses to build up his oeuvre, each new novel incorporating fragments from earlier ones. He received the Patrick White Award in 1999 and an Australia Council Emeritus Writer's Award in 2008.

narrative is devoid of sexual allusions; the novel is more idea- than character-driven; and it features what American literary critic Fredric Jameson calls an 'anonymous bliss'.

While the short stories *The Fat Man in History* (1974) and *War Crimes* (1979) offer readers a taste of Peter Carey's original and truculent style, *Illywhacker* (1985) demonstrates the full gamut of his imagination. His propensity for exploiting the bizarre and the sordid in his slightly allegorical stories has him labelled a fabulist. Carey's talent lies in his capacity to create a subtle mix of realism and surrealism that challenges the reader to question human nature. *Illywhacker* is a novel that, in Dionysian style, reveals a fertile, free-flowing imagination. Although it missed out on being awarded the Booker Prize, this novel gave Peter Carey's career an international impetus. It is a picaresque narrative about three generations of Australians told by a self-confessed pathological liar who admits his mendacity at the outset. Like Epimenides and his liar's paradox, Herbert Badgery shamelessly confesses to being 'a hundred and thirty-nine years old' and to being 'a terrible liar'. This unreliable narrator, nevertheless, accounts for a century and a half of Australian history: from the 1850s gold rush years with the lynching of the Chinese at Lambing Flat, the shearers' strike in the 1890s, the Great War, the arrival of aviation in Australia with the celebrated Charles Ulm, the Great Depression, the Second World War, right up to contemporary Australia. Herbert fits into the tradition of the picaroon, a pariah searching to belong and living by his wits, constantly on the move from place to place. His lies entertain the reader, who is invited 'to relax and enjoy the show'. During his richly eventful life, Herbert meets many colourful people, all experts at lying. *Pets* was the original title for this six-hundred page epic that culminates in the poetic metaphor of 'the Best Pet Shop in the World', representing the multicultural ghettoisation of the country. Domestication as a theme is omnipresent in *Illywhacker*, as it illustrates the postcolonial condition of Australians who, according to Carey, have 'historically ... mostly behaved as pets'. After being under British protection for several decades, Australians finally turned to the United States in 1941 knowing that they could be relied on for protection, before giving in to the Japanese economic conquest. If the author refuses this subjugation, it is because notions of dependency, servility and passivity inherent in domesticity restrain the creative imaginations of his compatriots.

Not to be outdone in originality, David Ireland wrote an audacious novel, to say the least, entitled *Archimedes and the Seagle* (1984). The story, which does not lack humour, is told by – believe it or not – a red setter dog. After all, why not go against fictional conventions that have a story told from the viewpoint and with the voice of a person? Here David Ireland claims his right to poetic licence.

As a rival in boldness, Antoni Jach experimented with the novel to see if a writer could entertain by evoking boredom. This Melburnian of Polish descent made the tedium of daily life the subject of his first novel, a veritable challenge for any writer who knows that action-packed novels usually become bestsellers. Published at the time when the republican debate was prevalent in Australia and before the 1999 referendum confirmed Australia's attachment to the British Crown, *The Weekly Card Game* (1994) explores the dynamics between changelessness and the willingness to change with a sociological study of Australia as backdrop. The story begins fifteen years earlier when Bernard Poe and his mates, Harry, Tim and Roger, congregated on a Friday evening around their first weekly card game. Vying with her husband, Dolores organised high-flown discussions every Monday for her friends. Employing a neutral tone and minimalist style, the novelist shows, with sardonic humour and a keen eye for everyday details, which is peculiar to the Nouveau Roman, how an Australian couple gradually fall into a weekly suburban routine that acts as an ennui-proof cocoon. From one ritual to another, Mr and Mrs Poe cram their social schedule with a range of activities they repeat *ad nauseam* week in, week out until, after several years, they suggest 'the possibility of a change'. Readers can listen to Antoni Jach's bittersweet symphony while their hearing is made more acute by the distress of their own humdrum lives. The author further erodes the qualities of the traditional novel with *The Layers of the City* (1999), an erudite novel that places Paris at the centre of a story devoid of plot (as it is classically understood) and characters. Jach's omniscient narrator is a *flâneur* who explores the topographical meanders of the City of Lights. While contradicting the Jamesian adage that the writer must show and not tell, this book gives the feeling that there is a universal plan in which chance plays no part. The neo-baroque *Napoleon's Double* (2007), the plot of which takes place in Europe and Australia, is a scholarly graphic novel influenced by the ideas of Pascal, Spinoza, Voltaire, Rousseau, Borges, Lacan and Alain Badiou. The illustrations in this novel allow Jach to stimulate the conscience, titillating the reader with questions about the nature of the novel and its capacity or incapacity to represent things adequately.

Some creative writers like Alan Wearne challenged the idea that novels should be in prose. Written in verse form, *The Nightmarkets* (1986) is Wearne's endeavour to emulate poet Les Murray's highly original work, *The Boys Who Stole the Funeral* (1980). Murray's 140-sonnet verse novel relates the story of two boys who steal the body of an old soldier from the morgue and take him back to his native land. With *The Nightmarkets*, Wearne develops a stanza-structured story that chronicles Melburnian life in the 1960–1980s, as well as the historical and political events that marked the lives of the characters Ian Metcalfe and Sue Dobson. In this work, the use of stream of consciousness places it within Joycean-style modernism.

What if the novel were only in prose? Would the form be more easily identifiable? We cannot be so sure when we read *The Orchard* (1994) by Drusilla Modjeska. This hybrid book sits somewhere between an essay and a novel by combining, in jumbled order, fact, fiction, biography, myth and essay. Its syncretism of genres disturbs the literary critic by making categorisation difficult. This method was also deftly used by the 2003 Nobel Prize winner John Maxwell Coetzee (known commonly as J.M. Coetzee) when he wrote *Elizabeth Costello*, his first Australian-inspired book. Originally from South Africa, Coetzee has lived in Adelaide since 2002 and became an Australian citizen in 2006. He amazes the reader with a series of eight didactic pieces that are essays rather than novels. His literary device of inserting philosophical documents reminds us of *Sophie's World* (1995) by Jostein Gaarder. The sixty-year-old eponym is an Australian woman writer who travels the world delivering her knowledge through a series of lectures incorporated in the narrative of *Elizabeth Costello*.

In *True History of the Kelly Gang*, Peter Carey* indulges in a ventriloquist act that results in an ungrammatical colloquial narration with minimal punctuation. This is a device that, all things considered, does not overly disconcert readers, who unconsciously reconstruct the linguistic orthodoxy while reading. The novel was awarded the 2003 French prize for the Meilleur Livre Étranger (the best foreign book). Ania Walwicz also tried challenging the content of the traditional novel with *Boat* (1989) and *Red Roses* (1992), two pieces that deconstruct traditionally accepted syntax and grammar in order to oppose the formality of linguistics and, more importantly, the many forms of authority. In this way, language fails to accurately mirror the fragmented and diffracted reality of the postmodern era.

The effect of fragmentation comes across as a structural element in *Diary of a Bad Year* (2007) by Coetzee. Inspired by postmodernism, this singular work relates the story of a highly celebrated South African writer who has immigrated to Australia and is introduced as 'C' (for Coetzee?). Paradoxically, this seventy-year-old, who was invited to write for a collection of essays entitled *Strong Opinions*, opposes postmodernism. In a subplot, the reader learns of the burning desire he has for Filipina Anya although she

Panoramic view of Peter Carey

Born in 1943 in Bacchus Marsh in Victoria and trained in advertising, Peter Carey was noticed in the 1970s for his unbridled imagination expressed in disturbing and anti-authoritarian short stories. A writer who keeps moving forward and avoiding well-worn paths, the majority of his novels are born of an original idea that he fleshes out. Among his Australiana narratives, *Bliss* (1981) depicts the double resurrection of an advertising executive; *Illywhacker* (1985) is a family saga narrated by an arrant liar who claims to be 139 years old; *Oscar and Lucinda* (1988) relates a duel between two compulsive gamblers; *True History of the Kelly Gang* (2000) retraces the legend of Ned Kelly told by the bushranger himself; *My Life as a Fake* (2003) blends the Ern Malley hoax with the Frankenstein myth in order to probe creation; while *The Chemistry of Tears* (2012) is a story Carey concocted by stringing together disparate elements. Many novels straddle American and Australian cultures, as exemplified by *The Unusual Life of Tristan Smith* (1994) which shows the relationship between two imaginary countries that bear a strong resemblance to Australia and the United States. Alternating the voices of two brothers, Butcher and Hugh Bones, *Theft: A Love Story* (2006) pursues the theme of cheating within the artistic milieu with a two-voiced narrative which takes the action to Sydney, Tokyo and New York. *Parrot and Olivier in America* (2009) presents the Old World colliding with the New, and his latest novel *Amnesia* (2014) tells the story of an Australian journalist working on the biography of a notorious hacker who jeopardises the American prison system. *The Tax Inspector* (1991), a darker novel, tends to be seen as out of place in his *oeuvre*.

It seems that New York-based Carey tries to come to terms with the trauma of exile through his fiction, which often exploits the idea of being in two places and contains hard-to-pin-down characters without ties, like orphans, and displaced people, be they fugitives or exiled. His work, twice rewarded with the Booker Prize, has been the subject of several academic monographs and has gained international recognition.

is devoted to her lover Alan. Another subplot tells her life story. *Diary of a Bad Year* interweaves several plots and narrative voices that upset the established order of reading in such a way that a vertical reading is still possible when Coetzee invites us to read horizontally from one page to the next.

If the postmodern bent of writers like Peter Carey, David Ireland and Gerald Murnane is clear, it is even more so in the works of Michael Wilding and Murray Bail. Michael Wilding, the Australian David Lodge, has never hidden his interest in postmodernism and post-structuralism by questioning the relationship between language and reality. In his most metafictional novel, *Wildest Dreams* (1998), for example, Wilding includes himself in the narrative by telling of the rise and fall of a writer who is part of the Sydney literary scene and comments on the influence that high-profile international writers have had on his writing. *Academia Nuts* (2002) is a metanarrative about the tribulations of Henry Lancaster, a lecturer specialising in how to write novels. *National Treasure* (2007) exposes the strange world of fiction writers and publishers.

Following the example of Michael Wilding, Murray Bail built his reputation with short stories as well as novels. *Homesickness* (1980), *Holden's Performance* (1987) and *Eucalyptus* (1998) are three allegorical works that obliquely offer a critique of Australian society. *Homesickness* shows how a feeling of national identity is in fact an artificial undertaking. *Holden's Performance* illustrates a society governed by a system of concocted values, while *Eucalyptus*, which won the Miles Franklin and the Commonwealth Writers' Prize, is based on the archetypal structure of a fairy story to denounce an oppressive patriarchy. In this story, Mr Holland and his only daughter settle on a property in western New South Wales. Because Ellen is a beautiful sexually mature young woman who attracts men, the patriarch – with a passion for eucalyptus and wanting to keep his daughter to himself – imposes a quasi-chivalry test on suitors seeking permission to marry her. The challenge is to show that the person is the father's equal in being able to identify and correctly name all the species of eucalypts. This ecological novel is structured in rhizomes whose ramifications give rise to anecdotes, short stories and digressions.

Literary frauds and identity feuds

In the influential sphere of postmodernism, no one should be surprised to see the authorship of novels questioned as a result of dishonest identity games. The first literary deception in Australia could be traced back to the Ern Malley affair which perhaps dealt the final blow to the modernist movement. In the 1944 autumn volume of *Angry Penguins*, a request by Ethel Malley to publish sixteen poems with the title 'The Darkening Ecliptic', a work by her dead brother Ernest Lalor Malley whom she presented as an efficient insurance salesman, attracted the attention of the editor-in-chief Max Harris. He enthusiastically included the poems in his journal. And they had good press! But a few weeks later, the *Sunday Sun* discovered the fraud and denounced it as the brainchild of two well-known poets and academics: James McAuley and Harold Stewart. There was no more an Ern Malley than an Ethel Malley. These jokers had spent an afternoon in October 1943 compiling all the newspapers and books within reach and selected at random a mixture of ludicrous sentences and trite quotations flirting with the absurd. They tried to prove that experimental *avant-garde* poetry verged on absurdity and that it was difficult to distinguish what was a product of art and what was the work of would-be poets. Max Harris was eventually charged with obscenity and the controversy went on for two decades. While Harris did not try to repudiate his editorial choices, he prophesied in his defence: '... time tells the story, and time will reveal that the myth is sometimes greater than its creator'. The classic illustration of this phenomenon is the Frankenstein myth that eclipsed its author Mary Shelley. As history continuously repeats itself, Ern Malley also left authors McAuley and Stewart behind in the dark. Though the seriousness of Australian criticism was strongly challenged through these stringent checks, the Malley hoax was beneficial in that it nourished literary creativity, such as by becoming the inspiration for Peter Carey's *My Life as a Fake*.

In *My Life as a Fake*, Ern Malley returns as Bob McCorkle. The story more or less runs along the same lines as the hoax. Sarah Wode-Douglass, head of a London journal of poetry, accepts a trip to Malaysia offered by John Slater, a renowned modernist poet with whom she has a somewhat strained relationship. Neglected by John in Asia, Sarah unexpectedly meets Australian Christopher Chubb, the unfortunate famous author of the hoax which had discredited David Weiss and his journal *Personae* in the 1940s, by making a collage of bits of sentences gleaned at random from readings and signed by an imaginary Bob McCorkle. The hoax aimed at eclipsing *avant-garde* poetry turned sour as the journal's editor was taken to court for obscenity. From then on, Peter Carey moves away from historical fact and elaborates on the plot. Wracked by shame, Weiss ends up committing suicide. Then to Chubb's great surprise, his invented character appears in the flesh. A man claiming to be the famous Bob McCorkle accuses Chubb of stealing his life and his work. In revenge, this man kidnaps Chubb's baby and disappears in South East Asia where he writes his brilliant manuscript 'My Life as a Fake'. When Chubb tries to catch Sarah's attention with Bob McCorkle's manuscript, he tells her of his life and the way in which his monstrous literary creation came back to haunt him and claim a past. Unable to give him a birth certificate and the childhood Bob so desperately wanted, Chubb pays dearly by pursuing this creature for fifteen years to find his daughter. When he finds McCorkle dying in Malaysia, he realises how futile his quest is and faces his adversary's superiority when he meets defeat. Chubb dies before selling Sarah the manuscript.

Other notable publications that used deceit and hoax as the bases of stories are *Double-Wolf* (1991) by Brian Castro and *The Hoax* (1997) by Sophie Masson.

Since the first literary fraud in 1944 with the Ern Malley Affair, which seemed to have discredited modernist poets, the Australian publishing world experienced a long period of lull before the storm in the 1990s when a new series of scandals fuelled interest in debates about author identities and the actual authors of texts. Such literary frauds, the most famous being the Demidenko affair,* were positive in more broadly questioning larrikinism as a distinctive trait of the Australian tradition, while giving way to postmodern ideology that emphasised chameleon identities. Following the example of Helen Demidenko/Darville's *The Hand That Signed the Paper* (1994), *Forbidden Love* (2003) is another fictitious story sold as being based on a real event. This hoax story by Norma Khouri was intended to be a poignant eye witness account of a victim's tragic story. The narrator, Norma, recounts how her best friend Dalia was executed by her own father for falling in love with a Christian. This autobiography was unexpectedly withdrawn from sales in July 2004 because of its falsified content. In fact, like *The Hand That Signed the Paper*, there would not have been a scandal if the author had written 'novel' on the title page.

In a long line of identity litigation, it was revealed that Marlo Morgan, who wrote *Mutant Message Down Under* (1994), was no more Aboriginal than Sreten Bozic, a Serbian writer who passed himself off as Banumbir Wongar – an Aboriginal man from Arnhem Land. In addition, the so-called young female novelist Wanda Koolmatrie was none other than a European man, Leon Carmen. Colin Johnson, who changed his name to Mudrooroo, also became a bone of contention in academic criticism adding to other literary frauds. Suspicion about his background was intense from 1965 until it was confirmed in 1996. This immediately divided the academic world. While some were ready to be charitable and put forward diverse motives, others could not disregard the author's dishonesty and condemned him to oblivion.

All things considered, Colin Johnson is reproached mainly

Close-up of the Demidenko affair

Australian criticism, which is occasionally inclined to dispense overly high praise, was led astray by the Demidenko scandal. *The Hand That Signed the Paper* received the Vogel Literary Award in 1993, a prize that brought the unpublished manuscript out of obscurity. Publishers Allen & Unwin were committed to publish the story in 1994. The following year, this purported autobiographical fiction, supposedly written by Helen Demidenko, was awarded the Miles Franklin by its committee in spite of the almost negligible aspects of Australian life in the story (the action takes place in Russia during the Second World War). Then it received the Australian Literature Society Gold Medal. The literary judges had cause to regret this, since accusations of anti-Semitism, a usurped identity and plagiarism were brought against Demidenko who was, in fact, Helen Darville.

At first, Darville enjoyed her impersonation when offering the media and readers a string of clichés intended to pay tribute to her Ukrainian culture. Many surprises were in store for her audience and revelations quickly followed. At first, Australians learnt that anti-Semitic ideas ran through the entire work; next, the author's identity was a fake: despite her claims, Helen was not the child of a Ukrainian immigrant but of English migrants Harry and Grace Darville. More seriously, Darville had to defend herself against accusations of plagiarism when it transpired that she had reproduced extracts from such writers as Thomas Keneally and Robyn Morgan. No matter how difficult it was to dispute these charges, Darville's lawyers managed to pass the borrowed excerpts off as a widespread postmodern practice. As a cunning illustration of this scandal, an Australian daily newspaper published a cartoon by Tandberg showing a man asking his librarian if she has read all the books on the shelf behind her. In reply, the librarian holds up Darville's novel and says: 'No, but I have read the abridged version'.

This affair, which was the source of a great deal of commentary, was beneficial in provoking debates about authorship, the status of fiction, ethics and literary judgement.

for his lack of legitimacy. This is the principal complaint made by the Aboriginal community, with Anita Heiss as its main representative. In her book *Dhuuluu-Yala: To talk straight* (2003), Heiss interprets the deceptive Aboriginality of Johnson as usurping Aboriginal cultural heritage, if not as a form of neo-colonialism. But this literary scandal poses the broader problem of representation rights. Should the representation of Aboriginal people be left exclusively to themselves? In other words, is it necessary to be Aboriginal to depict Aboriginal characters, their lifestyles or to evoke their culture? If so, let us be prepared to deprive Australian literature of some of its great titles like *The Chant of Jimmy Blacksmith* (1972) by Thomas Keneally, *The Savage Crows* (1976) by Robert Drewe, *The Seal Woman* (1992) by Beverley Farmer, *Remembering Babylon* (1993) by David Malouf, *The Custodians* (1997) by Nicholas Jose, *Serpent Dust* (1998) by Debra Adelaide, *Journey to the Stone Country* (2002) by Alex Miller, *Three Dog Night* (2003) by Peter Goldsworthy, *Wanting* (2008) by Richard Flanagan, and others. Should restrictions be made in other areas that would apply to ethnic groups? And why not forbid a man writing about female subjects or vice versa? Should we reproach Janette Turner Hospital for having slipped into a man's skin to be the narrator of *Borderlines* (1985) and J.M. Coetzee for giving his voice to the female protagonist in *Elizabeth Costello* (2003)? Perhaps David Ireland should have been prevented from adopting a dog's perspective as first-person narrator of *Archimedes and the Seagle* (1984).

For a few years, the establishment of protocols that were to be scrupulously followed seems to have found approval in the entire Aboriginal literary community. These protocols let Aboriginal people keep strict control of the representation of their people in literature. While they are instrumental in stopping any form of inexact representation (erroneous, caricatured, biased or partial) of the Aboriginal community, these protocols can hardly not be associated with a type of tacit censorship that silences non-Aboriginal writers who wish to express their views of Indigenous people. Perhaps the Aboriginal literary community does not subscribe to the concept of the novel genre as perceived by Western society: the novel as an alternative to reality, a world or mode of representations that generates dreams, fantasies and illusions. According to New Criticism, the reader has no more of a mission to seek truths in the literary text than the novelist has to expound them. Reducing the fictional literary text to a catalogue of counter-truths would be misunderstanding the verbal state of literature. The novel belongs to *fiction*, namely the mode of being of the non-true or the non-real, in contradistinction to the false, the fake, the counterfeit or the untrue, which are all antithetical to authenticity and truth.

The case of Colin Johnson is interesting in that he is irrefutable proof that a person can speak convincingly about things and conditions that are normally foreign to them. Although not of Aboriginal descent, he spoke about the community and its conditions and did not have to ask for permission to publish. Consequently, Anita Heiss' claims for representation rights are more political than literary. In line with political correctness, the proposed protocols represent a form of censorship to control authors' minds and their creativity. This pressure subjects the individual to the law of the collective and goes back to a commonly accepted Aboriginal view of literature, that is a means of expression that opens out onto the socio-political sphere to serve a community. Non-Aboriginal writers who depict Aboriginal conditions in their writings are reproached for possessing an incomplete knowledge of the culture, for placing token Aboriginal people in their stories, or for distorting their image. Certainly, freedom of expression can at times damage the content, but restricting expression carries just as many risks, if not more. These protocols seem to have hindered Aboriginal authors wishing to depart from their geographic and cultural concerns in order to liberate their expression.

The private sphere and the novel of introspection

The Australian private sphere is defined as much in terms of inclusion as exclusion, of rapprochement as distancing, of communication as non-communication. At the end of the 1960s, the Australian family began to disintegrate when feminism exposed serious family secrets: paedophilia, violence in marriages, family dramas, incest and so on.

The family is often the source of difficulties in the works of Elizabeth Jolley, a British writer who came to Western Australia in 1959 with her husband and three children. Her stories are often written like fables betraying an Oedipus relationship between father and daughter and a turbulent relationship with the mother. For example, in *My Father's Moon* (1989), Vera seduces her surrogate father and betrays her mother. Jolley's characters are often isolated, misfits whose fates are sealed when they end up in enclosed spaces, such as the retirement home in *Mr Scobie's Riddle* (1982) and the boarding house in *Milk and Honey* (1984). With Jolley, the sacrosanct private sphere shatters as a result of committing unnatural acts such as the sexual abuse of children in *Love Story* (1997). The subject is not an original one, as Kate Grenville had evoked these dark secrets in two of her novels. The first, *Lilian's Story* (1985), is based on an actual, colourful person, Beatrice or 'Bea' Miles (1902–1973), a woman noticeable for her stoutness and presented here as Lilian. Her eccentricity, brought on by the incestuous advances of her father, caused her to be placed in an institution which proved unable to control her. With *Dark Places* (1994), Grenville rewrites Lilian's story from the point of view of the guilty father, Albion. This is why American publishers titled the book *Albion's Story*. Rodney Hall's *Captivity Captive* (1988), which is part of a trilogy along with *The Second Bridegroom* (1991) and *The Grisly Wife* (1993), fits into this type of sordid story, captivity being a significant theme in Hall's writing. The plot of *Captivity Captive* is based on the historic murder of three members of a family on a farm in New South Wales in 1898. According to

Xavier Pons in *European Perspectives*, 'paternal authority represents [in this novel] the law – European law – on which white Australia was founded'. Acceptance of the law leads to alienation, while non-acceptance is dangerous. When pushed to its paroxysm, this authority, represented in the book by the father, becomes despotic. Much more than an expression of perversion, the transgressive taboo of incest, present twice in *Captivity Captive*, is tantamount to 'a denial of filiation', to the denial of blood ties. This complete destruction of the family breaks the father/child relationship by dispensing with generational barriers.

Tim Winton* is unquestionably one of the main novelists to write about the private sphere. His first novel *An Open Swimmer* (1982) sets the tone for his fictional output that mixes realism and *le roman intimiste*: a genre focusing on the private world of people's feelings and relationships. In this initiatory and highly descriptive novel, Jerra Nilsam and his childhood friend Sean go fishing on the Western Australian coast. It is worth noting that the accent and particularities of Australian English, known as strine, are faithfully transcribed in the dialogues. Set against a Socratic quest, *An Open Swimmer* defines human frailty. Beach culture plays a major role in Winton's work, because the beach itself epitomises an outlet for Westralians who want to come to terms with the vast desert expanses in their region.

With *Dirt Music* (2001), a novel in eight parts written in short chapters, Tim Winton evokes the difficulties of living as a couple in the fictional city of White Point. Jim Buckridge's re-formed family is a fiasco and his *de facto* relationship with Georgie is shaky. Georgie Jutland, the eldest of four girls, is an unsatisfied woman tired of her partner. She falls for Luther Fox, a foreigner and poacher living on the fringe of a river community. The novel highlights the author's interest in mundane daily life and dysfunctional families, which he touched on first in *That Eye, The Sky* (1986).

The disintegration of the couple is a popular theme in Australian novels. In her eighth novel *The Sugar Mother* (1988), Elizabeth

Panoramic view of Tim Winton

Born in 1960 in Scarborough, Western Australia, and from a modest background, Tim Winton spent his childhood in suburbia and on the west coast, as described in his autobiography *Land's Edge* (1993). Very quickly he became the darling of Australian readers, who enjoy his rich prose, which evokes the south-western landscape of his native land. Four-time recipient of the Miles Franklin among other prizes, Winton partly owes his wide appeal to his populist convictions. He can be defined as a writer who has a close affinity with the people and especially the land that he holds in high regard in his stories. He has written short stories, children's literature and novels, including: *An Open Swimmer* (1982), *Shallows* (1984), *That Eye, The Sky* (1986), *In The Winter Dark* (1988), *Cloudstreet* (1991), *The Riders* (1994), *Dirt Music* (2001) *Breath* (2008), winner of the 2009 Miles Franklin, and *Eyrie* (2013).

Influenced by contemporaries like Les Murray, Patrick White and Helen Garner, Winton writes about sensitive subjects such as: Aboriginal rights, ecology and the environment (such as the protection of ancestral whales in *Shallows*) and Aboriginal reconciliation – in short, the national heritage. Making marginality central to the Australian psyche seems to be the guiding principle of this regional writer. As a direct consequence of feeling marginalised on the less densely populated edge of the continent, his protagonists represent the average citizen who grows up on the edge of society. His characters are often alienated outsiders, modest individuals, questioners and questers, if not dysfunctional family members. Alienation is seen as a result of modernisation. His archetypal protagonist is a nomad of modest working-class background in a relatively hostile environment.

Winton's novels, defined as coastal narratives, invariably depict in vivid descriptions a rural community functioning in harmony with the beach culture. The author is thus seen as an alchemist who makes something extraordinary of the ordinary and evokes nostalgia for a golden age, 'a contemplative melancholy', to use his own words.

Jolley is interested in the institution of marriage and infidelity evoked through the escapades of fifty-year-old Edwin Page, who yields to the charms of a younger woman. Another example is Peter Goldsworthy's *Three Dog Night* (2003), a psychological novel in which the value of love is measured against the yardstick of trust within a couple. Lucy and Martin Blackman, a closely knit couple of psychiatrists, return to Australia after staying in London for ten years. Renewing his old friendship with a surgeon, Martin learns that Felix Johnson is facing death after being infected with hepatitis C. As a last wish, Felix wants to spend time with Lucy. This request takes the form of a dinner, then an escapade into the bush and, very soon, Martin, consumed with jealousy, regrets his indulgence. *Three Dog Night* is probably the most accomplished novel by Goldsworthy whose training as a doctor informs this five-part psychological drama. In these pages, medical jargon is mixed with notions of psychoanalysis and psychiatry, though Freudianism is denounced in the same breath. There are also tensions between a couple whose relationship is disintegrating in *The Philosopher's Doll* (2004) by Amanda Lohrey. Ruled by her biological clock, Kirsten, a young sturdy thirty-year-old, wants to experience the joys of motherhood by conceiving, but her partner Lindsay resists the idea of a family. This novel explores the dynamics between reason and emotion, biological determinism and free will, instinct and reflection.

The Slap (2008), Christos Tsiolkas's fourth novel, is clearly at odds with the offbeat rebellious voice, the narrative stamina and the hyperactivity of his previous characters and the confronting subject matter that is the hallmark of his fiction. However, as most obsessions die hard, *The Slap* is yet again an indictment of contemporary society, delving into the secret lives of sex-obsessed characters looking for cop-outs in a drug-infested Australian culture. Plot-wise, the content and structure of the book smacks of soap opera culture, which informs the narrative from cover to cover. The novel opens with a family and friends get-together in a suburban Melburnian backyard. Coincidentally, the crowd of merrymakers hosted by Hector and Aisha showcases a carefully well-balanced sampling of Australia's multicultural society. The party turns sour because a seemingly domestic incident – a non-family related adult has slapped Hugo, a spoilt kid raised by an overprotective mother – triggers off a nonsensical psychodrama which is blown out of all proportion and climaxes in a far-fetched lawsuit. Tsiolkas exploits this domestic scene to imagine a narrative which ties neatly together the various viewpoints of seven guests present at the barbecue: Hector, Anouk, Connie, Rosie, Manolis, Aisha and Richie.

Georgia Blain also has a taste for family dramas. In *Closed for Winter* (1998), Elise is disturbed from her earliest days by the unexplained disappearance of her sister. In *Names for Nothingness* (2004), Sharn is a sixteen-year-old mother who has to look after her child Caitlin by herself until Liam comes into her life. Years later, the couple are faced with Caitlin's involvement in a religious sect, a painful experience which brings them closer together. The family, often split in Blain's work, is a source of psychological suffering. Motherhood is a burden, filial relationships are tense and fathers, often withdrawn, are never a great help. Charlotte Wood shatters the private sphere outlining the problem of violence in marriage in *The Submerged Cathedral* (2004), a novel in which Ellen is the victim of abusive Thomas. Wood's parents' love affair became the starting point for this intriguing novel, which a critic from *The Bulletin* likened to a Debussy piano prelude: 'Wood's writing is made of the same stuff as Debussy's music: exquisite and sometimes dissonant chords; delicate, slow notes; a gentle, passionate witness of the patterns submerged within the real order of things; of longing and elegy. And of love.' The roles are reversed with Matthew Condon since *The Pillow Fight* (1998) opens with the newlyweds Christine and Luke, the latter sporting a black eye. This realistically constructed novel deals with an almost sadomasochistic relationship between a professional diver and a casino employee. Any excuse becomes a pretext to stir up the antagonism that gives structure to the couple's intimacy. Throughout the story, Luke takes the impulsive violent blows dealt out to him by his lady-love.

Fire, fire (2004) by Eva Sallis echoes Elizabeth Jolley's *Milk and Honey* (1984). Both novels deal with the relationship between Europe as the centre and Australia as the periphery, the breakdown of the nuclear family and the disintegration of social ties in situations of isolation. In *Fire, fire*, a couple of German artists settle in the Australian outback in the 1970s and lead a self-sufficient life with their children whom they educate themselves. But Acantia Houdini, who gradually becomes insane, turns into a cruel woman and drives the family into disarray.

London-born Alex Miller has won the Miles Franklin twice with his introspective novels *The Ancestor Game* (1992), a Socratic quest set in Australia and China, and *Journey to the Stone Country* (2002). The latter begins in Melbourne with a marital drama. Professor Steven Küen leaves his wife Annabelle for one of his female students. Distraught, the forty-year-old wife packs her bags and meets her friend Susan Bassett in Townsville to escape from the betrayal and to make a fresh start. Taking advantage of her new freedom, Annabelle discovers nature and her real self. She falls in love with Bo Rennie, an Aboriginal man of the Jangga people who cannot leave his traditional community and believes a mixed union to be unfavourable. Written in a stilted style, *Journey to the Stone Country* eventually segues into a novel of reconciliation.

Julia Leigh's first novel *The Hunter* (1999) was widely talked about and eventually adapted to the silver screen by Daniel Nettheim. The eponymous character is a scientist introduced to the reader by the letter M, short for Martin David. He leaves on a mission to Tasmania to obtain a DNA sample of the Tasmanian Tiger. Although the thylacine was officially recorded as having disappeared since 1936, it seemed that Jarrah Armstrong, an expert in bioethics, saw one before vanishing himself into thin air.

M calls on Armstrong's wife Lucy and her children Sassafras and Bike as a starting point in the search for both Jarrah Armstrong and the Tasmanian Tiger. Tracking the thylacine becomes an allegory for an introspective search during which human instincts gradually resurface.

The ailing mind and body: Madness and mutilation

The treatment of psychological disorders of all kinds and, more largely, of the deterioration of the mind, gradually made its mark in Australian novels in the early 1970s and gave rise to a series of books concerned with mental health issues. David Ireland's *The Flesheaters* (1972) and Walter Adamson's *The Institution* (1976) set the benchmark for total institution fiction, a subgenre which flourished as of the 1980s. Peter Kocan's two you-narration novellas *The Treatment* (1980) and *The Cure* (1983),* Carmel Bird's *The White Garden* (1995), as well as Amy Witting's *Isobel on the Way to the Corner Shop* (1999), fall neatly into this new trend. Total institution fiction can be defined as literature concerned with characters confined to reclusion in total institutions and living in very close quarters with other inmates, all of whom are placed under one supervising and all-powerful authority that is the keystone to an administratively structured organisation. No matter how useful a purpose these institutions serve, most characters would feel constrained by them.

As a rule, total institution fiction is largely concerned with a self-contained and isolated microcosm evolving within the precinct of a building whose spatial territory is tightly controlled, carefully organised and aptly segmented into a pattern of sub-divisions that fulfill a specific function or into zones that provide either more freedom or constraints. Walter Adamson must be credited for being the most explicit about depicting the institution as a society of captives sealed off from the outside world. In terms of power politics, the control the medical personnel have is in inverse proportion to the inmates' freedom. This centripetal pattern of

Close-up of *The Treatment* and *The Cure*

Peter Kocan went down in the history of Australian fiction for having written companion novellas inspired by his experience as an inmate at Long Bay Correctional Centre, then confined in Ward 6 for the criminally insane in Morrisset Psychiatric Hospital. At age 19, he attempted to shoot the then-leader of the Australian Labor Party, Arthur Calwell. Diagnosed as a borderline schizophrenic at trial, he was condemned to life imprisonment, a sentence commuted to ten years of treatment that gave him an insider's knowledge of psychiatric institutions.

Published in the early 1980s when asylum narratives were starting to make their mark in Australian fiction, *The Treatment* and its sequel *The Cure* chronicle Len Tarbutt's institutionalisation as a nineteen-year-old youngster confined in the maximum-security cell of a mental hospital to serve a life sentence. On another level, these two second person semi-fictions can also be interpreted as a national allegory of Australian penal settlement, which explicates the ruler-ruled relationship through the establishment of a panoptic repressive system. The asylum becomes a place of confinement in which the inmate becomes, to borrow Michel Foucault's words, an object of information but never a subject in communication in a system that ends up taking the power out of the hands of the individual. Illustrating Foucault's theory in *Discipline and Punish*, the inmates – who are under constant surveillance to the point of getting paranoid – are disempowered and thereby reassure their masters of their harmlessness. Even if they are not actually observed round the clock, this all-pervasive dominating watchful gaze of authority is persuasive enough to make them act as if they were.

Foucault's theories exposing micro power structures as part of a huge labyrinthine system enslaving people and controlling their behaviours were influential in postcolonial studies and anti-psychiatry. Both books demonstrate that the subjection of individuals made vulnerable serves the purpose of legitimising and enforcing paternalistic protection, all in the name of goodness and of a more civilised world.

biopower is patently illustrated in Amy Witting's *Isobel on the Way to the Corner Shop* in which patients gain more freedom as they move out into B, C and D grades. Another instance of this feature is the ward system in Kocan's novellas: if medical staff notice some significant improvement, inmates can be transferred from MAX to REFRACT and even all the way to the less-controlled REHAB. The dialectic of total institutions in terms of biopolitics and governmentality can be summed up as a binary process whereby 'the ruler looks in the mirror and sees a liberator; the ruled looks at the ruler and sees a tyrant' (Thomas S. Szasz). This explains the inevitable depiction of a plenipotentiary administration run by a father figure who generally dictates the slavish – if not sheepish – inmates into steady discipline. With the exception of Adamson's Professor Longbeard, who does not come across as tyrannical, Dr Ambrose Goddard burdened with a God complex in *The White Garden*, the all-powerful ward doctor dubbed Electric Ned in *The Treatment* and Witting's Dr Stannard, described as an authority figure, are to some extent many literary avatars of Ireland's Dr O'Grady, whose nickname, O'Grady Says, is a giveaway of his authoritarianism. The treatment given by god-like doctors to helpless patients insulated from the outside world – a treatment which is in a large part uncaring, despotic and cruel – can be construed as an oblique giveaway of these authors' jaundiced view of psychiatry and human nature at large.

Like Ireland or Adamson, Peter Kocan, Carmel Bird, and Amy Witting have all chosen to denounce the negativity, injustices and occasional destructiveness of the claustral world of total institutions in their fiction while giving a voice to the oppressed and powerless. It is hard to say whether these authors are trying to undermine the credibility of total institutions by implying that they mean more harm than good to inmates or whether they are making insanity (traditionally passed over in silence) less alarming and more familiar to readers through literary exposure. They could also be using mental health issues to deconstruct the influence of biopolitics and its mode of government. If their motivations remain unclear at the end of each narrative, there is nevertheless a consensual view that insanity is a fluctuating state that oscillates between quaintness and abnormality. What these creative writers surely help people realise is how relative insanity is.

Novels published at the beginning of the twenty-first century began to explore the possibilities of psychiatry as exemplified by the following stories: *Café in Venice* (2001) by Dorian Mode; Elliot Perlman's *Seven Types of Ambiguity* (2003); *Cape Grimm* (2004) by Carmel Bird; *Three Dog Night* by Peter Goldsworthy; Rodney Hall's *Love Without Hope* (2007) and *The Memory Room* (2007) by Christopher Koch, a novel in which the writer depicts the borderline personality of journalist Erika Lange. While the world of psychiatry and its pathologies have a relatively marginal place in the works of these writers, they are the core of Peter Kocan's *The Treatment* (1980) and *The Cure* (1983).

Institutionalised at the very time when anti-psychiatry became prominent and widespread thanks to David Cooper's *Psychiatry and Anti-Psychiatry* (1967), Peter Kocan is likely to have been influenced by the views of British psychiatrists R.D. Laing and David Cooper, who took the work of Hungarian-American Thomas S. Szasz one step further. Among anti-psychiatric tenets, there is the idea that doctors and medical staff at large are reading too much into people's behaviour. Constant vigil and fear of being misinterpreted result in an edginess that segues into psychosis. A cast of screws, whose role is to give and restrict access to areas of the psychiatric hospital by locking and unlocking doors, monitor the inmates and, if need be, report suspicious behaviour, thereby ensuring constant vigil in *The Treatment* and *The Cure*.

As the institution novel *par excellence*, *The Treatment* denounces the mediocre and inhumane conditions of life in a psychiatric environment with bitter criticism of the staff involved and the psychiatrist nicknamed 'Electric Ned' because of his immoderate use of ECT (electro-convulsive therapy or shock treatment). It also denounces excessive medication and the institutional prison regime, with male nurses acting as the screws of a systematised and quasi-panoptic organisation. To avoid the morose and distressing atmosphere, inmates have the choice of committing suicide or escaping. In some edifying passages, the informed reader can detect manic-depression or bipolar disorder causing Len Tarbutt to switch from a depressive decompensatory state to one of exaltation. Even though *The Treatment* contains humour, it shows an aversion to institutionalisation. Such anti-psychiatric resentment exemplifies the typical reaction of former inmates. *The Cure* is another total institution novella narrated again by Len from an internal viewpoint. Transferred to a less restrictive ward, young Tarbutt gives a detailed account of institutional life and the eccentricities of each criminal patient. In this sequel, the narrator emphasises sexual promiscuity, unhealthy living conditions created by the inmates themselves, and talks about his own loss of virginity. The novel, which ends with two attempted suicides, emphasises the inmates' distress.

In *The Best Man for This Sort of Thing* (1990) by Margaret Coombs, the main character Helen Ayling looks back, at times lightly, at other times severely, at the treatment she had to endure and the follow-up sessions with a psychiatrist to overcome post-natal depression. More serious pathological conditions have also been the subject of other publications such as *Memoirs of Many in One* (1986), a novel by Patrick White about schizophrenia in which he 'edited' the story narrated by Alex Xenophon Demirjan Gray, an elderly Greek woman. Poet Anthony Lawrence takes up this psychotic condition in his one and only published novel *In the Half Light* (2002). The young narrator James Molloy suffers from synaesthesia, a confusion of the senses that results in the production of several passages of rich lyrical tonality.

Although the deterioration of the mind is no new theme in Australian literature, exploration of psychology and psychiatry is far from evident. Some scholars questioned the lack of success of psychoanalytical theories in Australia, asserting that a hedonistic culture is hardly conducive to intellectual discussion. If it is true that poor understanding of psychoanalysis* is partly responsible for its rejection, it should be acknowledged that there is also, in a way, a refusal to concede authority as embodied in the father of psychoanalysis. In the face of this observation, this period paradoxically witnessed a real trend for novels emphasising the mind.

Despite the lack of wide appeal of psychoanalysis in Australia, there are still, among novelists, some passionate followers willing to incorporate the workings of the mind and the brain's interpretative function into the structure of their stories. Proof of this is seen in three psychoanalytically informed works worthy of interest: *Julia Paradise* (1986), *Double-Wolf* (1991) and *Toccata and Rain* (2004). Except for *Toccata and Rain*, psychoanalysis, like psychiatry, is treated more or less negatively. This is shown in descriptions of a milieu deemed hostile and by the discrediting of some theories and practices.

Julia Paradise by Rod Jones is the first Australian novel to have a plot based on psychoanalytical culture. This short fictional work, inspired by the case of Dora, whose condition enabled Freud to highlight the symptoms of hysteria, questions the credibility of psychoanalytical treatment through a process of transference and counter-transference. Psychoanalyst Kenneth Ayres treats Julia Paradise who is suffering from hysteria. With a few psychoanalytical sessions using hypnosis, he manages to bring out the traumatic events of her childhood. She had repeated incestuous relationships with her father from the age of thirteen onwards. But the plot intensifies when her husband Willy Paradise casts doubt on Julia's story by giving Ayres contradictory information. Who is telling the truth? Is Julia's confession true or is it a sort of subterfuge to seduce and whet the appetite of her psychoanalyst who seems to have a perverse liking for young girls?

Close-up of psychoanalysis in Australian novels

While psychoanalytic theories spread through two major channels in France, medical institutions and literary circles (with prominent creative writers like Georges Bataille, Michel Leiris, Pierre Jean Jouve, Philippe Sollers and Catherine Clément), Australian novelists have not shown similar enthusiasm in championing and drawing on Freudianism in their works. And yet, their most obvious common denominator is perhaps tale-telling, as Melbourne-based novelist Antoni Jach hints at in *The Weekly Card Game* (1994). Whether fiction and psychoanalysis can be readily assimilated on the grounds that they share a history of tales is a different story altogether. Within the realm of fiction, tale-telling taps into fancy for the most part, even though some narratives may be history- or reality-based. However, tale-telling in psychoanalysis relies heavily on facts – be they personal, medical, or scientific. On the basis of such a deep kinship, some Australian writers – like Christos Tsiolkas and his use of incorporation and the oral-sadistic stage in *Dead Europe* (2005) – have unconsciously or implicitly drawn on psychoanalytic theory to build up or flesh out their narratives.

Writers such as Brian Castro, Antoni Jach, and Philip Salom have been very stringent in their use of psychoanalytic culture, which they consciously included in their works of fiction. For instance, the urge to confess, analyse and be analysed, which repeatedly resurfaces in *The Weekly Card Game*, translates into as many opportunities to mention Freud and his brainchild in a most apposite fashion. Other writers like Rod Jones and Peter Kocan have been quite loose with the handling of references and definitions. Rod Jones goes so far as to quote Freud from an apocryphal source, *Psychotherapy of Hysteria*, as an epigraph for his novel. As for Kocan, he gives the misleading impression that psychoanalysis and psychiatry are interchangeable terms. The terminology muddle just serves to underscore the clearly delineated tendency to present psychiatry, psychoanalysis and psychotherapy as a mixed bag of theories. When not amalgamated with medical practice, Freudian psychoanalysis is debunked, if not simply dismissed, in Australian fiction.

Is a patient being cared for when the carer is not normal? Can we trust the confession of an unreliable narrator? These are some of the questions raised in this novel. *Julia Paradise* concludes with an admission of powerlessness and the failure of psychoanalysis as a form of therapy. The anti-psychoanalytical position of this novel is strongly and more subtly suggested than in *Double-Wolf*, a book written in denunciatory mode.

Double-Wolf by Brian Castro* is certainly the most Freudian Australian novel, precisely because it seeks to shake the foundations of psychoanalysis. In this postmodern story trying to untangle the misrepresentation of reality, Castro considers how Freudian theories about infant sexuality, interpretation of dreams and the castration complex based on the case of the Wolf Man are invalidated by the case history's apocryphal nature. In fact, the story of Sergei Wespe is simply the product of a fertile imagination. In *Double-Wolf*, Wespe is an unknown writer, the author of psychoanalytical crime thrillers, who hides behind a pseudonym and who may have invented his entire story. In this imaginary scenario, Sigmund Freud is portrayed as a con man. As in most of Castro's novels, *Double-Wolf* continuously moves from the past to the present and back, and from different places between Australia and Europe. The irreverence of this literary speculation upset Jungian critic David Tacey, who denounced Castro's tendency for anti-psychoanalysis. This sentiment is understandable given the far from glorious portrait of Artie Catacomb, an impecunious swindler who reinvents himself as a psychoanalyst so that he can abuse his patients in every way possible. Artie ends up being the ghost writer for the Wolf Man by writing his memoirs. Freud is depicted as a highly unscrupulous man who knowingly would have used a literary work to lay the groundwork for his pseudo-scientific theories. Castro even goes so far as to scoff at psychoanalysis by devising language games about associated ideas with the use of collocation (association of words) and paronomasia (punning). These Freudian lapses,

Low-angle shot of Brian Castro

Born in 1950 in Hong Kong to Chinese-Portuguese parents, Brian Castro settled in Australia in 1961. According to him, his works are not readily accessible even though they have been judged highly successful (nearly all his novels have been awarded prizes). His prose, didactic in nature and sparkling with wit, is contained within complex narrative structures. As Deborah Madsen has remarked in the volume edited by Nicholas Birns and Rebecca McNeer, *A Companion to Australian Literature Since 1900*, Brian Castro's 'work systematically deconstructs the notion of cultural authenticity'.

The author, who lived for a while in Hong Kong and then in France, labels his novels 'cosmopolitan', an adjective that suits seven of them: *Birds of Passage* (1983), *After China* (1992), *Drift* (1994), *Shanghai Dancing* (2003), *The Garden Book* (2005), *The Bath Fugues* (2009) and *Street to Street* (2012). *Pomeroy* (1990), *Double-Wolf* (1991) and *Stepper* (1997) are different. The first is a post-structural detective story that questions the relationship between language and reality; the second is an anti-psychoanalytic novel and the last is a spy novel written at the request of his publisher who wanted to see him try a more commercial genre. Castro's novels often praise diversity: disparate places, a chronology that mingles past and present (as in *Birds of Passage* and *Double-Wolf*), a mixture of several cultures, a wise dosage of fact with fiction (particularly disconcerting in his fictitious autobiography *Shanghai Dancing*) and a questioning of stereotypes, in particular in *The Garden Book*, where he denounces certain racial prejudices.

Castro – rather cerebral in conceiving his plots – was well positioned to theorise about his writing in two collections of essays in which he touches on some aspects of Asian culture: *Writing Asia and Auto/biography: Two lectures* (1995) and *Looking for Estrellita* (1999). The author advocates the shattering of the national monolith of the Australian identity in order to embrace the richness of the melting pot of cultures on offer. Castro's *The Bath Fugues* was shortlisted for the 2010 Miles Franklin Award and he received the Patrick White Award in 2014.

integrated in a divided, jerky narrative within a succession of short chapters, reveal the way Brian Castro's analytical mind works.

Toccata and Rain, poet Philip Salom's second novel, is the unusual story of an eccentric forty-year-old called Simon. With the display of his artwork – a phallic piece made of metal – in the backyard of his Melbourne suburban home, he succeeds in gaining media attention. One evening, he gets a call from a certain Margaret, based in Perth, who recognises him as Brian Tyrell, her missing husband. After undergoing medical treatment, mainly psychoanalytical sessions and hypnotic trances, Brian/Simon tries to fill in the gaps in his life story by making a palimpsest of each story. The informed reader recognises in the subtext the theories of Sigmund Freud, Jacques Lacan, Jean-Martin Charcot and Fritz Perls. Constructed as a fugue, *Toccata and Rain* plays on the articulation of memory and identity that the main character has lost. From this perspective, identity is a 'pure and simple fiction of the mind', as expressed by Stéphane Ferret, in a world that, according to the thesis of universal mobilism, 'is not made up of continuing but of becoming' in which 'beings are not but always become others'.

The 1980s was a time of prosperity for Australian women writers, who were given special attention by publishers and readers alike. Their growing number coincided with the increase in women's studies, which opposed the phallocentric definition of woman from a man's perspective in his representations and his language. The swing of the pendulum came at the end of the 1990s when the novel genre was once again mainly male dominated. The masculinity crisis (a direct consequence of the loss of reference points, the redefinition of man's role, alienation produced by individualism, and gender confusion) questioned the stereotype of the 'Aussie battler'. In Australian literature, this person had been represented up until then as the European struggling against life's vicissitudes and obstacles. Perceived in his most intimate vulnerability, man is no longer as solid as a rock, remaining insensitive against all odds. The stories of women writers are made up of representations of an often wounded male body and Jillian Watkinson is no exception in trying to depict the fragility of manhood. In *The Architect* (2000), not only is the eponymous character Jules Van Erp seriously burnt and mutilated (he loses an arm) in a motorbike accident, but he has two sons who are also victims of injuries: Che Lai has suffered deep burns and is heavily scarred and Mark is a paraplegic due to a horse-riding accident. In this novel, man's suffering makes him dependent on welfare. In *The Last of the Sane Days* by Fiona Capp, Flight Lieutenant Rafael Ball is forced to suspend his activities after an unexplained abdominal disease. He is unable to re-establish a good relationship with his father and the two men commit suicide. The four men (Ross, Ian, Kelvin and Peter) in *Transplanted* (2002) by Sarah Myles are also presented as fragile. One is defeated, another mutilated, a third has precarious health and the fourth is assassinated. These women novelists like to weaken their male characters who are often physically seriously injured. Another example is young Silas, who suffers episodes of self-mutilation and seeks psychological help from Daniel Lehaine in *The Blind Eye* (2001) by Georgia Blain. It could be believed that these disparaging representations of the male are the result of a feminist campaign that aims at sapping what it perceives as male supremacy. In fact, this is not so, since these female concerns about the vulnerability of the flesh and the precariousness of the body do not exclusively weaken masculine identity. They find their counterpart in unflattering representations of the woman by female novelists such as Margaret Coombs, Anne Derwent (who published *Warm Bodies*, 1986), Kate Grenville* and Penelope Rowe, author of *Tiger Country* (1990).

According to Chantal Kwast-Greff, literary representation of the woman in novels like Grenville's *Lilian's Story* (1985) is often

Low-angle shot of Kate Grenville

Born in 1950 in Sydney where most of her education took place, Kate Grenville finished her studies in the United States after a long stay in Europe. Besides her interest in the short story, she has published seven novels that fall into two categories. Firstly there are those that explore the private sphere, like *Lilian's Story* (1985) – which the jury placed first for the *Australian*/Vogel National Literary Prize – and its sequel *Dark Places* (1994), then *Dreamhouse* (1986) and *The Idea of Perfection* (1999), which all evoke the disintegration of marriage bonds and the breaking up of the nuclear family. Then there are stories dealing with colonial history like *Joan Makes History* (1988), a rewriting in parody form of history according to a feminist reading with a contemporary perspective, and *The Secret River* (2005), which gained her the Commonwealth Writer's Prize in 2006, and *The Lieutenant* (2008).

Grenville takes a gentle humanist look at the world in a prose tinged with feminism. She tirelessly relates, in a manner both comical and gothic, the destinies of women who are unattractive physically and sexually inadequate. Her female characters try to take control of their destinies by escaping from the shackles of society. The author likes to connect her works either by borrowing a character from a previous book – this is exactly what unites *Joan Makes History* and *Lilian's Story* – or by exploring more fully a theme she is fond of.

Grenville, who denounces patriarchy and phallocracy, does not hesitate to raise sensitive subjects like homosexuality and incest in her novel ironically entitled *Dreamhouse*. However, her radical stance is not for everyone. Shortly after the publication of *The Secret River*, she attracted the wrath of two historians who felt she was passing her novel off as a 'work of history'. Despite this controversy, the author resumed the exploration of Australia's contact history by retracing the beginnings of the novel in a documentary book *Searching for the Secret River* (2006) and by releasing a further sequel: *Sarah Thornhill* (2011).

stereotypical. It aims at being impressionable, sensitive and artless. These women tend to place themselves as victims of an oppressive patriarchy. When they are not harming themselves, they are often suffering from psychic problems. Sometimes madness pursues them; sometimes they are afflicted by flaws that deform the body. Problematic diet issues, like anorexia and bulimia for instance, contribute to destabilising the body. To this self-inflicted mistreatment is added violence by men who want to dominate women, who are unable to fight back. Physically and morally damaged, these women end up denying their humane aspect and seeing themselves as objects. In the master/slave relationship in which they are subjugated, sexually and otherwise, to men (although they can also be under the iron rule of women), their docility results in submission and, consequently, acceptance of paternal law.

Therefore, the female characters in this literature, when faced with violence, compensate physiologically for not reacting physically by somatising their suffering: 'the deformed body functions as a sign, reaction and language, a sign socially interpreted as madness' (Kwast-Greff). It would seem that the subjugation of women is the consequence of a slave mentality commanding them to be virtuous, and virtue in this case is chiefly epitomised by the lovable and loving 'yes' woman. More than victims, these women, moved 'by their own desire to be manipulated', seem to be their own torturer.

Kwast-Greff naturally qualifies these female characters as 'wax dolls' since they are easy to manipulate; then as 'blood dolls' from their propensity to repeat their torments in self-mutilation. The position of women writers remains, however, too ambiguous since it is difficult to determine if their main female character is dominated or indomitable, persecuted or persecutor. In these books, the woman is often the object of male predation, a tendency that so-called 'grunge' fiction seeks to overturn.

Grunge fiction and urban space

Grunge fiction brings to the fore urban protagonists tortured by spleen and nihilism, who try to fill the void of their existence with outlets such as drugs, alcohol, music and sex. Whereas the characters' sexuality is often presented as an outlet, no other generalisation can be made about this genre involving an equal number of women and men from both the working and middle classes. Most of the works are first novels written mainly in the last decade of the twentieth century and by authors under the age of thirty using the confessional mode, with the exception of *Monkey Grip* (1977) by Helen Garner, a pioneer of the genre. *Praise* (1992) by Andrew McGahan revived the trend, which he consolidated three years later with *1988* (1995), a novel that retraces the events prior to *Praise*. Because of the stylistic mediocrity of these works – *Monkey Grip* being an exception – and their extreme realism that depicts erotic scenes rather crudely, many commentators denigrated the genre as unserious and judged it commercial because it borders on pornography.

My contention is that grunge fiction is the expression of a *fin de siècle* mentality presented as the avatar of the French Decadent movement that, at the end of the nineteenth century, could not be exported to Australia because of government literary censorship from the 1880s to the early 1970s. A century later, like 'the return of the repressed' in psychoanalytical terms, this genre has kept many characteristics of the Decadent movement, such as egocentrism, disenchantment and ennui compensated by a sharp taste for strong feelings, debauchery and perversity defying the middle classes.

Above all, these stories reflect the disintegration of love. The male characters in this literature are individualistic and detached from everything: people (references to friends or family are rare), their environment and the self. This separation breeds a disquiet that they try to assuage with violent erotic behaviour.

Sexuality, described as a far from romantic activity motivated by the search for instant gratification, becomes something sterile and mechanical as shown by the circularity of *Loaded* (1995) by Christos Tsiolkas.* In this heavily autobiographical first novel, Ari, a young nineteen-year-old homosexual Greek, recounts a day in his dissolute and stormy life that he spices up with unbridled sexuality, illicit substances, alcohol and a deep passion for music.

Male sexuality is largely depicted as imperious, promiscuous and performance-driven, while female sexuality finds its fulfilment in imaginary constructs as much as in fictional reality with domination-based scenarios, whether female characters appear empowered or disempowered. *Eat Me* (1995), which author Linda Jaivin claims to be 'comic erotica', reads like the archetypal scenario of a pornographic film: a succession of fantasies that climaxes in an unbridled orgy. The sexual practices are varied, from classic heterosexuality to the weirdest deviations: stuffing, sadomasochism, exhibitionism (and its counterpart, voyeurism), fisting, transvestism and felching. For most grunge fiction characters, deviant practices are experienced as an expansion of the boundary lines imposed by the body to feel themselves coming alive again in an attempt to fight off the stresses and strains of modern life.

Unlike pornography, grunge fiction does not praise phallocratic ideology. It simply illustrates the psychological maelstrom in which the characters find themselves. They experience ruptures, romantic deprivation, emotional instability, the incapacity to concentrate on an object of desire and a propensity for wanting to realise their fantasies. Stripped of its meaning, sexuality is no longer an intimate experience but an experiential activity. The characters' frenzied search for sexual activity makes them pioneers and prisoners of the 'erosphere' (Emmanuelle Arsan), a self-contained world in which self-oriented pleasure has become a substitute for the mutual satisfaction of a fruitful relationship, while instant and short-lasting gratification has replaced the slow-paced investment in a long-lasting fulfilling commitment.

Low-angle shot of Christos Tsiolkas

Born in 1965 in a working-class Greek neighbourhood of Melbourne, Christos Tsiolkas is known as the *enfant terrible* of Australian literature. Some of the recurring themes in his work which gave him this heretical reputation are homosexuality, anti-Semitism, racism, perversity, loose morals and pornography.

After a bachelor's degree, he tried his hand at journalism and films before publishing *Loaded* (1995), which was later adapted to the screen. Tsiolkas then produced *The Jesus Man* (1999), a novel that did not receive the success anticipated. The writer tells part of the story of three brothers: Dominic, Luigi and Thomas Stefano. Thomas, unbridled sexually, is in some way the literary avatar of Ari in *Loaded*, except that he tries to conciliate his sexual inclinations with the negative judgement religion passes on same-sex desire. Influenced by pornographic culture, this young bisexual, who is interested in the 'mechanics of sex', mirrors the contradictions inherent in the author whose ambivalence oscillates between romanticism and lust, gay culture and homophobia, affirmation and denial of homosexuality. It is clear in *The Jesus Man* that homosexuality is not easy to live with: after being surprised sexually abusing his young brother Luigi, Thomas ends up committing suicide while Sean, also a homosexual, meets the same fate.

Tsiolkas' third novel *Dead Europe* (2005) propelled him once again to the fore of the literary scene. Narrated in the first person, *Dead Europe* is the story of Australian Isaac Raftis, a young talented thirty-six-year-old photographer of Greek descent, who leaves his mother Reveka and his gay partner Colin to organise the opening of his exhibition in Athens.

Rewarded with the Australian Literary Society Gold Award and the Commonwealth Prize, *The Slap* (2008) exposes urban middle-class conservatism. His latest novel, *Barracuda* (2013), is yet another exploration of the triangulation of ethnicity, class, and identity within contemporary Australia, this time through the eyes of Daniel Kelly, a working class teenager whose swimming scholarship enables him to attend an independent school.

As with novels of initiation, these grunge narratives very often end with a self-revelation that leads to disenchantment. Ari, the homosexual protagonist of *Loaded*, considers his life at the end of his adventures and quickly realises that it is extraordinarily banal. Nora in *Monkey Grip* becomes aware of her loneliness and returns home. The eponymous heroine of Justine Ettler at the end of *The River Ophelia* (1995) struggles against submissiveness and breaks away from the influence of her dominating lover Sade. These drifting characters realise that their search for ephemeral pleasure condemns them to an endless quest. The confusion, which their deadpan humour reveals within the suburban desert, is to some extent a symptom of angst, the spleen of wealthy Western societies caused by an existential anxiety at the approaching end of the millennium.

Candy: A novel of love and addiction (1997) by Luke Davies takes up the grunge spirit with its admixture of drugs and sex to depict the intensely close relationship of a young couple of heroin addicts in Sydney as they plummet into the depths of hell to feed their addiction. There is no real sexual predation and Candy's problems and those of her partner, even if they are grunge-like characters, originate in a family malaise. Both youngsters kill time by finding refuge in artificially induced trances and in unrestrained sexuality.

It seemed probable, with new horizons opening up at the start of the third millennium, that grunge fiction would be extinguished. Perhaps this new swing of the pendulum will bring back hope to novelists and pave the way for a whole gamut of possibilities for utopian writers. Unlike grunge fiction, true utopian literature does not emphasise sexual relationships since the central target is not the individual – who comes across as a mere statistic – but the community.

Silent tyrannies: Australian utopias and dystopias

In an increasingly insecure world, it seems almost natural to see the resurgence, in the 1980s, of interest in a utopian way of life. Whereas Michael Wilding set his utopian experience beyond the Australian frontier in *The Paraguayan Experiment* (1985), as indicated by the title, most Australian novelists chose their own country as the geographic location. Gerald Murnane's *The Plains* is a contemplative intellectual novel in the tradition set by Thomas More. Utopias represent perfect worlds located in far-off countries that incarnate alterity and whose descriptions refer either to diegesis (if they are imaginary fables) or to mimesis (imitations of reality). In all cases, the mechanism of projection is at the heart of the utopian process in the form of the extra-territorial (in space) or the extra-contemporary (in time), a very useful distancing between fantasy and reality. In Australian novels with utopian impulses, the island continent represents the setting or the blueprint for a model of society that either implicitly reflects the Australian population or opposes it. It is not impossible that these utopian aspirations dating from the creation of Australia took the opposite course to the dissatisfaction of the first settlers, sentenced to transportation against their wishes or fleeing the British social class system. Because unexplored lands were becoming fewer, contemporary utopias were set up in imaginary geographic locations (see Rodney Hall's utopian cities in *The Last Love Story* and Peter Carey's in *The Unusual Life of Tristan Smith*) and in real places that belong to a bygone era (as in *Out of Ireland* by Christopher Koch) or uchronian settings (as is the case with *The Plains** by Gerald Murnane).

After encouraging numerous fantasies in the minds of explorers in search of *Terra Australis Incognita*, a country that would counterbalance the continental mass in the northern hemisphere, Australia was fertile soil for establishing a utopian project as soon as its existence was discovered. Set 'in a lost space and in an isolated dimension propitious for nourishing the overabundant imagination of a "different" world, the ideal society proposed by Australia is not the object of a discovery but of a creation' (Enrico Nuzzo). While every Australian citizen from birth by *jus soli* could

Close-up of *The Plains* by Gerald Murnane

Gerald Murnane's third novel *The Plains*, published in 1982, challenges classifications. The author has concocted, in concise prose, a novel of exploration that exploits the themes of discovery, nature, displacement and country, among others. Located in the centre of the largest island in the world, the plains are defined as a self-sufficient reclusive world, a secret alterity that comes from the ineffable and the indefinable. Although this microcosm of inhabitants of the plains has its own history, culture and political life, it is still a future nation looking for its own particular identity.

The protagonist is a promising filmmaker who set himself the task of interpreting the flat countryside of the central region of Australia by making a documentary called 'The Interior'. After scrapping all the generic traits, the male character tries unsuccessfully to define the specifics of the Australian panorama. Years go by and the filmmaker, like most artists who had tried before him, becomes bogged down in a creativity that never comes to fruition, allowing the book to be read like a parable about the persistence of desire. Murnane carefully develops a topography of the mind with his model of imaginary countries and succeeds in making us doubt the reality of our existing world.

Described by the author as a 'caesarean book', *The Plains* was originally part of a larger manuscript than the rather small one hundred or so pages of the final version, a reduction that gives the feeling it is incomplete. The persistent exploration of the filmmaker and the detailed notes he takes form part of this definition of a draft and of the wish to procrastinate its completion in order to be able to prolong the desire. The filmmaker suffers from writer's block and the pages of the scenario remain blank with the search for truth turning out to be unfruitful because it is impossible. The inherent nature of this highly distinctive landscape is imperceptible for it lies beyond the visible, beyond the accessible and the possible, and is therefore untranslatable.

acutely sense this insular phenomenon, Christopher Koch was probably much more deeply influenced by the condition having been born in Tasmania, the island of the island continent. Set apart from the world, Australia's vulnerability was not lost on its inhabitants. Protection, security and stability were guaranteed as long as it retained allegiance to a protecting military power, Great Britain at first, and then the United States. The country's isolation led Australians to think that they evolved in a hermetic and sanitised bubble – a defining characteristic of insular utopias – uncorrupted by outside influences and where evil could not reach them. At least, this is the impression that comes from almost all of Koch's novels where Australia is seen as being innocently preserved from the flow of world history. Insularity implies, therefore, voluntary or involuntary isolation, a withdrawal which makes the feelings of solitude and boredom rest heavily on the shoulders of the inhabitants, a feeling that forces them to escape from the tightly constricting space of their gilded prison. This gives rise to the *topos* of Australia as a prison frequently present, time and time again, in the novels of Christopher Koch.

Koch's story tries to mirror Australian reality as it was in the mid-nineteenth century. In *Out of Ireland* (1999), the construction of Australia, and more precisely of the future Tasmania, is at first presented as a utopia. The first salient traits of this *Mundus alter* reveal a city difficult to reach, only by sea. The authorities have erased its past with a double denial of history. Firstly, a colonial power that is organised around the 'idea of centrality' (*pensée de la centralité*), to use Christian Marouby's term from *Utopie et primitivisme*. Secondly, a system of transparency which vouchsafes for order in the city and allows the internal structure of the colony to be compared with Jeremy Bentham's Panopticon. But the portrait of Australia as a utopia imperceptibly transmogrifies not into a dystopia but into 'a utopian satire' (Northrop Frye).

In classical utopias, 'appearances and reality must overlap' (Marouby). Consequently, if the island purports to be a reassuring place and a picture of perfection, one should be able to read happiness on the faces of its citizens. In Koch's work, the mock utopian society is built on the imperfection of its population made up on the whole of convicts responsible for a latent sense of insecurity. In Koch's Eden-like space, the island of Tasmania, which desires happiness as evidenced by references to Boeotia/Arcadia in *Out of Ireland*, shows signs of hostility: barbarous 'savages', noxious vegetation and an aggressive foreign population. Influenced by reason, the project to set up a utopian community opposes the asocial tendency of man looking after his own interests. The collective must be controlled by strict rules. This reasoning in *Out of Ireland* is pushed to the extreme and generates a penal world of coercion organised in concentric circles.

In the greatest utopian tradition, the existence of imaginary archipelagos of the republic of Efica and the Grand Voorstand in *The Unusual Life of Tristan Smith* (1994) by Peter Carey is geographically vouched for by illustrative maps in the novel. Although these insular spaces seem to share the same globe as real nations like France and England, we cannot help but think that Efica can be read as Australia and the imperialistic Voorstand as the United States of America.

The Last Love Story (2004), a novel subtitled *A fairytale of the day after tomorrow*, is a science fiction story structured around the romantic idyll of Judith Scott, living in the middle section of a divided city, and the older Paul Bergson, born in the northern part called the 'Slow City' but living in the southern part since the city's bipolarisation. Rodney Hall's novel sets the action in the immediate future, close to anthrax attacks, the twin towers of 9/11, the 2002 Bali bombings and an imaginary insurrection responsible for this geographic division between the north and the south which occurred on the 'Great Day'. These twin cities, separated by a river but joined by the Friendship Bridge, face one another as if assessing their contrasting aspects. They evoke historic cities of Europe and the Middle East. In the north, a dystopian regime: austere and paranoid; in the south, a utopian society: prosperous, free but already unobtrusively corrupt. Judith, a young intellectually challenged twenty-two-year-old, falls in love with Paul, a modest electrician, to the displeasure of her mother who does not approve of the relationship that eventually takes a resolutely tragic turn.

All things considered, Australian utopias, like all others, impose silent tyrannies on readers because it is easier to transform large structures like an entire society in the imagination than in reality. If a philosopher as sensible as Emile Cioran can ask in *History and Utopia*: 'How can so many men coexist on such a small space without destroying each other, without mortally hating one another?', it is because the utopian mystery is difficult to penetrate and shrouded in paradoxes. Utopia is geographically distant, but should remain a target to be aimed at. It is a model of society suggested obliquely, but one that should be emulated. Finally it is perceived as a paradisal space ruled by a coercive administration. In fact, the utopian ideology is seen as a totalitarian idea. Happiness is a moral duty, the norm becomes the rule, sociability is presented as a way of life and isolation from the world is an abiding feature. After all, when seriously considered, the impossibility to complain, compliant behaviour, communal conformity and confinement are all defining traits of prison life – of institutionalised tyrannies.

Terror Australis: Exploitation of fear in the political novel

In the previous section on utopias and dystopias, contemporary Australia – claiming to be a harmonious egalitarian society, regulated and coherent – seems to present itself as a space conducive to paranoia. This would explain the historic misunderstanding cultivated in the country regarding Asians, especially the Japanese and Indonesians. From a psychoanalytical viewpoint, paranoia, a pathological state especially developed among insular people, is a defence mechanism. The isolation of these utopian spaces makes islands vulnerable as well as resistant, acting as a rampart against all forms of aggression thought to be coming from the outside. Faced with anxiety about invasion, contamination and degeneration, islanders have no choice other than to overprotect themselves by keeping at a respectable distance all exogenous elements. This fantasy of physical inviolability and sanitised space so characteristic of literary utopias appears as overcompensation for a deep fear of annihilation, a direct consequence of the porous nature of frontiers. Dreams of perfection, prelapsarian society and paradisal beatitude (at times transposed to an urban setting) also respond to the need to isolate original sin that ought to be expelled from the *hortus conclusus*, the enclosed garden. To achieve such perfection, everything has to be regimented, channelled, arranged, codified, regulated and unified to obtain perfect homogeneity supervised by an omniscient patriarch. This explains the recourse to different coercive systems of surveillance, from the panopticon organisation in *Out of Ireland* to the latest technology in *The Last Love Story*.

It is generally thought that exploitation of fear is naturally more evident in a dystopia. In her strongly political novel *The Reading Group* (1988), Amanda Lohrey gives a dystopian vision of a two-tiered Australian society whose individuals, upset by the disintegration of the social fabric, end up losing their identity. According to Paul Salzman, 'the atmosphere of threat and paranoia' is 'created by what is essentially a projection of the political atmosphere of the late 1980s'. More recently, Andrew McGahan's fifth novel *Underground* (2006) is a dystopian political fiction, if not a satirical exploration of the abuses of the Howard government's war on terror and the draconian security measures that gradually turned Australian democracy into a military state. John Howard is disguised as Bernard James whose twin brother Leo narrates the story. If *Underground* had the boldness to attack official Howard government policy at the time when the latter was still in power (John Howard was replaced by Labor Prime Minister Kevin Rudd in November 2007), it was strongly disappointing compared with the success of his earlier novel *The White Earth*, which won the Miles Franklin in 2005. Far-fetched developments, cardboard characters and a plot lacking in credibility are the main factors that make reading *Underground* disappointing.

In the same vein, Richard Flanagan's novel *The Unknown Terrorist* (2006) also speaks about terrorism, but indirectly. Twenty-six-year-old Gina Davies, the lover of Tariq and a professional striptease artist working in the Chairman's Lounge in a seedy inner suburb of Sydney, becomes the main suspect in a terrorist plot that aims to destroy the Sydney Olympic Stadium on the eve of Mardi Gras. As with *Underground*, this novel deals with the instrumentalisation of fear, not through political power this time, but by the fourth estate. By becoming the scapegoat of the media capitalising on the sordid event, Gina finds herself – in an ironic twist for a stripteaser – stripped of everything and completely disgraced.

The exploitation of terrorism in Australian literature is not new. At the start of the 1980s, it became a topical subject for novelists such as David Malouf, who wrote *Child's Play* (1982) and Jennifer Maiden with her novel *The Terms* (1982). However, after the 9/11 attacks, terrorism was heavily exploited by the great names of the contemporary novel with varying success. While the endeavours of McGahan and Flanagan were not convincing, those of Janette Turner Hospital* and Adib Khan achieved honours in this area.

Abid Khan's fifth novel, *Spiral Road* (2007), interweaves aspects of identity in the author's earlier works and Islamic terrorism to catch a glimpse of the dilemmas faced by Masud Alam, a fifty-year-old man born in Bangladesh who has been living in Melbourne for several years. His past as a militant student catches up with him when he returns to his native land to look after his father, who is suffering from Alzheimer's disease. Masud discovers that his brother Zia and his nephew Omar have radical ideas and are harbouring destructive plans. Masud's dilemma will be choosing which side he belongs to.

Hailed by critics, Janette Turner Hospital's *Due Preparations*

Panoramic view of Janette Turner Hospital

Janette Turner Hospital has led a nomadic life since her early childhood. Born in 1942 in Melbourne, she settled in Brisbane in 1950 and took up a teaching career before her marriage in 1965 to Clifford Hospital whom she followed to Boston in the United States.

Since her first novel *The Ivory Swing* (1982), rewarded by the Seal – a prestigious Canadian literary prize – she has been translated into many languages. As an expatriate, she has lived in Canada, the United States, Britain, India and France, gathering experiences that have fuelled her prolific writing: *The Claimant* (2014), *Forecast: Turbulence* (2012) *Orpheus Lost* (2007), *Due Preparations for the Plague* (2003), *Oyster* (1996), *The Last Magician* (1992), *Charades* (1988), *Borderline* (1985), *The Tiger in the Tiger Pit* (1983), a detective story *A Very Proper Death* (1990, using her pseudonym of Alex Juniper) and three collections of short stories.

Her novels, containing many autobiographical elements, often relate the unfortunate destiny of educated women and are a reflection of her strong taste for an itinerant lifestyle in the postmodern world. Even though she is seen as adept at internationalism, Hospital has her roots deeply entrenched in Australia. As a novelist, she considers that she can write about anything she wants to as long as she researches in detail subjects in which she has no expertise. Although she has published mainly novels, she has a particularly strong inclination for the more exacting form of the short story, which demands more rigour on the part of its creator. Her novels take their inspiration from the complexities of life experiences, her own and of people she meets along the way.

Enjoying the status of a distinguished professor in several faculties, Hospital has reaped university honours and literary prizes overseas. In 2003, she received the Patrick White Award for lack of recognition in Australia for her work. It was not until mid-2009 that *Rainforest Narratives*, a full-length study of her writing by David Callahan, was published.

for the Plague (2003) is another novel about Islamic terrorism. It recounts a fictitious plane hijacking, Flight 64 Air France leaving Paris for New York on 8 September 1987. The destruction of the plane in Iraq costs the lives of more than four hundred people. However, in an act of leniency, the terrorists spare a few children like Lowell Hawthorne, Samantha Raleigh and Jacob Levinstein, who live with this painful memory for about ten years. Some want to know who the supporters and participants of the tragedy were; others repress the trauma. *Due Preparations for the Plague* is both a spy thriller and a psychological crime novel and takes up the ethical question of evil set against international terrorism, a phenomenon perceived as a scourge and likened to the plague. The novel almost becomes a conspiracy theory. What if the Central Intelligence Agency was involved in this sordid matter? Did the mysterious American, Salamander, order or direct the hijacking? For what purpose? Hospital's *Orpheus Lost* (2007) continues in the terrorist-novel vein by depicting terror and suspicion in the love relationship between Michael Bartok (alias Michka) and his partner Leela-May Moore. An expert in mathematics, she will do her best to find and save Michka who vanished into thin air.

Crime thrillers also nurture political themes since their authors, who have for a long time been considered as belonging to an infra-literature, use their literary marginalisation to denounce imperfections in the system. English-born Fergus Hume gained instant success with his detective story written in Australia, *The Mystery of a Hansom Cab* (c. 1886). Shane Maloney, one of the best known writers of the genre, introduced humour in his six novels so that their subversive nature is more readily accepted. Unlike most detectives portrayed as ageless in most crime novels, Murray Theodore Whelan is an atypical Hercule Poirot who does grow old throughout his adventures and over time. Maloney, inspired by popular culture, is unfortunately often guilty of overusing formulaic phrases.

Historical truth recreated

It is generally accepted that a work of imagination is built on reality, which contributes to the psychology of the characters, the historical context, the fictional setting, the authenticity of certain situations modelled on the author's life and so on. As the substrata of all literature, real-life minor events have multiple uses. When they are not inspiration for the basic structure of the plot, they are the engine that enables the narrative to unfold. They also take the reader back to a pre-text and an after-text when they do not legitimise the story. But more than that, facts give the text substance so that the reader can read it literally or symbolically. Using real but insignificant events in Australian historical novels could be construed as a compensatory strategy. It enables writers to give historical weight to more than two centuries of European occupation of a country that some people would deem too new. With this in mind, the national historical novel fits into three main movements: convict fiction, contact-history fiction and the pioneer saga. It should be noted that contemporary novels again draw from this breeding ground, which had not been exploited since the end of the Second World War.

Australia is very often viewed as a far-off country at the *end* of the world. Its populations are represented in fictional space as evolving at the *edge* of the world and on the margins of world history. But it is another story altogether on the national scale. The period of colonisation, which was painfully set up with convicts in chains, has indelibly branded generations of Australian novelists, especially since the 1980s because of discussions held in 1988 during the bicentenary of the arrival of the First Fleet – the maritime convoy of the first British convicts under the command of Captain Arthur Phillip. Writers like Peter Carey, Kate Grenville, Colin Johnson, Christopher Koch, Richard Flanagan, David Malouf* and Roger McDonald appropriated these colonial episodes according to their respective sensitivities and, in this way, gave an impetus to the publication of a huge number of historical novels.

Panoramic view of David Malouf

David Malouf was born in 1934 in Brisbane where he lived until he left for Europe in 1959. When his father died in 1968, he returned to Australia. He became a lecturer at Sydney University before publishing his first poems and his early novel *Johnno* (1975). He rapidly became known as a poet, novelist, short story writer, essayist, playwright and librettist. In 1978, he dedicated himself to writing and decided to spend his time between Australia and Tuscany in Italy. After four short novels were published (*An Imaginary Life* in 1978, *Child's Play* and *Fly Away Peter* in 1982, then *Harland's Half Acre* in 1984, a story partly inspired by the life of Australian artist Ian Fairweather), *The Great World* (1991) brought him international success with the award of the Commonwealth Writer's Prize and the Prix Femina Étranger. *Remembering Babylon* (1993) further confirmed his reputation as a great writer when it gained the Los Angeles Times Fiction Prize and the IMPAC Dublin Literary Award. In 2000, after publishing a novel (*The Conversations at Curlow Creek*, 1996) and a collection of short stories (*Untold Tales*, 1999), Malouf received the Neustadt International Prize for Literature. It was not until 2009 that the author published another novel, *Ransom*.

Most of his novels are set in Australia and pose questions about metamorphoses in life. According to Malouf, his native country needs to be re-imagined, constructed verbally in the form of literary and cultural representations. He is precisely serving this myth-making process, which informs the Australian ethos, in the imaginative space of his fiction. By combining mind and body, the individual and nature, past and present, place and identity, his books substantially treat polymorphic exile inherent in the Australian and postcolonial condition. The historical novel for him is a means of mentally appropriating history and of incorporating it in the collective unconscious. His homosexual identity is hinted at through the recurrence of the motif of two men united by family ties or friendship.

In 1987, David Malouf was made an Officer of the Order of Australia for contributions to literature. His many prize-winning works and the quality of his writing make him an outstanding Nobel Prize candidate.

The historical novel is Christopher Koch's preferred genre. In *Out of Ireland*, he recounts the misadventures of Robert Devereux, an Irish political prisoner exiled in the Bermudas and later in Van Diemen's Land (now Tasmania) where he comments incessantly on the outlying location of this British colony. *Out of Ireland* offers a double depiction of Australia. On the one hand, there is *Australia Felix* with the *hortus conclusus* theme: a paradise blessed with its pristine vegetation; on the other hand, it is a damned land with the classic image of the infernal nightmare based on Dante's *Inferno* functioning as hypotext in this palimpsest. Besides a poetic tone, the two works share the same narrative schema: a triptych about forms of condemnation, expiation and liberation. The author takes on the existential concept of the Middle Ages, of living as a pilgrim whose one aim is to reach God and paradise. In short, Koch's and Dante's stories deal with a soul in search of salvation in a profane insular world which takes on a sacred quality with the addition of an allegorical religious dimension. The island becomes a pure and purifying symbol. More than just a world for the damned, it is the incarnation of the expiatory antechamber in paradise that leads to deliverance. Koch depicts a merciless prison universe based on privation and coercion. Peopled with the dregs of British society (convicted criminals, villains and harlots) and controlled by a ubiquitous administration, the colony is also held as being responsible for persecutions inflicted on Australia's first inhabitants. Terror and debauchery reign in Van Diemen's Land: sadism, drunkenness, pederasty, insecurity and paranoia are the prisoners' daily lot. Koch depicts for us the persistent anxiety of the characters that are, or say they are, spied upon. This novel confirms the idea that Australian history has its roots deeply grounded in repressed violence.

Jack Maggs (1997) evokes a weighty heritage by having England haunted by its colonial past. Peter Carey's eponymous character is an orphan driven to the brink of criminality by a merciless British system. Maggs is thrown into prison and transported to Australia in accordance with the tradition of convict literature. He returns to England full of illusions only to be disillusioned. The metaphor of somnambulism perfectly conveys the idea that sleepwalker Maggs is imprisoned by his dream of an idealised mother country. Written in the style of a Victorian melodrama, the novel is a postcolonial re-writing of Charles Dickens' *Great Expectations*, Jack Maggs being a reinvented version of the convict Magwitch. This narrative takes up a common theme in Australian literature, the theme of loss lived out as a traumatic experience giving rise to a feeling of abandonment. According to David Malouf (and Jack Maggs is a typical example), Australians like being seen as orphans in the Pacific abandoned by a wicked stepmother, namely perfidious Albion.

Gould's Book of Fish (2001) and *The Secret River* (2005) are two other works that fit into the colonial literary genre. *Gould's Book of Fish* by Richard Flanagan,* is presented as a reconstruction of the *Sketchbook of Fishes in Macquarie Harbour* by William Buelow Gould, a work the main character Sid Hammet has lost. Sentenced to life imprisonment, Gould is a convict ordered to sketch all the fish of Sarah Island, to which he was transported in the late 1820s. This Commonwealth Writers' Prize-winning novel, which also reads like a fable of the colonial period, is a fine illustration of historiographic metafiction. *The Secret River* by Kate Grenville is written in the tradition of the colonial literature in vogue in the nineteenth century. It takes up the archetypal plot of the convict who is offered a new life in Australia at the end of his sentence. William Thornhill, destitute in London at the end of the eighteenth century, was, like Daniel Defoe's Moll Flanders, reduced to thieving in order to survive. His infamy does not go unnoticed but he escapes the death penalty by being transported to New South Wales with his pregnant wife Sal and their child. Upon arrival, they grow poles apart. William mistrusts the Aboriginal people and is given a patch of land on which he establishes himself. His wife makes contact with the Indigenous people more easily

Low-angle shot of Richard Flanagan

Born in 1961, Richard Flanagan grew up in Rosebery, a Tasmanian mining town, and graduated from the University of Tasmania. He expanded his erudition and honed his narrative techniques when trying his hand at nonfiction in the mid 1980s to early 1990s before the publication of his first novel, *Death of a River Guide* (1994).

When not taking up the cudgels for noble causes, Flanagan, like Patrick White, is a stylist whose transnational and nationalist novels have gained belated recognition from the Australian literary establishment.

Despite the fact that *The Unknown Terrorist* (2006) is not the best of his works, Flanagan had brilliant success with haunting and powerful tales such as *Death of a River Guide* (1994), *The Sound of One Hand Clapping* (1997), *Gould's Book of Fish: A Novel in Twelve Fish* (2001) and *Wanting* (2008), which received a few awards in Australia, England and the United States, as well as being shortlisted for the Miles Franklin. His literary masterpiece to date is *The Narrow Road to the Deep North* (2013) for which Flanagan was awarded the 2014 Man Booker Prize. The novel is largely based on the story of his father, Archie Flanagan, who survived the Burma Death Railway and passed away on the very day his son completed the typescript. This POW narrative focussing on the adventures of Dorrigo Evans is a humane and moving account of wartime experience which, to some extent, is illustrative of Flanagan's 'late style' – to quote Edward Said's phrase.

Like Christos Tsiolkas, Flanagan went into journalism after his bachelor's degree and proved to have a taste for opinionated pieces and controversial topics, mostly related to politics and the environment. His most influential essay on logging company Gunns was instrumental in curbing the selling-out of Tasmanian forests and won the 2008 John Curtin Prize for Journalism. A multi-talented artist, Richard Flanagan turned *The Sound of One Hand Clapping* (1997) into a feature film in 1998 and, a decade later, co-wrote the script of *Australia* (2008) with movie director Baz Luhrmann. In 2015 he was appointed to the inaugural Boisbouvier Chair in Australian Literature.

but yearns for London, where she was born. When the wheel of fortune turns in his favour, Thornhill sees his business prosper.

When Kate Grenville just missed out on the 2006 Miles Franklin, it was awarded to another novel about the colonial period, an avatar of the pioneering saga. *The Ballad of Desmond Kale* (2005) deals with the wool industry when Merinos contributed to the rise of the Australian economy in the same way as the goldfields. We see in this seventh novel by Roger McDonald, which fits into the colonial novel tradition, an analogy between sheep and men who had to show endurance in order to withstand particularly hostile conditions and respond to the demands of an imperial centre. Two men, an Irish political prisoner Desmond Kale and the Reverend Matthew Stanton, Protestant to the core, are shoulder to shoulder in trying to gain the fleece market worth its weight in gold. As there is no sheepfold without land, McDonald places great importance on the literary representation of the geographical landscape.

The legend of Ned Kelly keeps us in the centre of rural Australia at a time when its society was composed of squatters and selectors. *A priori* the rebellious attitude of Edward Kelly (1855–1880) is characteristic of a more general battle fought in particular by the Irish against the tyrannical British colonial system of the nineteenth century. The story of this Australian Robin Hood – for some a true national hero, though his deeds and misdeeds still divide the Australian people – has caused a lot of ink to flow from the pens of novelists. As if to mark the centenary of the death of this agitator of Irish ancestry, Australian writers published six novels about Ned Kelly between 1980 and 2000, celebrating his gallant last stand in front of a large group of policemen. This notorious brigand was the eldest of a large family of siblings and was just eleven years old when he had to take over as head of the family after his father's death. The untimely death of Ned, who was hanged within the walls of the Melbourne prison, is to some extent responsible for his being regarded as sacred and for his being lionised in literature.

The four major novelists who perpetuated early colonial larrikin literature by using the Ned Kelly story are: Jean Bedford, Bertram Chandler, Robert Drewe and Peter Carey. In *Sister Kate* (1982), Jean Bedford erodes the phallocentric myth of Ned Kelly by a succinct telling of his tribulations in the first third of this feminist novel, before finally concentrating on the short love life of his sister, the eponymous Kate, who meets a tragic end. Kate's partiality as narrator is found in the demonisation of authorities who put her brother in the position of a victim. In *Kelly Country* (1983), a science fiction novel containing a series of flashbacks and flash-forwards, Bertram Chandler uses the siege at Glenrowan for his political dystopia. His story rests on the fictional failure of Thomas Curnow to escape from among the hostages and reveal Ned's plans, which of course leads to the successful derailing of the police train and to the crushing victory of the outlaw whose exacerbated nationalism contributes to the foundations of a republic a few generations later. Not only does the homodiegetic narrator Duffin Grimes have the freedom to write about anything he wants to, namely to correct history, but he also measures 'the frightening possibilities' of power to intercede in the course of events in order to shape the future. *Our Sunshine* (1991) by Robert Drewe sticks more to reality as he traces the erratic career of the popular hero. The novel's title, which uses the nickname given to Ned by his deceased father John Kelly, suggests the humane sentiment infused in the diegesis is clearly an attempt to rehabilitate this young man persecuted by the authorities. Drewe's originality, taken up by Carey, resides in the perspective he adopts. By making Ned his narrator, he gives him a voice to justify his actions and allows the reader to identify with the character. Peter Carey continues the psychological approach chosen by Drewe and adds a few twists to the story in his version, *True History of the Kelly Gang* (2000). The 'true history' evoked in the title is ironic since, according to Carey, historical facts represent an infinitesimal part of the story. The novelist used the Jerilderie letter, one of the few historical writings by Ned Kelly, to give the correct tone to his book. It is based on a manuscript Ned would have left his fictitious daughter, conceived with a no less fictitious Mary Hearn – two unexpected twists Carey gave the myth.

Historical novels that swing between myth and reality are invariably inspired by true events on which the author's imagination and aims are grafted to produce a work of fiction. These more or less linear stories follow a set pattern of events that can thus be summarised: a brief description of Ned's childhood at Eleven Mile Creek in Victoria; the altercation in April 1878 with agent Alexander Fitzpatrick who tried to seduce young Catherine Kelly; the forming of the outlaw band (Ned, his brother Dan, their friends Joe Byrne and Aaron Sherritt), the insurrection and getaway; the killing of three policemen at Stringybark Creek; the first bank hold-up at Euroa (in northeast Victoria); their raid on Jerilderie in New South Wales when Ned dictated his legendary letter; the execution by Joe of his long-time friend Aaron; the escape of the teacher Thomas Curnow (held hostage in the Glenrowan Inn with other town folk), whom the Kellys deliberately allow to leave when the inn becomes a blazing inferno; Ned's failed derailing of a police train and the eventual death of the four bushrangers. Among the secondary elements sometimes added to the narrative structure are: the arrest of young Ned, charged with two counts of highway robbery; the influence of the outlaw Harry Power; the homosexual implications that underlie the bandits' cross-dressing; the Queensland Aboriginal trackers who have the task of flushing out the band of thugs; armour made from ploughshares to withstand attacks from the authorities; the arrest of the leader and his hanging after Judge Sir Redmond Barry had pronounced the execution order.

The myth, which according to François Laplantine in *Les trois voix de l'imaginaire* is 'by nature irreducible to one transcription', allows each novelist to enrich it by their own re/presentation while taking part in constructing the oxymoronic image of Ned

Kelly, a direct consequence of his polymorphic history. Half angel, half demon, ingenious crook and scapegoat, a villain with a heart of gold, dispenser of and answerable to justice, social outcast and political militant: it is difficult to accurately define this legendary figure of the Australian bush. And yet, like any mythical hero, he stands out by emphasising a moral or physical trait. Bedford and Drewe take the opposite stance to the journalistic propaganda of the period by showing the humane face of Ned. Chandler emphasises the character's boldness and ingenuity, while Carey plays on the paternal feelings that Ned Kelly could have had by imagining a daughter who, according to historians, never existed.

The Conversations at Curlow Creek (1996) is the second part of a diptych of the colonial period depicted by David Malouf. His tableau, inspired by the long line of Australian bushrangers, evokes nineteenth-century barbarity by using reported events. Adair, a British cavalryman, interrogates a man condemned to death the night before he is to be executed on the gallows. During his confession, the convict, who had become a bushranger, talks as much about the cruelty of the colonial era, relations with authorities and the difficulties experienced when the colony was being established, as he does about the more metaphysical concerns of time and death. With his characteristically elegant style, David Malouf writes his novel with great sensitivity, transcending colonialism and reaching down into the very core of existence. *The Conversations at Curlow Creek* is the companion to *Remembering Babylon* (1993), another novel about colonisation in the nineteenth century in which David Malouf discusses confrontation other than physical conflict with Aboriginal people. Thrown into the sea at the age of thirteen, Gemmy Fairley from Britain is saved by a group of Aboriginal people and spends sixteen years with them in northern Queensland. When Gemmy learns that there is a Scottish community nearby, he sets off to meet them and succeeds in changing their attitudes and their way of thinking. *Remembering Babylon* capitalises on the myths of the noble savage and the lost child, common in Australian literature. This book, considered as Malouf's *chef d'oeuvre*, does not however offer any resolution to the mysterious disappearance of Gemmy.

Poorly considered by its author but acclaimed by critics, *Doctor Wooreddy's Prescription for Enduring the Ending of the World* (1983) offers a new historical interpretation. Colin Johnson gives us his diagnosis of the evils suffered by the Aboriginal population in their contact with the colonial masters. Wooreddy, a member of the Bruny Island clan, avoids the government policy of being placed on a reserve with the help of the paternalistic and zealous evangelist George Augustus Robinson, who makes it his duty as a missionary to save 'these poor heathens'. Robinson's salutary mission makes him decide to take the Bruny people under his wing to Flinders Island, then on to the Australian mainland. In the novel, the noble savage myth is shattered in the final chapter by an Aboriginal uprising that makes Robinson's enterprise a disastrous failure. The story's content demonstrates every type of fragmentation: geographic division (the consequence of deportation and regrouping in reserves); the fragmentation of history (deliberately hidden historical episodes that Johnson tries to re-establish); the breaking down of social fabric; the dissemination of Aboriginal remains (thrown into the sea); and the tearing away of the Aboriginal people from their land and its close spiritual ties. There follows a spiritual division caused by evangelisation and worsened by the introduction of alcohol. Added to this is a psychic division that evokes an identity crisis symptomatic of schizophrenia for writers of dual heritage. Since they are placed between two cultures, these authors are divided to the point that they no longer know where they belong, giving rise to multiple metaphors for duality. A parallel theme is contamination, that exposes the physical and psychological suffering of these people. Traditionally, Europeans played the role of the aggressor responsible for many infections that decimated the Aboriginal people. In line with the bad omen announced in the opening lines of the novel, the atmosphere rapidly becomes nightmarish, since the dying population on Bruny Island are victims of the 'coughing demon', tuberculosis, imported by sailors. This suffering reads like an old familiar story, as persistent as sharp pain. For a long time, Wooreddy had felt his only salvation was to flee from the situation. But illness and poverty dogged him and finally caught up with him, making a widow of his wife Trugernanna.

Did Colin Johnson think he needed to make a clean slate of the past so that a new depiction of historical facts could be set in place? Or did he aim to fight against the fragmentation and contamination of the Indigenous people by Western invasion? It is true that Johnson's writing can be read as a prescription or a cure for the suffering of Indigenous people and the spread of Western evils. By fitting the pieces together, Johnson acts as a healing shaman. Because *Doctor Wooreddy's Prescription for Enduring the Ending of the World* belongs to political literature, this novel – in spite of Colin Johnson's usurped identity – is not like a poultice on a wooden leg. Quite the contrary; it strikes the imagination with its vast socio-political dimension – a defining trait of Aboriginal literature. The case of Colin Johnson invites us to reflect on the right to poetic licence. It is interesting in that it brings irrefutable proof that a person can talk about things and conditions outside their culture. For Colin Johnson, words were alternatively palliative (by their analgesic effect, they have eased Aboriginal suffering), curative (they have healed wounded souls) and preventive (since they prevent the repetition of evils). His writing, no matter how non-Aboriginal it is, nevertheless meditates on and mediates the traumatic past.

While these authors attempted to record historical events and wrongdoings in Australia, others like Thomas Keneally felt more at ease with tragedies on a global scale, like the Holocaust in *Schindler's Ark* (1982).* Awarded the Booker Prize, this novel was published at the same time as the Australian reading public became less concerned with fiction and more interested in real life minor events found in historical novels and life stories. Rodney

Low-angle shot of *Schindler's Ark* by Thomas Keneally

Published originally as *Schindler's Ark* in 1982 and later as *Schindler's List*, following the success of Spielberg's 1993 film, this novel is a 'faction': namely, a story of journalistic construction with a political crisis as its base, inspired to a large extent by facts within a historic framework. In fact, the idea of the book began in 1980 after Keneally visited a leather repair shop owned by Leopold Pfeifferberg, who told him of his experience during the Shoah.

Almost a documentary, this fully researched book is based on a series of interviews conducted with fifty or so of Schindler's survivors from seven countries: Australia, Israel, Germany, Austria, America, Argentina and Brazil. Thomas Keneally tried not to give a slant to historical truth, though he occasionally took liberties with it. For example, it is not clearly indicated if saving the Jews had been organised at Mrs Schindler's instigation. Also, Oskar Schindler's generosity was not altogether altruistic since there was some advantage in it for him: Jewish labour meant he was able to keep his factory running at a very low cost.

When Poland was occupied by the Germans, this German/Czech industrialist decided to employ intellectual Jews in his factory and thumb his nose at Adolf Hitler's final solution. It took many shady compromises, negotiations and transactions to achieve his ends and lessen the impact of the Nazis' extermination enterprise. As a tribute to his charitable acts when Oskar died in October 1974, the survivors of the Holocaust organised for his remains to be taken to Israel so that he could be buried in hallowed ground.

An ambiguous character, Oskar Schindler was not a saint, even if he went bankrupt in saving the lives of the captives. A great womaniser, he was unfaithful to his wife Emilie and even went so far as to stake the life of a Jewish servant, Helen Hirsch, during a game of cards with the camp's commandant Amon Goeth.

Hall explored the Nazi phenomenon more openly with *The Day We Had Hitler Home* (2000). It is not to be thought that Australian novelists are incapable of writing historical novels about universal subjects. Quite the reverse! Read for instance Sallie Muirden's novels written in a baroque postmodernist style and grounded in European culture, Spanish for the most part: *Revelations of a Spanish Infanta* (1996), *We Too Shall be Mothers* (2001), *A Woman of Seville: A novel of love, ladders and the unexpected* (2009). As additional examples, among the numerous historical novelists who have tackled universal themes, suffice to mention Frank Moorhouse's triptych about the United Nations (*Grand Days*, 1993, and *Dark Palace*, 2000, and *Cold Light*, 2010), and Roger McDonald's *Mr Darwin's Shooter* (1998) about the eponymous scientist. However, except for *Schindler's Ark* and a few other novels, I have taken the liberty to discuss in this concise literary history only the works that specifically address Australian concerns.

With *The Great World* (1990), David Malouf subverts the Second-World-War historical novel by considering real life minor events as significant as major historical events. In his historical novel focusing on the private world of people's feelings and relationships, global war is used as a backdrop for the writer to explore the cult of mateship. Children of the Great Depression, Vic Curran and Albert Keen, alias Digger, are joined in friendship forged by adversity in wartime during their internment in a Japanese prisoner-of-war camp in the early to mid 1940s. Digger, a taciturn dreamer with modest ambitions, is the exact opposite of Vic, a self-taught materialist who went from rags to riches. In spite of this, their unshakeable friendship survives the hardships and tribulations of life over the years up until Vic breathes his last. This rather sombre novel is haunted by death hovering over a chaotic chronology.

These novels that correct or denounce official versions of Australian history do not represent isolated cases. Other stories, including those written by certain Aboriginal novelists, carry on this tradition of a politically engaged literature.

Affirmation of the Aboriginal novel

There are two traditions in the writings of Aboriginal authors.* On the one hand, there are those who see in literature a means of putting down on paper and perpetuating an oral tradition by transcribing myths and legends in order to pass them on from one generation to the next so that they do not disappear. This is essentially the case of writers of autobiographical fiction such as Elsie Roughsey and Sally Morgan, famous for *My Place* (1987). On the other hand, there are those who, strengthened by diehard activism, try to create a political agenda with literature. Essentially, these include Aboriginal novelists such as Archie Weller, whose identity was contested in 1997 but who is still famous for his deeply pessimistic novel *The Day of the Dog* (1981); Vivienne Cleven of the Kamilaroi nation; Anita Heiss, a Wiradjuri woman; Terri Janke from the Wuthati and Meriam peoples; Melissa Lucashenko, who belongs to the Murri community; Kim Scott, worthy representative of the Nyoongar people; Tara June Winch of the Wiradjuri clan; and Alexis Wright, who belongs to the Aboriginal community Waanyi of the high plateaux to the south of the Gulf of Carpentaria.

Among the main injustices denounced by Aboriginal novelists are those committed in the name of the concept of *terra nullius*. These were the deep concerns of Terri Janke. A part-Aboriginal lawyer, Janke published her first novel *Butterfly Song* in 2005 and based it on her own life. After obtaining her law degree and on the request of her mother, protagonist Tarena returns to her ancestral land to recover a brooch in the shape of a butterfly sculpted by her grandfather out of mother-of-pearl shell and given to his wife as a love token. This mission raises a painful past and begins a litigation which, in many ways, symbolises the legal battle of Eddie Mabo (1936–1992) to have his land rights recognised by the High Court. Mabo died before hearing the verdict in his favour and seeing it applied legally as the Native Title Act, approved in September 1993. So the reader understands the moral of the story: that some

Close-up of several Aboriginal authors

Contemporary fiction by Aboriginal authors certainly is not thin on the ground. Among the award-winning examples is the work of Anita Heiss, a leading Aboriginal writer and commentator, whose smart and popular black chick lit fiction breaks the mould and challenges stereotypes. Her novels include *Not Meeting Mr Right* (2007); *Avoiding Mr Right* (2008); *Manhattan Dreaming* (2010); *Paris Dreaming* (2011) and *Tiddas* (2014). In *Mullumbimby* (2013), Melissa Lucashenko moves on from her earlier grunge realism to weave a strong, passionate story of place and community set in the author's traditional country. A sense of place and pride in Aboriginal heritage are also the distinctive traits of Dylan Coleman's novels. In *'Mazin Grace* (2012), she fictionalises her mother's life with an impressive closeness to local language (Kokatha) and customs, as part of everyday life in a remote community. Tony Birch draws on his own upbringing in inner city Melbourne in *Blood* (2011) and other works. His sharp writing is appreciated by those who might normally avoid books, particularly teenage boys. Jared Thomas, likewise, writes award-winning novels for young adults. In *Sweet Guy* (2005) and *Calypso Summer* (2013), he engages with the dreams and difficulties of young men with humour, insight and edge. Concerned with social justice, Larissa Behrendt turns to her own family and life experience in her novels *Home* (2002) and *Legacy* (2010). A distinguished law professor, Behrendt is a passionate advocate for Indigenous rights. This is also true of Fabienne Bayet-Charlton, whose *Watershed* (2005) was published before her untimely death in 2011. Bayet-Charlton spent her formative years in Coober Pedy and explored identity-related matters in her writing. Through her determination to observe and document, she became a valued literary artist.

All these novelists have managed to combine their creative writing aspirations with successful academic careers.

things, even if they appear to have no great value, must be given back to their owners. There is also strong activism in *Carpentaria*, by Alexis Wright,* the 2007 Miles Franklin winner. Will, the son of Norm Phantom and his wife Angel Day, fights till his last breath against the predatory capitalists of the Gurfurrit Mine who defend tooth and nail, and even illegally, their economic interests in the gulf region of Carpentaria. The author draws from allegory, myth and satire to give this postcolonial saga and mythopoetic narrative an operatic resonance which flirts with magical realism.

It is not only in novels that *terra nullius* has been denounced. Voices are more often heard in Aboriginal autobiographical stories and memoirs where they endeavour to strongly criticise the consequences of the neglect and non-recognition of Aboriginal people since the early stages of colonisation. In order not to be a victim of 'Aboriginalism' (that is, a European-centred model of representing Aboriginal people), writers have taken things in hand by publishing their life stories to affirm a past that people wanted to expunge by placing in limbo. These slices of life are published partly for a non-Aboriginal readership. The autobiographical Aboriginal story is a hybrid genre that sits between the novel and the memoir. To take up Fanny Duthil's analysis in *Histoire de femmes aborigènes*, the challenge with the majority of Aboriginal women writers from an oral tradition is to help them formulate the narrative so as to match the standards expected from a story published in the Western tradition. The formulating is either personal, as in the case of Elsie Roughsey's *An Aboriginal Mother Tells of the Old and the New* published in 1983, or the result of a rewrite with the help of a ghost writer. A prime example of this practice is Shirley Smith's *Mum Shirl* published in 1987 and written to a large extent by Roberta Sykes, whose Aboriginal identity was legitimately challenged.

Because these *hétérobiographies* (a term coined by Philippe Lejeune) are not reflexive, they pose the double problem of authorship and of the authenticity of the story whose form and

Low-angle shot of Alexis Wright

Born in 1950 in Cloncurry in Queensland, Alexis Wright is a rising star of the Aboriginal novel genre. As the place-name titles of her two novels indicate, Alexis Wright is a regional author who has a definite attachment to the land and gives pride of place in her writings to the lands of her group. Her first title, *Plains of Promise* (1997), is an expression used by the first explorers to describe the Gulf of Carpentaria, alluding to the beautiful grazing lands that the region offered livestock. Irony is subtly present throughout, since the explorers' discovery did not promise any benefit for the Indigenous people.

The same locale is taken up in *Carpentaria* (2006) and in her third novel, *The Swan Book* (2013), which is set in the chaotic future of climate refugees and condemned mankind. Aunty Bella Donna has managed to survive by fleeing to northern Australia where she rescues Oblivia, a mute Aboriginal girl left for dead after being gang raped. *Plains of Promise* brings to the fore another tragedy, the stolen generation, while *Carpentaria* explores land claims through a saga told by elders for the young generation against a background of conflicts arising from the mining industry.

Alexis Wright's militancy is serene but efficient. She has long been interested in her people's land rights as well as their social and cultural rights and has worked to achieve these in a number of administrative positions in defence of Indigenous people, while publishing many political papers including a manifesto available only in French, *Croire en l'incroyable* (*Believe in the Unbelievable*, 2000). A collection of seven short stories was published in French (*Le Pacte du serpent arc-en-ciel*, 2002) before *Carpentaria* gained her a host of literary prizes, including the prestigious Miles Franklin.

Respectful of Aboriginal protocols, she admits to not being completely free to tell her stories and realises that this editorial policy is not conducive to creativity. Following protocols implies restriction while at the same time poetic licence gives the artist infinite power and the feeling of being able to talk about any subject whatsoever. Married with three children, she is based in Melbourne.

content could have been manipulated. In fact, all the characteristics of an oral form of expression are found in these writings: a story rich in allusions and repetitions; associated patterns of ideas at times responsible for a few digressions; a cyclical concept of time that defies linear chronology; content that is rather anecdotal and tinged with magic realism that befuddles rational Western thinking; a narrator who partially confides in the reader; and the excessive use of direct speech where indirect speech would be expected. The experience of storytelling is certainly cathartic for a large number of Aboriginal women writers, but as they participate in the construction of history by telling their life stories they also edify their readers. Concerning the literary reception of these Aboriginal autobiographies, readers, whose cultural baggage is not exhaustive, do not always fully understand the subtext, especially the symbolic and spiritual overtones. In spite of the fact that Aboriginal literature has flourished since the late 1990s, publishers are generally still rather reluctant when faced with the protocols of editing and marketing, the uncertain profit margin and, in particular, sensitive subjects that may shock some readers.

Another injustice, a double one this time, is the stolen generations, a crime committed with the tacit consent of the Christian church, combined with the assimilation policy which encouraged the forced mixing of Aboriginal people as early as the 1930s. These abuses of power aimed at re-making Aboriginal people so that they could integrate into the European-society mould through education and evangelisation. While toponymy, violence and land claims are recurrent themes, loss appears to be a persistent leitmotiv in many forms: mourning, dispossession of lands, disappearance of ancestors and obliteration of reference points. In *Plains of Promise*, Alexis Wright tells the story of the lost childhood of Ivy, a young Aboriginal girl who was taken away from her mother and given a Western education on a mission in the south. Imbued with Aboriginal beliefs, the novel emphasises the moral and physical abuse inflicted on Indigenous people.

Because of deprivations, they end up feeling empty and this is expressed in an elegiac prose full of despair. *Follow the Rabbit-Proof Fence* (1996) is another book about the stolen generations. Doris Pilkington, also called Nugi Garimara, poignantly recounts how, as an adolescent, her mother Molly and two younger sisters escaped from the mission where they had been confined and walked many kilometres to get back to the Aboriginal camp they had been taken from by the authorities. Molly and her sisters were among the hundreds of thousands of Aboriginal children taken by force from their families between 1910 to 1970 and confined to white guardianship. Along the same lines, *Benang: From the heart* (1999), Kim Scott's Miles Franklin Award-winning novel, tells how the identity of the Aboriginal community is blurred under the assimilation policy and the lies perpetrated by a history that favours the European intruders. White-skinned Harley is the perfect product of this wish to dilute Aboriginal blood by imposing interracial union. Horror overcomes him when he learns that a member of his own family, his grandfather, was a supporter of this infamous policy. The son of an Aboriginal father and a Caucasian mother, Scott consolidated his literary reputation with a quite moving historical drama, *That Deadman Dance* (2010), which was also awarded the Miles Franklin prize. It relates the contact history of the Nyoongar people mainly through the eyes of Bobby Wabalanginy whose Aboriginal name translates as 'all of us playing together'. Bobby straddles his community and the world of settlers on the south coast of Western Australia while believing in a peaceful interaction of both cultures, until he is proven wrong.

Identity is at the core of Aboriginality. As a direct result of her mixed blood, Tara June Winch questions her origins in her first novel *Swallow the Air* (2006) which begins with a wretched description of the Aboriginal condition. Youthful May Gibson, the main character, suffers many setbacks in her life: her mother's suicide, an alcoholic aunt who adopts her, her drug-addicted brother Billy who runs away and so on. May decides to set out in search of her father, a mission that quickly morphs into a Socratic quest aimed at determining the authenticity of her Aboriginality. The poetic tone of the novel and the beauty of certain lyrical descriptive passages tend to make the reader overlook some awkward structures.

Vivienne Cleven is perhaps the most iconoclastic of this generation of Aboriginal authors. Her first novel *Bitin' Back* (2001), which oscillates between mascara and masquerade, broaches the question of transvestism with a truculent and original approach. At Mandamooka, an Aboriginal woman realises that her son Nevil Dooley – convinced that he is the novelist Jean Rhys – dresses in women's clothes. Nevil's mother, who is afraid of community disgrace, devises several strategies to keep her son from indiscreet eyes during the time he is going through his identity crisis. Cleven's second novel *Her Sister's Eye* (2002) also plays with identities – especially that of the character Archie Corella – but does not match the subtlety of *Bitin' Back*. For Melissa Lucashenko, there is no fixed Aboriginal identity. Perusing *Steam Pigs* (1997), the story of an urban Aboriginal woman looking for a way out of her problematic relationship with her lover Roger, the reader realises that it is impossible to give a precise definition of Aboriginality. Sticking to violence in a whodunit entitled *Hard Yards*, Melissa Lucashenko denounces the suspicious deaths of Aboriginal people held in custody.

It can therefore be said that a defining trait of Aboriginal literature is the presence of a significant political and social dimension. Often, Aboriginal discourse reads as a response to Western literary discourse. The European oppressor is sometimes compared to Ria Warrawah, an evil spirit who sows the seeds of violence and destruction upon the earth. Believed to be ghosts, Europeans are held responsible for illness, the ravages of alcohol, violence and abuses that have decimated the Aboriginal people. As a counter-reaction to this, a form of writing arose in the form of a repression/expression dynamic. By taking the role of the oppressed, the disadvantaged Aboriginal figure has become a leitmotiv of this literature in which the Indigenous are depicted as a broken people (spiritually or physically), reduced to the status of Object, hence the frequent use of the passive form in narratives. The slaughter and degradation of Aboriginal people gave way to a new form of abuse: exclusion. Aboriginal people are doubly marginalised since they live on the edge of Australian society, which is itself removed from Europe. Typically enough, the Aboriginal community in *Carpentaria* lives right on the edge of Desperance, a fictional town that strongly resembles Burketown. The theme of ostracism is not new in Alexis Wright's fiction, given that she has already tackled it in *Plains of Promise*.

The disenchanted generation

Contemporary Australian literature somewhat addresses the *zeitgeist* through its warts-and-all depictions of ordinary life in the absence of hope, established authority and happiness. David Foster is probably the author who began this generation of disenchanted authors, but others, like Andrew McGahan with his first novel *Praise* (1992) and *1988* (1995) and Christos Tsiolkas with *Loaded* (1995)* rapidly followed. David Foster, a highly trained scientist, has dedicated himself entirely to writing since 1972. As the author of satirical novels verging on black humour, he is the writer of anomie *par excellence*. Often, his inspiration comes from classical myths and legends that he transposes into today's society. Although they are interesting, his works are too disparate and somewhat eccentric to gain much academic critical acclaim even though four of his novels have won awards: *The Pure Land* (1974), *Moonlite* (1981), *The Glade Within the Grove* (1996) and *In the New Country* (1999). It has to be said that his cynical depiction of contemporary Australian society puts him out of favour with many of his fellow citizens.

Even before Andrew McGahan was known, Peter Carey had tried to write a dark novel, *The Tax Inspector* (1991), which attracted

Close-up of *Loaded* by Christos Tsiolkas

The clever mix of sexuality and ethnicity pervading *Loaded* paved the way for the emergence of gay multicultural fiction. This 150-page novel, divided into four sections that follow the four cardinal points, is an exploration of sexuality and class identity tinged with nihilistic anger. By the same token, Ari's sexual odyssey also offers a literary mapping of the city of Melbourne.

Unlike Patrick White or David Malouf, Christos Tsiolkas has chosen to openly explore his gay identity in his writings, which in *Loaded* comes in the form of two homosexual stereotypes: Ari, the introverted macho who remains discrete about his sexual preferences with the people he has contact with, and his best friend Johnny, the extroverted effeminate kind who at times dresses up as a woman to become Toula. Ari uses all forms of drugs to excess, their effect being sometimes euphoric, sometimes atonic. Drugs and music enable the main character either to connect with people or to remain aloof. It is worth noting that Tsiolkas' subsequent novels (*The Jesus Man*, *Dead Europe*, *The Slap* and *Barracuda*) further pursue the introspective study of his homosexuality.

Even though Tsiolkas has lived with his partner for more than twenty years, he has chosen to speak about polygamy and the incapacity to love. *Loaded* shows this sentimental ambivalence that has Ari torn between love and hatred. Manifestations of love include Ari's frantic search for sexual partners (fuelled by his libidinal energy), the extent of his friendly devotion to Johnny and his perfect integration within the Greek community. As a counterpoint, Ari's chronic bouts of misanthropy, his overt racism and his eschatological desires exemplify aspects of his polymorphic hatred. At the end of the novel through a belated self-revelation, Ari becomes aware of his shallow and insignificant life while thinking about an epitaph he would like to leave behind when he dies: 'he slept, he ate, he fucked, he pissed, he shat. He ran to escape history. That's his story.'

disapproval from the critics who found difficulty in accepting these incestuous paedophilic stories about the Catchprice family. Right in the middle of the seedy suburbs of Western Sydney, Mort Catchprice (Sophie's husband) shamefully abuses his son Benny who later repeats this deviant sexual predation. But there is more to this novel than just a gruesome sex case. Its life-affirming value lies in the eponymous character's bravery – Maria Takis being a tax inspector of Greek descent who seeks to protect the underdog.

Stories of the last twenty years are more introspective, more centred on the individual, more claustrophobic than ever in settings that are rather shabby and essentially urban. Sonya Hartnett, given to oppressive atmospheres, had made a name for herself with *Of a Boy* (2002), which just missed out on the Miles Franklin. The book opens with the abduction of the three Medford children, an event that affected young Adrian and even fuelled his paranoia. He becomes the object of every type of humiliation before meeting a disastrous end. In *Surrender* (2005), Hartnett, a specialist of unhappy childhoods, takes up the theme of the mistreatment and misfortune of a small lonely boy by introducing the *doppelgänger*, the double in literature. Finnigan, a young wild boy, comes to haunt and torment young Anwell who is confined to bed. In a similar vein, *Spirit Wrestlers* (2004) by Thomas Shapcott has the same theme as Hartnett with a young boy, Johann, under the negative influence of the undesirable Ivan, a young Russian immigrant who turns out badly. *Sixty Lights* (2004) by Gail Jones takes up the theme of destitute children by making her main character Lucy Strange an orphan who lost her parents in cruel circumstances. Throughout the novel, the influence of Charles Dickens, especially that of *Great Expectations*, is unambiguously evident. This novel, punctuated and framed by death (that of her parents and her own) and with joyous times peppered with difficulties, is reminiscent of *chiaroscuro* paintings.

To this same stream of novels about destitution can be added *Fantastic Street* (2003) by David Kelly and *The Secret Burial* (2003) by Penelope Sell. Nature was not kind to Alex, the protagonist cum narrator of *Fantastic Street*: he has an unattractive physique, a tormented mind (he has to control his latent homosexuality) and has had a miserable childhood in a poisonous atmosphere marked by family violence: bullied by his stepfather. Living in a Brisbane suburb, Alex's sardonic humour nevertheless enables him to cope with adversity. *The Secret Burial* is an initiation novel that shows the difficult conditions in which Elise has grown up. After the death of her alcoholic mother as a result of an accident, Elise and a willing neighbour secretly organise her mother's burial so that she and her young brother are not taken into custody by government officials. Prematurely thrust into the adult world, Elise takes the place of her mother, up to the point of assuming her identity.

Academic A.L. McCann was not to be outdone. His first novel, *The White Body of Evening* (2002), paints a sordid picture of Melbourne. The unflattering depictions of his characters present the metropolis as corrupt. Even abroad, when in the course of the story the main character Paul Walters goes to Vienna, the pessimism remains. In *Subtopia* (2005), a realistic initiation novel, McCann's story is no less pessimistic, but it contains more autobiographical elements. We recognise the author in Julian Farrell, the young narrator who denounces the inertia of the Melbourne suburbs of the 1970s. His thirst for adventure is quenched when he leaves to live in Berlin and New York as an expatriate. In fact, it is no exaggeration to say that *Subtopia*, which is connected in part to urban literature, opposes the long tradition of the bush story written in the rural tradition. In the city, community spirit has given way to individualism within a vast sterile expanse with characters prone to existential angst, a feeling of loss, vacuity, pessimism and despair. At the same time, this striking contrast shows to what extent man has alienated himself from Mother Nature. The neutral tone of the story and the rather plain style justly reflect this nameless banality.

With *Dead Europe* (2005) whose controversial subject-matter verges on the heretical, Christos Tsiolkas has lived up to his reputation of being consistently daring, if not controversial, with the contents of his novels. *Dead Europe* reads like a grim fairytale with Gothic-laden aesthetics, and one of the worst kinds at that, featuring bloodcurdling and repelling subject matter: vampirism, coprophilia, zoophilia, hustler sex, teenage prostitution, paedophilia, incestuous sex, racism and anti-Semitism for instance. Admittedly, the novelist's dark thoughts and themes have a knack of deliberately confronting readers. Europe is on the decline, metaphorically dead, as the title puts it. Isaac's travel to Greece is a perfect opportunity for readers to witness the dramatic changes in post-Cold War Europe, which has become a haunted and decadent land, corrupted by vice and plagued with cancerous evils. *Dead Europe*, which focuses on the adventures of Isaac Raftis, who gradually develops a taste for vampirism in an Old World steeped in tradition and superstitions, falls within the purview of the fantastic. Parallel to the main plotline, moreover, is the story of Lucia and Michaelis Panagis who have been cursed. After visiting his mother's home village, Isaac – who feels that he has inherited this family curse – morphs into a vampire, thus causing the likely and the unlikely to merge. By meshing homosexual desire with the vampire fiction genre, Tsiolkas has taken up the Victorian Gothic trope which presents homosexuality as a curse in his exploration of the politics of desire, while his status as a major author arguably brings aspects of gay culture to the attention of more readers.

The almost misanthropic content of M.J. Hyland's second novel did not prevent her finding favour with the jury of the Hawthornden Prize, a prestigious British prize worth £10,000. *Carry Me Down* (2006) is a story set in Ireland in the 1970s and narrated by eleven-year-old John Egan who sets about dissecting the adult world he sees as being corrupted by lies. As a general rule, it has to be noted that it is somewhat rare for these pessimistic novels to be noticed by critics. It is likely that Mandy Sayer's novel *The Night has a Thousand Eyes* (2007) will not mark an epoch. In her novel, Roy Stamp's children run away from home when they realise that their father has killed their mother.

Written in a much more morbid tone is the third novel by trained lawyer James Bradley. *The Resurrectionist* (2006) is a gothic crime thriller that reeks of death, as it deals with the sordid activities of grave looters and anatomists. The story is liberally inspired by William Burke and William Harem, two British criminals who killed people and sold their remains to the anatomists in Edinburgh. In 1826, Gabriel Swift, an obscure amoral character, is the apprentice of a London anatomist Edwin Poll who procures corpses illegally. *The Resurrectionist* dissects evil by tracing Gabriel Swift's descent into hell. He is deprived of his status as apprentice and becomes involved in a gang of grave looters.

This *esperectomic* generation of writers (i.e. plagued with the ablation of hope) questions the direction in which the contemporary Australian novel is heading, for it is clear that most of these stories promote the emergence of a novel that is devoid of style, affectation, complexity, originality and fantasising.

Epilogue

The Australian novel, particularly English in character in its early stages, initially complied with colonial British influences. When the first waves of settlers arrived, the European-educated novelists brought with them a cultural baggage that was to prove inefficient in transcribing Antipodean reality. Before Federation, writers maintained the hope that British culture would prosper and assume a new form on much more fertile Antipodean soil. But this Anglomorphism was largely a waste of time and effort since the emerging literature, long perceived as part of British literature, could not easily be compared to older forms of literature.

Half a century later, the Australian novel intermittently began to declare its distinctiveness by praising nationalistic values of egalitarianism, mateship, democracy, independence and endurance in the bush. This would serve as the basis for establishing a federated nation at the turn of the twentieth century. Thus, the bush became the nation's mythical cradle. For a time, this literature was deeply concerned with regional and national issues before finally embracing the wider world towards the end of the 1920s with the publication of the first war novels.

The essentially narrow British readership of this early period increased and diversified at a time when literary criticism, split into rival factions, tried to separate the wheat from the chaff by setting up a canon of literature that aimed at establishing reliable indicators for the Australian reading public. Authors who were not favoured by the critics, like Miles Franklin, had to leave Australia and live overseas to have their works published, or they were forced to use a pseudonym to bypass the literary cliques who set themselves up as the gatekeepers of Australian fiction.

In the 1950s, novelists started to move away from the ubiquitous and outdated realist model and paved the way for new artistic trends such as modernism. At the same time, the large-scale influx of migrants, most of whom were refugees from postwar Europe, and the subsequent abolition of the White Australia Policy broke the cultural homogeneity represented in novels up until then. While this opening out to the world was gradual, writers worldwide were resolved to leave their mark on Australian literature in the 1970s and 1980s. The experience of multiculturalism enabled new voices to be heard and challenged the commonly accepted literary representations of Australianness, all the while promoting new cultures by giving the Australian novel a multi-ethnic flavour. By drastically changing the nature of writing and subverting the norms of the novel genre, novelists laid the emphasis on creativity. However, the bicentenary of Australia's colonisation in 1988 temporarily slowed down these literary inventions by reminding writers that they needed to explore the more traditional historical beginnings of their homeland.

The highly popular novel, boosted by its own success, was to opt for a new direction. Taking into account a full awareness of commodification, fictional prose released by the large publishing houses was now subjected to oversimplification. The aim was to make a lot of money and sell as widely as possible! By pushing this logic to its limit, the graphic novel, in which the story is enhanced by images, represents the ultimate shift in the changing genre.

The Australian novel was thus redefined at every stage. From modest documentary value in the colonial era, it rapidly displayed a mimetic trend and then, at the start of the twentieth century, a political nationalistic ambition. In reaction to the wearisome realism inherited after the Second World War ended, the novel became an anti-mimetic object and was used as part of a political and sociological mission for multiculturalism. In the liberating 1980s, novelists embraced other possibilities by focussing on an aesthetic ambition which vied with the resurgence of mimesis and politics.

With the influence of literary criticism and its tendency to label writers, authors fall into two contrasting categories. The *nationalist novelists*, subdivided as regional writers (like Thea Astley, Miles Franklin, Helen Garner, Dorothy Hewett, David Ireland, David Malouf, Olga Masters, Frank Moorhouse, Gerald Murnane, Mandy Sayers, Tim Winton and Alexis Wright) and national writers (such as Peter Carey, Kate Grenville, Colin Johnson and Katharine Susannah Prichard), are opposed to *transnational novelists*, specialised in treating universal topics, like Shirley Hazzard, Hannah Kent (who wrote her way to fame with *Burial Rites*, 2013) and Sallie Muirden. Some writers fit into both groups: Brian Castro, Richard Flanagan, Rodney Hall, Janette Turner Hospital, Antoni Jach, Thomas Keneally, Christopher Koch, Roger McDonald, Christina Stead, Christos Tsiolkas and Patrick White. So writers find themselves caught between the temptation to exploit national heritage and the desire to broaden subject choice by giving in to the international trend – two polarities where every advantage has its disadvantage. On the one hand, the nationalist authors who are proud to contribute to the building up of a national identity feel that their narrow subjects confine them to a niche market of sorts. On the other hand, the internationalist novelists who enjoy a larger readership and greater freedom of expression run the risk of alienating themselves from their fellow citizens. What a cruel dilemma!

To conclude this panoramic overview, I have to admit I have often had reactions of astonishment, if not incredulity, from my interlocutors when I have spoken about my research into Australian literature. The reason is simple: people seem unaware of its existence, as if Australia were off the literary map. I hope that *A Brief Take on the Australian Novel* will change the situation and allow many readers to dive into a postcolonial literature that, especially since the 1980s, is no longer emerging. The budding days of Australian literature are over. Prospering in fresh soil, the increasingly vigorous Australian novel is now in full bloom.

SPECIAL FEATURES

Documentaries

Patrick White (1912–1990): Australia's only Nobel Prize-winning author

Born to Australian parents, Patrick White grew up and was partly educated in Sydney before he was sent back to England to benefit from patrician schooling. The pull of home prompted him to break off his studies and return to his native island when he came of age. After jackarooing in rural Australia for two years, he entered King's College (Cambridge), started to write sporadically, and ended up having twelve novels published during his lifetime.

Shortly before winning the Nobel Prize for Literature, Patrick White's vanity preened itself a little when he reported in a letter to Marshall Best that Anthony Burgess made the following statement at the 1970 Adelaide Festival: 'A country is only remembered for its art. Rome is remembered for Virgil, Greece for Homer, and Australia may be remembered for Patrick White.'

A fascinating oxymoronic figure

Patrick White is a fascinating oxymoronic figure in Australian literature with a taste for dualities, ambiguity and ambivalence. Born fortuitously in London while his parents were on their honeymoon, he came from a family of wealthy pastoralists whose forebears first settled in Australia in 1826. Despite his patrician education and his upper-class background, he defined himself as a socialist who more than once barracked for the Australian Labor Party and empathised with ordinary people and the subaltern (mainly the Jews and Aboriginal people). No matter how reclusive he was – first establishing himself in Castle Hill for 18 years and then moving to 20 Martin Road in the centre of Sydney because he felt suburbia was gradually swallowing him up – he occasionally went public to speak on behalf of the environmentalists and the republicans, especially once he gained international recognition. While he tried to export himself to Europe and the United States as a transnational writer, he also made a valuable contribution to Australia's literary heritage by drawing his inspiration from a series of national icons (Ludwig Leichhardt, Eliza Frazer, Sidney Nolan, etc.) in his fiction. White's general attitude was fairly equivocal, fuelling his public image of being an insider-outsider – if not an exile at home.

One must admit that the distinguished dweller in Centennial Park had a rather strained relationship with Australia, demonstrating its literary prestige worldwide while repeatedly flaying its cultural values and popular beliefs. He did exclaim in his published correspondence edited by David Marr that:

> Sometimes I get fed up to the teeth here in the country, where the type of Australian one encounters is the most uninspiring, unintelligent, deadening specimen to be found on earth. Although you will meet charming people here, I detest the average Australian, who is little more than a cheap imitation of the American. (16/03/1931)
>
> How sick I am of the bloody word AUSTRALIA. What a pity, I am part of it; if I were not, I would get out to-morrow. As it is, they will have me with them till my bitter end, and there are about six more of my un-Australian Australian novels to fling in their faces ... (08/02/1958)
>
> What is so amazing is that Australians have changed so little; we are the same arrogant plutocrats, larrikins, and Irish rabble as we were then. At least the graziers have been damped down. (28/12/1973)

'Australia's most unreadable novelist'

After his secondary schooling in England, White travelled in the United States before returning to Australia after the Second World War. Living in seclusion, he gradually built himself a romanticised and charismatic writer's persona that would adroitly paper over the cracks of his strong personality. With character-driven novels constantly churning round in his head, Patrick White fuelled his romantic literary reputation of being a compulsive writer, one working under duress and who has a taste for painstaking work and a honed prose. Nevertheless, he quickly gained the reputation of being 'Australia's most unreadable novelist' and, being highly sensitive to other people's opinions about his work, he never missed an opportunity to spread the word, thus consolidating the ivory tower he had erected for himself and establishing himself as an *écrivain maudit*. This reputation was confirmed in 1956 when 'the great Panjandrum of Canberra' described White's prose as 'pretentious and illiterate verbal sludge'. Not only did A.D. Hope's notorious broadside leave a deep scar on White's mind, but it dealt a severe blow to the novelist's self-esteem and probably enhanced his fragility, sense of insecurity and taste for self-deprecation.

The wider critical reception of his works

Given the almost 50 monographs that have been published worldwide at regular intervals between the year he was awarded the Nobel Prize and today, it is no wonder that anyone intent on studying White will spend much more time reading the available mass of critical material than White's literary production. The fact that the bulk of these monographs were published outside Australia and written by non-Australian scholars attests that White may have had solid grounds for feeling he was a writer chiefly praised abroad and misunderstood at home. This feeling of being neglected would account for his establishing the Patrick White Award, given to under-recognised authors and whose untaxed cash prize increases in value over the years. By way of indication, Brian Castro was awarded $24,000 in 2014. However, the first attention White received early in his career came from two Australian scholars whose monographs were published in Australia.

It therefore seems rather peculiar that there has been talk

about the fragility of White's significance and of his waning critical reputation, of the decline in numbers of Patrick White scholars (possibly explained by the fact that after so many publications attached to his name, academics seeking to break new ground may opt for a less-studied literary figure), and of public disinterest. Sales of the *The Hanging Garden*, his thirteenth novel posthumously released for the centenary of his birth, might contradict this latter assumption, unless readers prove not to fancy an unfinished novel nor dare go against White's will requesting the destruction of any remaining work in progress.

White's ambivalence

White's uncomfortable in-betweenness expressed in terms of sexual, social and cultural identity is possibly the key to his ambivalence – his most defining trait. *The Twyborn Affair* (1979), which critically confronts the politics of sex while revealing the author's private inner world, is exhibit A for displaying the politics of ambiguity and sexual indeterminacy that clearly comes through in his autobiography, *Flaws in the Glass* (1981):

> I can't remember being much worried by evidence of sexual ambivalence. I indulged my sexual inclinations at an early age. What disturbed me was the scorn of other boys, not for my sexuality, which they accepted, and in some cases enjoyed, but for a feminine sensibility which they despised because they mistrusted. It is much the same situation when predominantly masculine men despise women for subtleties the male lacks, while making use of their sexuality.

Socially, no matter how close to the people White wanted to be, he is no Tim Winton. He held no populist beliefs, roamed the world on frequent travels and moved deftly in high society. As for the cultural identity malaise he experienced in his youth, it is symptomatic of the postcolonial condition of twin allegiance – a no-win situation in which people feel they can never belong.

Seeing himself as 'a man of divided loyalties' for being brought up in Australia and in England, White bitterly recalls that at his British school he 'was accused of being a cockney or colonial, and back in Australia, "a bloody Pom". Language troubles have widened the split in my nature.' These various splits or dualities in his nature account for the strong sense of fragmentation that defines some of his characters, particularly in the three novels that deal with mental illness and multiple identities: *The Aunt's Story* (1948), *The Twyborn Affair*, and *Memoirs of Many in One* (1986).

Reading White's self-analysis – to which he was consciously prone in both his autobiography and correspondence – will give a clear indication of how tormented his soul was. White led a life of seclusion from childhood, when his impaired health prevented him from taking part in physical activities with his classmates, throughout his teenage years as a Cheltenham school boarder in England, to his young adult life when he hid his homosexual proclivities from his close friends and from the objects of his affection.

The Murphy novel: Journeying into White's mind

The Twyborn Affair, written at a time when White's physical health began to decline, was shortlisted for the prestigious British Booker Prize but the author, out of generosity for the new generation of talented writers, pulled out of the competition. The book critically confronts the politics of sex while revealing the author's private inner world. *The Twyborn Affair* is quintessentially a social comedy verging on a comedy of errors in which the traditional gendered dichotomy is subverted in order to blur clear-cut distinctions between what is meant to be masculine and feminine. The starting point for *The Twyborn Affair* is the portrait of Herbert Dyce Murphy, an English gentleman transvestite, which White saw in the National Gallery of Victoria.

All the core ingredients that are central to White's introspective novel – namely, gender-bending, disguise and homosexual references – are contained in this *donnée*. *The Twyborn Affair* quickly became the 'Murphy novel', which was commenced in early 1977 and completed by the end of the following year. The author regarded *The Twyborn Affair* as one of his four best novels and the most autobiographical of all his novels at that. As he explained to Manning Clark, 'All my novels have been to some extent autobiographical, but the present one is more explicit than the others. There are still plenty of disguises of course, otherwise it would be the kind of humdrum documentary expected by Australians.' Being his most personal book, in which his homosexuality is fully explored, *The Twyborn Affair* can be construed as the author's coming out, since White thought it was best to talk embarrassing things out rather than having other people expose them. The publication of *The Twyborn Affair* even prompted him to write his heretical autobiography in which he is even more outspoken about his sexual inclinations. In a letter to Graham Greene, White even predicted when writing this 'abrasive novel' that it 'will probably earn me complete social ostracism in Australia'. When *The Twyborn Affair* appeared in November 1979, he was proven wrong. The critical reception of the novel was a complete success, benefiting from commendable reviews and good sales.

In order to document this novel of multiple identities, White returned to the Monaro to capture the landscape of his early jackarooing days back in 1930. The biographical lineaments that one classically finds in fiction are scattered throughout the book. For instance, White's exploration of the South of France and his visit to the Parc Hôtel in Hyères were disguised in his fiction as the Golsons' Grand Hôtel Splendide des Ligures in Saint Mayeul. In addition, he has incorporated Greek history as a homage to his lifelong partner Manoly Lascaris, with whom he shared over forty years. What is more, the erotic scene observed by Monsieur Pelletier has its roots in White's childhood, when water was associated with sexual boyishness. The element of water is crucial here in terms of sexual and Freudian imagery, being as much a male symbol of fertility as a matrix of sorts. White makes it clear that the gender of the desired person is of little importance when it comes to lust. Sexual tension has overwhelmed Aristide Pelletier to such an extent that he must release it through a pleasure-seeking interlude of autoeroticism.

White's flawed and fragmented self

Psychological realism in *The Twyborn Affair* is not only achieved through recalling and drawing on actual personal experiences but also by having recourse to projection. White's commentators have noted that while the bulk of his characters expressed fragmented aspects of his self, Eddie was the most complete expression of himself. Even though White wanted to steer clear of Freudian psychoanalysis, he seems to be in tune with the Freudian axiom according to which the psychological novel is the result of the writer's habit to split his ego and project fragments of his own self onto the various characters: 'I see myself not so much a homosexual as a mind possessed by the spirit of man or woman according to actual situations or the characters I become in my writing'. Patrick White impersonates his male and female characters so that his 'flawed self' may finally retrieve original unity and a sense of completion by imaginatively embodying both sexes at once.

This mental androgyny, scattered throughout the text in a multifaceted protagonist, may account for the fact that most critics found it difficult to wring meanings out of *The Twyborn Affair.* This tripartite psychological novel shows the progress of an ambiguous gender-bender character, bearing a new name for each part of her/his life. The protagonist – the son of Judge Edward Twyborn and his spouse Eadie – is first Eudoxia, the sexual partner of an ageing Greek man, then Eddie Twyborn going through bisexual experiences. The situation is further complicated when Eddie Twyborn becomes Eadith Trist, the notorious madam of a sophisticated London brothel. In this new instalment, the protagonist has assumed a new guise – that of a woman – all the while sustaining an unflinching power of seduction. Despite these multiple identities, Eudoxia, Eddie, and Eadith are one and the same person born to the world as masculine.

White's unflattering portrayal of women in his works has set him up for charges of misogyny, a misunderstanding he tries to clear up in *Flaws in the Glass*: 'In life I have known far more admirable women than admirable men. ... Of course my women are flawed because they are also human beings, as I am, which is why I'm writing this book.' White's first queer protagonist, equally sharing feminine and masculine sensibilities, reflects his own ambiguous mindset. The protean character E – for enigmatic, Eudoxia, Eddie, or Eadith – struggles against prejudiced minds to set free 'the woman in a man and the man in a woman', to quote *The Twyborn Affair*. In terms of name symbolism, the young Twyborn is obviously born twice, first as a man and later as a woman, Eudoxia – which is, in his eyes, and as his name indicates, the 'good norm', the perfect blend that sustains mobile and volatile identities in terms of gender and sexuality. The trouble is, where White craves fluctuation, nuances, ambiguities and complexity, society begs for binary systems, dichotomous solutions, and single gender-marked identities.

Eddie Twyborn's gender bending, bisexuality and ever-shifting nature do not enable readers to pin down the representation of his elusive male beauty. Having said this, E's ambiguity points to a modern concept of male beauty epitomised in a mix of feminised and manly traits – a concept lately advertised as 'metrosexual'. In this respect, it could be argued that Patrick White was well ahead of his times. The indecision of choice has left him with an abiding interest in sexual indeterminacy and in the politics of ambiguity that both inform *The Twyborn Affair*.

Christopher J Koch (1932–2013): A Doubleman

By guest author Noel Henricksen

'Double! All was double!'

This insight is Robert O'Brien's: he is the central character of *Across the Sea Wall*, Koch's second novel, one of his best, and probably the least well remembered of his works.

In Koch's fiction, 'all is double'. His easily read narratives are built on foundations of dense allusion and abstruse mythology; sensitively realised characters with metaphysical twins; faery kingdoms, seances, *doppelgängers*, and a mysterious doubleman borrowed from Scottish legend. His novels teem with Gnosticism, Manichaeism, Platonism, spiritualism, mysticism – all of which is strange, given Koch's aversion, expressed in his 1996 Miles Franklin Award acceptance speech, to 'depressing terms ... always ending with "ism"'.

Koch saw duality in his life, no less than in his fiction. He believed his doubleness had been inherited from his family's roots in Australia: Johann Christian Koch, victim of a mid-nineteenth-century schism within the Lutheran Church, and Margaret O'Meara, a Catholic peasant girl from Tipperary, sentenced to seven years' Australian transportation for stealing clothes. His genealogy confirmed this doubleness, incorporating Protestant conservatives and Irish Catholic radicals; social stalwarts like architects, Justices of the Peace and city councillors, with swashbucklers, seafarers, and adventurers.

Almost Keats' fate: The legacy of criticism

In 1955, Koch sailed to England on the *Surriento*, impulsively detouring through India. It provided the experience on which he based *Across the Sea Wall*. It was eight years after the proclamation of Indian independence, and Koch discovered confraternity with Indians, sharing their Indo-European cultural heritage, and a doubleness wrought by colonial allegiance to a distant 'mother country' – lives lived in 'the half-light of a dying British Empire'. In India, the young Australian Catholic encountered Hinduism and some of its myriad gods. He became familiar with the *Bhagavad Gita*, and subsequently immersed himself in *The Gospel of Ramakrishna* and books written by Nirad Chaudhuri and Heinrich Zimmer.

Superficially, *Across the Sea Wall* describes the chance meeting, on a cruise ship, of a disgruntled clerk and a migrant with an unhappy past, and the subsequent collapse of their untenable relationship. Beneath the account of their liaison, the reader discerns an Australian's confrontation with godhead that is not based on peace and goodwill, but is, rather, awesome, intractable, unaccommodating and devastating.

According to Koch, Robert O'Brien is a man 'of rather ordinary nature'. Less charitably, contemporary critics saw him as 'very limited and undeveloped', 'aimless and rather lazy', 'fairly uninteresting and unimportant', 'a callow self-pitying youth that only a mother could love'. An indifferent scholar and an unexceptional public servant, O'Brien is 'drifting' at the start of the novel into the existential narcosis of 'all the other dreary little nine-to-five men'. He does, however, embody a spark of Augustinian restlessness which carries him from the spiritual somnolence of 'boring' Australia – exempt from wars, social convulsion, totalitarianism, militarism, violence, poverty and squalor – into India, with its double smell of 'excrement and incense', material penury and spiritual abundance, circumambient noise and otherworldly stillness. Into the world, too, of Ilsa Kalnins, one of the most consummately crafted of Koch's characters, a Latvian war-child who is also the incarnation of the goddess Kali. India and Ilsa: both are strange countries. Kalnins and Kali: each is 'of double aspect', voluptuously accommodating, coldly unresponsive. Both are dancers: Kalnins with her exotic performance; Kali with her cosmic dance of arbitrarily mixed creation and destruction.

Koch would repeat this device in subsequent novels, with no

diminution in its potency, creating parallel worlds populated by analogous pairs, humans and deities: the gods of Indonesian *wayang* in *The Year of Living Dangerously*, for example; Christ, Baldur and Lakshmi in *Highways to a War*; Prometheus and Cerberus in *Out of Ireland*.

Critical response to *Across the Sea Wall* was hardly adulatory. The most enthusiastic appraisal was written by Kenneth Slessor, Koch's friend. Reviews were generally indifferent. At worst they were scathing. In a particularly virulent piece, 'Groaning on the Groyne', Alan Roberts wrote:

> I read this novel as I presume Mr Koch wrote it – with a dogged determination to finish it even if it killed me. This is the author's second book, and there seems no reason to doubt that he will go on grinding them out for as long as his publishers continue to make him advances. This is a prospect which gives me little pleasure, for I believe that Mr Koch is a dull, pretentious writer who lacks the novelist's gift. If he is to continue writing he should get himself some real characters for whom he can feel deeply; learn economy, and not try to expand a short story into a book. At the moment he has neither the theme nor the stamina for ninety thousand words. He should come to terms with the limitations of his own talent. He will never write literature with a capital 'L' and he should face this and learn his trade.

'I am not a fanatical nationalist,' Koch told Adrian Mitchell in 1985, 'but what people think of my work in Australia is what matters most to me ... My optimism had been somewhat sapped by the mostly hostile reception for *Across the Sea Wall* in Australia.' Koch told me that 'the reception here was so negative in many quarters that [he] found it quite shattering'. In 1992, Les Murray recollected visiting Koch in the aftermath of antipathetic reviews, finding 'a very bitter, sad man ... He'd given up writing novels; he'd broken his pen; he'd retired, hurt, from the whole business.' Richard Connolly told me (in 1995):

> When first I met him [in 1963, he was] a happy young man with the future seemingly at his feet – a bright future, and not just happy but in the best meaning of the term happy-go-lucky. That changed in 1965 after the publication of *Across the Sea Wall* ... His personality, or at least his outlook on life, was brutally altered by that savage and quite unmerited doing over ... I was close witness to the suffering and despair that it caused in Koch, who said bitterly to me that he would never write again, and maintained that attitude for a long time after.

With all of his other novels being reprinted regularly, I often suggested republication of *Across the Sea Wall*, saying that it would prove to be one of the foundations for a reputation which would outlive us both: no, he would reply morosely, I have never had good luck with that book.

Koch became inordinately sensitive to criticism. Writers or journalists were now likely to describe him as 'rebarbative' rather than 'intense'. And for a time he opted for safer employment, as a producer in the Education Section of the Australian Broadcasting Commission in Sydney. He would be ten years with the national broadcaster, a time of calm after turbulence, stability after decades of volatility.

Young years

As a schoolboy during the war years, Christopher Koch had been uneasy about his German origins. His education had been generally unsettled. He was initially enrolled in Clemes College, a Quaker school with an Anglican tone and a British imperial spirit. It was A.D. Hope's school, with fresias, violets and moss, lines of cypress and box hedges, stone urns and a Greek temple. For six months he attended the very suburban Bowen Road State School, constructed to cater especially for children of workers in the Electrolytic Zinc Company. Following frequent and bitter arguments between his Anglican father and Catholic mother, he was transferred to Saint Virgil's College: there, a quiet, introspective boy, he was traumatised by the teaching methods of the Christian Brothers, 'Irish Jansenists', some of them so brutal that they 'just about destroyed [his] ability to learn anything'. Ultimately, he became a student at the Hobart High School, which he described as 'civilisation after barbarism'.

For a time, Koch had combined a drudge job in a Hobart book shop with the furtive discovery of iconoclastic writers like Lawrence and Joyce. He had completed a degree, majoring in English, Philosophy and Ancient Civilisations; renounced Catholicism; flirted with anarchism; married a Lithuanian refugee; and published a handful of lyrical poems. He had worked for the Heart of Oak Insurance Company in London, addressing and sealing envelopes; as a clerk in the London office of BHP (Broken Hill Proprietary Company); and as a teacher of delinquent and special needs children.

In this time he had written two novels, the second of them generally damned, the first (occasionally) lauded as the work of a literary prodigy. *The Boys in the Island* was published when Koch was twenty-six. The novel germinated from a poem he'd had published in *The Bulletin*, on 26 May 1954: 'The Boy Who Dreamed the Country Night'. The book was considered part of a three-pronged assault on pre-*Tree of Man* fiction: a reaction against its 'flat, dreary naturalism' and 'glum social documentation'; an assertion of prose that was 'essentially poetic'; a statement of the importance of 'myth, metaphor, and the use of symbol'. Koch's lyrical prose and the novel's spiritual, almost mystical, dimension inevitably invited comparison with the works of Randolph Stow and Patrick White – to the extent that Koch felt compelled to assert his literary independence.

Essentially, he said, his novel concerned 'the search for Paradise'. The search was that of Francis Cullen, 'an Everyman, a perfectly ordinary youth who happened to harbour an intense world of dream – the sense of the Otherworld'. Cullen's pilgrimage zigzags, as one promise of transcendence cedes to the next. His life is built on the dialectic between the expectation of mystical experience and the 'sadness of reality' – the promise of transcendence and the 'sluggish safe light of domestic steadiness', intimations of exhilaration and ensuing disillusion, illumination that dances before his eyes in a 'silent frenzy' and 'day-nude reality'. 'You Catholics,' one character tells Cullen, 'you see God at the end of every road'. Cullen's Otherland *is* situated 'ahead', at the end of the road, at the vanishing point of myth-tinctured telephone poles, or the terminus of north-bound railway lines: assorted destinations and different doorways to a mystical otherworld.

Predictably – one is reminded of Bernini's Saint Teresa – the promise of ecstasy is found in romantic love and, in this novel of Koch's youth, in the awakening of love. Heather Miles is a country girl, and a 'foreign country'. She is pretty, with 'vivid, hill-blue eyes', the wide-set country eyes of 'someone who looked over distances'; her hair smells of gully-ferns; on a summer Saturday, she and Francis swim together, and kiss awkwardly with 'water-cold, leaf-tasting lips'. Through his love for her, Cullen anticipates the taste of heaven, a religious experience where hop-kilns are temples. Inevitably, though, infatuation gives way to disenchantment.

The Boys in the Island is a novel within a novel, a story of the development and devolution of young love. Intrinsically, this element justifies the entire book. No Australian novel surpasses it in its sensitive evocation of young love. For Francis Cullen, disillusioned with love, and Tasmania, paradise is ultimately the 'Mainland'. Arriving in Melbourne, he finds a city which, in fulfilment of his dreams, is a constellation of illuminations, a criss-cross of gleaming rails, the 'giant highway of his city dream', 'winter darkness shot with icy lights, and the sulphur smell of menace'. Life in a shabby St Kilda boarding house and employment in the concrete basement of a biscuit factory promptly dispel his illusions. The city falls from its state of grace to become 'warrens of little houses and the long factories ... weltering in the grease of a limitless boredom, terrible as war'. This is the culmination of his pilgrimage. No beatific vision, no mystical communion with God: instead, drunkenness, violence, shame, lust, cruelty, betrayal, despair, and the 'portent of some future degeneracy'.

The book is not irredeemably pessimistic. There are suggestions in its concluding pages that there will be a resurgence of Cullen's desire for Otherland. 'I continue to believe that the longing for Paradise is implanted in each one of us,' Koch wrote, 'and that in the words St Augustine addresses to God in his *Confessions:* "You made us for yourself, and our heart is restless until it rests in you."'

The *Year of Living Dangerously*: The novel that became an Oscar-winning film

In 1968, Koch, as Federal Education Program Officer (Radio), was seconded to UNESCO to advise on the introduction of educational broadcasting in Indonesia. It was three years after the bloody coup of 30 September; Jakarta was 'a city of rumours and subterranean tensions', Sukarno was under house arrest, and the apprehension of erstwhile members of the Partai Komunis Indonesia continued. Three years earlier, his brother Philip had been the ABC's correspondent in Indonesia, at the epicentre of *konfrontasi* and coup, and a close observer of Sukarno, the 'short, posturing man in his be-medalled, splendidly tailored uniform and black *pitji* cap ... in those confrontation days of 1965, as he built up his "crush Malaysia" campaign and then ran headlong into the Thirtieth of September communist coup attempt which tumbled him from grace'.

For Koch, these were gifts. He read appraisals of the coup by John Hughes, J.D. Legge and Cindy Adams. And he studied a book which would transform *The Year of Living Dangerously* from a historical novel into something greater: *On Thrones of Gold,* James Brandon's study of *wayang kulit.*

In 1972, Koch resigned from the ABC. With 'no career, no

money and no certain future' he became a dedicated writer. The result was a consummately crafted novel, written simply and lucidly, resonant with literary and mythological allusion.

His novel's relationship to Indonesian history, Koch saw as analogous to the kinship between *War and Peace* and the Napoleonic Wars, or *A Tale of Two Cities* and the French Revolution. As James Joyce had underpinned *Ulysses* with Homer's *Odyssey*, so Koch's novel runs parallel with the (*Mahabharatan*) *wayang* play, *The Reincarnation of Rama*; despite Koch's description of the juxtaposition as 'a game that is probably of more importance to me than to the reader'.

From *wayang*, Koch had access to a wealth of symbols; to dualities like light and darkness, good and evil, illusion and reality. Here was rich mythology, relatively unmined. 'More than a puppet-master', the *dalang* is God, his puppets cast shadows on a screen which becomes heaven, Mahabharatan cosmic confrontations run parallel to human conflicts, and tension is established between the physical world and Otherland. Through *wayang*, Koch has built a multilayered narrative. As *The Year of Living Dangerously* opens, the reader is subtly introduced to the three interconnected 'worlds' in which the book will proceed: the Wayang Bar in the Hotel Indonesia in Jakarta, frequented by foreign correspondents, where Wally O'Sullivan – a mountain of flesh and correspondent for a Sydney daily – is enthroned; the reception room of Istana Merdeka, the presidential palace, where an imperious Sukarno is surrounded by a deferential circle of journalists; and Dwarawati, where Kresna is king.

The heroes of *wayang* are reflected in the novel's characters – appropriately enough, given that Sukarno saw himself as a shade of the Bima, one of *Mahabharatan* Pandawa brothers. So Guy Hamilton, newly arrived in Jakarta, is an incarnation of the 'hero Arjuna'. Billy Kwan, an Australian-Chinese achondroplastic dwarf and cameraman is synchronously Semar, the familiar spirit of Java, and a dwarf-god who serves Arjuna. Kwan becomes

Hamilton's conscience, nurturing his humanitarianism and enabling his discovery of Eden.

Hamilton's glimpse of paradise is aptly consonant with *wayang*. In *The Reincarnation of Rama*, there is a Hermitage Scene: 'a religious teacher or seer ... receives in audience Ardjuna [who] asks that "the will of the Almighty" be revealed to him: the holy man offers peace of mind and a heart filled with joy'. In *The Year of Living Dangerously*, Hamilton has been covering the Long March of *PKI*-adherents processing from Yogyakarta to the capital. On the road outside Bandung, he is threatened by the insurgents, and he confronts the prospect of death at the hands of the mob. He is spared. His escape from death initiates a new life. Suddenly, shops in the kampong are suffused with preternatural colour and mystery. Mankind, through Hamilton's shriven eyes, has become innocent. His fellow-creatures, in turn, smile and consecrate his new direction: '*Slamat datang*' – may your journey be blessed.

Koch's novel attracted considerable interest from Australian filmmakers, causing Koch to approach Peter Weir, then best known for his 'atmospheric' adaptation of Joan Lindsay's *Picnic at Hanging Rock*. Collaborating with Weir, Koch worked on a screenplay. His marriage had 'blown apart', so it was not the most equable of times for collaboration. The Koch-Weir screenplay proceeded through 'a number of drafts'. Weir presented it to CBS. According to Koch, CBS 'wanted Peter Weir, ... wanted the novel; but not the script. As Americans so often do, they plainly had plans to debauch the property along commercial lines.' CBS commissioned Alan Sharp, a 'former novelist' to restructure the screenplay. Koch judged the new screenplay a 'talentless betrayal' of his book. Doubtless with good reason: Sukarno's Indonesia in 1965 had been transformed to the more contemporary Iran under the Ayatollah Khomeini. Weir found Sharp's script unacceptable and CBS intractable: the association disintegrated, and concurrently, an enmity developed between Weir and Koch. In Weir's words, 'Conventional wisdom has it that one should avoid a situation where the novelist is to adapt their own work ... Chris' draft was impossibly long – several hundred pages – and he was reluctant to change anything ... It was not a fruitful collaboration.' The playwright David Williamson was contracted to disentangle the imbroglio and prepare a final screenplay. He solicited Koch's advice 'on which Billy Kwan speeches should go into the Kwan voice-overs', to enhance narrative clarity. Despite the multiplicity of writers, the final script was powerfully coherent, and the reviewer for the *Sydney Morning Herald* praised the film as 'seamless'.

Just as reviews of *Across the Sea Wall* had made Koch temperamentally fractious, suspicious of critics, hostile to academics, so this experience jaundiced his subsequent dealings with film directors and producers. Royalties, though, were lucrative.

Researching my book, *Island and Otherland*, I chanced across a reference to a film version of *The Boys in the Island*. I asked Koch about it, only to be told that it did not exist. The website *IMDb* suggests that it did, but was released (in 1990) only in the Netherlands and Japan, and on VHS in Greece. On negotiations for filming *Out of Ireland*, Koch was more candid: the budget was large, a contract had been signed, the screenplay had been written (poorly) by John Banville, the cast included Liam Neeson and Kate Winslet, and production was scheduled for January 2003. No film eventuated. In June 2002, Koch was in discussion with two London film producers, about a film version of *Highways to a War*: consultations inexorably degenerated into 'terrible things'.

Despite Koch's anguish, he seemed more and more to write novels which were halfway to screenplays. *The Memory Room* seems hardly to have come from the same mind responsible for the evocative, allusive, profound and beautiful earlier books. Koch's final novel, *Lost Voices*, is a reprise of a lifetime's familiar motifs and preoccupations: slow-moving at best, melodramatic at worst, it pauses frequently to describe settings with dogged meticulousness, like the italics between a play's act and scene numbers and its dialogue.

Conflict, confrontation, controversy

On 9 September 1985, Neil Davis, an Australian photojournalist, was killed in Bangkok, while filming an attempted coup for NBC News. He had been a combat cameraman for more than twenty years, beginning in Borneo during *konfrontasi*, and remaining in Vietnam to film the arrival of North Vietnamese troops at the presidential palace in Saigon. Koch read his obituary in the *New York Times*, and realised that Davis had become 'a myth in other people's minds'. Seeing the metamorphosis, cognisant of contemporary mythopoeia, Koch had the idea for his next novel. Only the idea! In the 'Author's Note' Koch insisted – almost defensively – that his protagonist, Michael Langford, was 'a composite: mostly invented'.

In 1987, Koch was to be contracted to write a script for a television mini-series based on *One Crowded Hour*, a biography of Davis, written by Tim Bowden. He accepted, travelled through South-East Asia (with Bowden and the head of the South Australian Film Corporation), returned to Australia, and quarrelled with the producer over the screenplay. The agreement was cancelled, the project stalled.

The novel continued. Koch intended to create 'one large tapestry': two interlinked stories, intermixed passages from mid-nineteenth century Van Diemen's Land and South-East Asia during the Vietnamese and Cambodian Wars. Proving unwieldy, the novel became a diptych: the composite novels were *Out of Ireland* and *Highways to a War*. The first revolves around Robert Devereux, a Young Irelander transported to Van Diemen's Land, having advocated violent resistance to the British Government. In the second, his great-great-grandson, Michael Langford, works the farm Devereux established in Tasmania's Derwent Valley, becomes a celebrated photographer in the Vietnam War, has a similar commitment 'to lost causes', is crucified in Cambodia's paddy fields, mythologised, and apotheosised after his death.

Two stories, genealogically linked: two novels, dialectically joined by parallels and mutual illuminations: the diptych is unified by 'echoes', enhancements, psychic recurrences and salvages from a Jungian reservoir of ancestral memory. The past permeates the present – in dreams, and through the persistence of Otherland's spirits, domestic gods, house fairies, dryads and druids.

Twice, Christopher Koch received the prestigious Miles Franklin Award: for *The Doubleman* in 1985, and for *Highways to a War* in 1996. Winning the second Miles Franklin Award ought to have been a triumph. Sadly, it was limited, and on two accounts. Most obviously, from the podium, there was Koch's alienation of academics and deconstructionists ... at best imprudent. Worse, there were murmurings in the audience that *Highways to a War* owed more than a slight debt to Tim Bowden's *One Crowded Hour.*

Koch told me, in September 1998, that Bowden had circulated among the guests at the award ceremony, accusing Koch of having plagiarised from his book; that these charges became the basis for an article in *The Australian* accusing him of plagiarism; and that it marked the end of the long-standing Bowden-Koch friendship. The borrowings may have been unconscious, but they could thereafter be judged empirically by readers. Koch might argue that there is 'an odd paradox in regard to the creation of a character ... If you don't draw on characteristics from real people, the character won't have life'. But Koch's book shares many incidents, words and descriptions with Bowden's biography. And some of the parallels are unnervingly blatant. Luke Slattery and Evan McHugh, writing in *The Weekend Australian* (6–7 July 1996), cite example after example of Bowden's Neil Davis morphing into Koch's Michael Langford.

If the novel as a genre survives and an Australian literary canon persists, it will probably show few correspondences with those books chosen by the judging panel for the Miles Franklin Award. Nevertheless, Koch's literary output deserves longevity. At his best, he writes as a poet, wastes few words and achieves profundity through allusion and suggestion, reverberation and echoes.

Both the author and his characters search for a country beyond their comprehension. Paradoxically Koch's evocation of place has been judged masterly: from canal-side kampongs in Old Jakarta, plank walkways crossing the mud, gimcrack shanties of flattened oil cans and cardboard, coconut oil cooking smells, gamelan music pulsing through equatorial heat, to a narrow Irish laneway winding between bramble-topped banks, past rude cottages, towards the violet and purple mountains of Clare. Especially, and perennially, Koch's words bring to life the beauty of his island homeland, Tasmania: with words, he paints dolerite pillars and grim cliffs assaulted by elemental grey seas, uncharted Gondwanan forests, emerald-green hopfields, the mauve and mystical twin peaks of Mount Direction. Graham Greene, having read Koch, wrote that 'I feel now that Tasmania is part of my memory'.

Publishing matters

The world of Australian publishing is a web of paradoxes difficult to unravel, and it requires close scrutiny. People involved in producing books are somewhat disheartened and plead poverty. They claim that publishing is at a crisis point even though publishers are earning more money than the music and the performing arts industries combined.

Moreover, it seems that Australian literature doesn't sell readily and yet Australians have always been reputed voracious readers, even in the absence of a viable local book industry. Also paradoxically, while authors and publishers secretly hope to conquer international markets as a result of world agreements, protectionism in the form of territorial copyright regulations still dominates the local publishing scene. And finally, it is not unusual for writers, who aspire to be able to live from the sales of their books, to realise more money with the receipt of reproduction rights and copyrights in the form of public and educational lending rights (PLR and ELR) than cashing the publisher's meagre royalty cheque. This documentary aims at clarifying the issue.

1788–1864: An Anglo-modelled culture subjected to the imperial centre

Since books were not produced on Australian soil during the colonial era, they were regularly imported or brought in by travellers from Great Britain – which obviously helped maintain a close connection with the Mother Country. While the small Australian readership continued to develop a strong taste for British literature, the first Australian novel had had difficulty in making its mark, all the more as it was published anonymously.

Whereas the stories of colonial writers such as Marcus Clarke and Rolf Boldrewood were assured of being serialised in contemporary newspapers, most stories needed to be exported to England to become novels, sometimes after undergoing extensive modifications to the original manuscripts. From hesitant beginnings, literary creation from the Antipodes was dependant on the imperial centre's opinion of its content and written style. British publishers saw the colony of New South Wales, where many of the population could read and write, as a developing market for their books. There is no need to point out that the English monopoly of Australian publications did nothing to support local publishing houses. For the hardiest, who wished to brave the colonial readers' cool reaction towards local publication, there were mainly vanity press publications. They could barely hope to sell many copies by subscription in order to alleviate their investment. Not only did the colonial writers have to pay tidy sums of money to be printed, and so to be read, but there was not one Australian author who could live from his art alone. In 1831, when the first Australian novel was published, books began to be imported regularly from the Mother Country, maintaining a link with the imperial centre.

1865–1938: The beginning of a literary press

In 1865, the first edition of the *Australian Journal* appeared in Melbourne and became the main means of disseminating information about Australian literature. This approach was soon adopted by other local newspapers in Sydney and Melbourne and even country towns. Serialised novels were commonplace. January 31, 1880, marked a decisive change in publishing with the creation of the Sydney-based *Bulletin*, a weekly review that aimed at promoting Australian writers. The Bohemians of the *Bulletin* were formed, leaving in their wake a dynamism that gave strength to literary debate. In contrast to the more traditional criticism in Melbourne, that of the *Bulletin* was new and more creatively aggressive. The newspaper promoted many literary talents, including the most famous poet Banjo Paterson, who wrote the words of 'Waltzing Matilda' in 1895.

Even with the advent of the twentieth century, books were still being imported in large numbers from England offering choice and information to Australian readers. Bred in British culture, they gradually forged for themselves a scholarly literature that appealed to them with the appearance of several literary magazines such as *All About Books for Australian and New Zealand Readers* (which first came out in December 1928). These aimed at encouraging literary consumerism particularly from Britain. This tendency was energetically counterbalanced by the influence of nationalistic literary critics, like Nettie Palmer, who did their utmost to separate the wheat from the chaff. They wished to dissipate any confusion between the diffusion of great literature and the commercialisation of lesser works. Criticism, which was then in its early stages, was strongly divided. While some critics were highly descriptive in their reviews summarising plots and, in the process, making few – if any – literary judgments, others felt it was important to educate readers and to give them a taste of 'good' literature judged on form and not content.

1939–1969: Specialised journals as resonators

At this time, it was a struggle to show that there was an Australian tradition – the revival of nationalism could not be accomplished without the support of literary criticism established over the decades by the increase of outlets for expression. The birth of *Southerly* in Sydney in 1939, noted for its eclectic content with R.G. Howarth as its editor-in-chief, was soon followed by *Meanjin Papers* in 1940 in Brisbane, edited by C.B. Christensen who opted for an aggressively Australian political editorial. Five years later, it became *Meanjin Quarterly*, but in Melbourne. In 1954, *Overland*, under the socialistic auspices of Stephen Murray-Smith in Melbourne, took up the famous Furphy formula in the masthead of the newspaper without its adverb 'offensively': 'temper, democratic; bias, Australian'. Such a slogan indicated many of the rather radical viewpoints contained in this publication which was associated with social realist writers. Traditional in structure, *Quadrant* (1956) came soon after with the literary sensitivity of its editor, the poet James McAuley. Much later, the more elitist *Australian Literary Studies* (1963) quickly surpassed and dominated all other journals. Although published by Laurie T. Hergenhan at the University of Tasmania before being transferred to the University of Queensland in 1975, this journal had been inspired by McAuley's work. *Australian Book Review* (1978), a magazine specialising in intelligent discussions about published books, quickly became the main reference in surveys. The following year, Tasmania was busy with the publication of *Island*, another literary magazine. Within forty years, the development of a plethora of literary journals spectacularly encouraged the growth of the book industry in the period between the two World Wars. This was noted by academic Richard Nile in *The Making of the Australian Literary Imagination* (2002). Nile indicates three major stages in publishing: from 1900 to 1919 with the publication of more than 900 easy-to-read Australian novels; from 1920 to 1969 when even more literary titles were produced; and from the 1970s onwards, a time when the novel became more economically available to a majority of people.

It was the right time for these publications specialising in books, for no book industry could survive without promoting or reviewing fiction. Considerable efforts by Australian academics to generate dynamic competition via the press were heading in the right direction and compensated for deficiencies of literary programs both on radio and television. In spite of this, the Australian book industry could not compete with the large well-oiled commercial machinery of London and New York publishers. In addition, there were not enough writers of international stature to incite real literary interest. But without democratising books, this would not be possible. Fortunately from 1963, Penguin in Australia gave Australian literature a privileged place in its listings, publishing the main Australian titles as paperbacks.

1970–1979: A cultural renaissance

The 1970s saw the end of Australian censorship impacting on the commercialisation of books in Australia. Many literary titles worldwide were blacklisted because of content that would shock the most prudish sensitivities. Among the *non grata* books due to their sensational content or their political ideology were: James Joyce's *Ulysses* (banned in 1929) followed by *Dubliners*, D.H. Lawrence's *Lady Chatterley's Lover*, Vladimir Nabokov's *Lolita* and Philip Roth's *Portnoy's Complaint*.

At this time, both literature and cinema benefited from the pro-cultural policy of the Whitlam Government (1972–1975). With unprecedented financial assistance for culture, money being the sinews of war, there was a marked increase in the number of publishing houses and literary prizes that stimulated sales. In 1973, the Labor Government set up the Literature Board of the Australian Council that boosted literary output by granting writing scholarships and financial assistance for publishing on merit. From 1973 to 1974, the commission supported fifty-four fictional works. Initially called the Literary Arts Board, it was renamed in 1996 as the Literature Fund.

At the same time, the highly precarious status of the writer had to be strengthened. Programs that aimed to make up for financial loss to authors, caused by partial or total photocopying of their works and library loans, contributed to putting butter on their bread. The Copyright Act of 1968, which was later amended, is the cornerstone of the legislation of author's rights. It states that, besides fair dealing, any representation or reproduction of a work, whether partial or in its entirety, is illegal without the consent of the author or his or her legal successors. Copyright expires seventy years after an author's death and is more or less applicable worldwide with the Berne Agreement.

Not without some provocation, the giant photocopy company Xerox financed a publicity campaign to inform people how easy it was to reproduce a complete book – boasting that caused indignation in the literary community who immediately joined together to defend their livelihood. With no further delay, photocopying became the *bête noire* of novelist Gus O'Donnell, who became a member and outspoken advocate of the Australian Society of Authors in 1965 two years after it began. In 1974 with help from Frank Moorhouse who gave his name to the contentious affair (the Moorhouse Case) as the offence concerned the reproduction of a story from his book *The Americans, Baby*, O'Donnell sued the University of New South Wales which, according to him, supported the copying of entire works within its establishment. In 1975, the Australian High Court recognised the University to be criminally responsible.

With this victory in sight, Copyright Agency Limited (CAL) was established in Sydney under the aegis of Gus O'Donnell in collaboration with Keith Kersey, Peter Holderness, George Ferguson and David Kindon – a committee whose main aim was to ensure authors' marketing rights were respected. On 20 March 1985, the Copyright tribunal decided that CAL would take two cents per page for the author. Thomas Keneally and Frank Moorhouse were the first to receive their cheque from CAL, which had amassed more than four million dollars in 1989. Paradoxically, it is not unusual for these indirect revenues to exceed benefits accrued from book sales. In 2002, CAL accepted to use the Digital Object Identifier (DOI), which is to the numerical document what the ISBN (International Standard Book Number: the administrative identity number) is to the book. In the future, this tracking system will probably enable income to be gained from electronic books. Since 2007, CAL has more than 11,000 members made up of more than two thirds authors and one third publishers and it handles more than fifty million dollars annually.

1980–1999: Globalisation of the book and the rise of the celebrity writer

With the respective implementation of Public Lending Right and Educational Lending Right schemes by the Federal Government in 1985 and 1994 (ELR being interrupted from 1996 to 2000), authors gain financially from their works harboured in libraries. The only impediment to benefiting from the Public Lending Right Act 1985 was that the work must be available for consultation in a minimum of fifty libraries in Australia. The 1980s saw globalisation influence what can be called 'the golden age of publishing'. While renowned writers (Christopher Koch, Peter Carey, David Malouf, Janette Turner Hospital, Thomas Keneally, etc.) were courted by the big English publishing companies (Jonathan Cape, Chatto & Windus, Faber, etc.) and were tempted by a literary career overseas, others resorted to literary agents to make a name for themselves on the international scene. By participating in the liberation of global trading, Australia realised how competitive and relentless the market was. With the cannibalisation (being absorbed or bought out) of young independent publishers by transnational firms specialising in books for entertainment rather than literary value, the media and publishing tended to combine their efforts to diffuse the dominant cultural models. Whatever the nationalists' views on the matter, it is to be feared that these conglomerates in the hands of foreign investors (Pan Macmillan and Random House controlled by the Germans, Hachette Australia by the French, Harper Collins by the Americans and Penguin administered by the British) will not give priority to the development of Australian literature. Moreover, patriotic consumerism, 'Australian Made, Australian Owned', is no longer current in the mainstream, although it occasionally raises its head. Out of a concern to improve productivity and to enter new markets, printing is being carried out in Asia: mainly in India, Singapore and, more recently, China.

To be prepared for any attempt at dumping of foreign

publications, the copyright law of 1991 set up two protective measures: the 30-day rule forces publishers to make available in Australia any book published in the world within a month; failing this, they lose market exclusivity. This measure reinvigorated local publishing by supporting Australian presses instead of foreign publishers. Accompanying this measure was the 90-day rule that obliged publishers to supply bookshops in less than 90 days; if this was not done, the owner would be able to import foreign editions.

In a nationalist leap in the 1990s, some companies such as Heinemann developed an aggressive marketing strategy to increase their pool of Australian authors. Every measure was allowed to ensure the best artistic choices: poaching authors by offering them a tidy amount of money as an advance; promises to establish good promotion tactics to attract fresh talents; and developing the loyalty of authors who would support their publishers throughout their various ventures. Publishing houses also emphasise the visual appearance of book cover designs made appealing by the use of four strong colours. Now, paperbacks and soft-cover novels are advantaged by luxury packaging quite unlike the sobriety of books during the 1970s with their fragile binding, monochrome covers and poor quality paper. It could be said that, in this marketing strategy, the content of the novel is less important than its aesthetic presentation: the author's photograph is often on the back or on the spine of the book, the cover is artistically attractive, and the pleasant, well-spaced text comes in a generous reader-friendly font.

Literature, which had to compete with the rebirth of Australian cinema, finally found its place. The conjunction of these two artistic activities brought about fruitful exchanges since this was the *belle époque* of film adaptations of great Australian classics by the best Australian movie directors. Fred Schepisi brought Keneally's *The Chant of Jimmy Blacksmith* (1978) and, more recently, White's *The Eye of the Storm* (2011) to the big screen. Bruce Beresford followed suit with Nene Gare's novel *The Fringe Dwellers* (1986). From the

1990s onwards, filmmakers seemed more inclined to adapt works by Aboriginal authors. This is the case of James Ricketson with his film *Blackfellas* (1991) adapted from the novel by Archie Weller entitled *The Day of the Dog*. Philip Noyce also brought Aboriginal stories out into the limelight by producing *Rabbit-Proof Fence* (2002), inspired by Doris Pilkington's story. This connection between literature and cinema has endured since the 1980s. Bruce Beresford adapted the literary success of Kathy Lette and Gabrielle Carey, *Puberty Blues* (1981), while the following year Peter Weir's *The Year of Living Dangerously* and Ken Cameron's *Monkey Grip* appeared. Added to these were film versions of Peter Carey's first novel *Bliss* (1985); Jerzy Domaradzi offered a film version of *Lilian's Story* (1996); Gillian Armstrong adapted *Oscar and Lucinda* (1997), Peter Carey's *chef-d'oeuvre*; Ana Kokkinos changing the title to *Head On* (1998) gave her interpretation of *Loaded* by Christos Tsiolkas; Kate Woods brought Melina Marchetta's novel *Looking For Alibrandi* (1999) to the screen and Sara Sugarman produced a film version of *Mad Cows* (1999) by Kathy Lette. Director Gregor Jordan was inspired by *Our Sunshine* for his film *Ned Kelly* (2003) and Neil Armfield superbly adapted the novel *Candy* (2005) written by Luke Davies. These cinematic versions broaden Australian writers' readership, reaching out to a different public. Reticent readers will more readily spend two hours in a movie theatre than a whole day reading a book. This combination of literature and film has also contributed to the popularisation of writers who benefited from increased media exposure. An example of this is Stephen Spielberg's adaptation in 1993 of *Schindler's Ark*, which brought Thomas Keneally unprecedented international recognition. His publisher capitalised on this and used the film title, *Schindler's List*, in re-publishing the novel.

Leading a life as a recluse in a world in which the writer is increasingly exposed in the media is to forego the possibility of becoming well known. As a result, popular newspapers frequently talk about the private lives of authors. Biographies of famous writers are numerous (like David Marr's biography of Patrick White). However, some literary monographs have the poor taste of mixing the lives of authors with analysis of their works.

2000–2009: The book as object – a commercial product

In the twenty-first century, publishing changed by adapting to demand. According to Antoni Jach: 'What is valued in Australian fiction by the mainstream publishers at the moment are the features of simplicity, clarity, accessibility and verifiability'. Today, there is a unified culture and the birth of what I call the marketing-modified book – a book reduced to a commercial product modelled on popular tastes. Without forecasting doom, it can be said that this formatting of writers and literary works according to the demands of the large publishing groups will eventually deal the final blow to the creative output of authors considered less accessible.

Today, it would seem that a writer as talented as Patrick White would not be accepted for publication by any of the large publishing houses. In 2006, the *Australian* attempted a similar experiment to the one carried out the previous year in England by the *Sunday Times* with a novel by V.S. Naipaul. Australian publishers had to read a slightly modified third chapter of *The Eye of the Storm* by Patrick White without knowing its source. It was presented as a typed manuscript of doubtful authenticity entitled 'The Eye of the Cyclone' from the pen of Wraith Picket – the author's anagram. The experiment was conclusive in that it seemed that no publisher recognised the famous extract and categorically rejected the typescript with rather unpleasant comments on the whole. Even though some recognised a certain talent in the phraseology, the publishers unanimously refused to publish it, claiming it would not be profitable. One might think that the huge commercial success of some potboilers would enable large publishing companies to publish a fine pen for a more restricted readership, but this is not so. This venal attitude of some publishers even extends to asking their established authors to lower their literary ambitions in order to gain a wider readership. For those who refuse, going with independent publishers is the only solution.

The independents, which previously could not guarantee broad audiences, now enter the playing field. Publishers like Giramondo and Text Publishing, directed respectively by Ivor Indyk and Michael Heyward, have published notable successes that have a relatively good run by courting great names in Australian literature. Another improvement is that readership has increased so much that, while every novel by Patrick White published after he was awarded the Nobel Prize sold no more than 30,000 copies in Australia, today a successful novel written by Carey, Grenville or Winton easily triples this modest print run. Peter Carey is an exception; even though he teaches every now and then, he is one of the rare Australian authors who enjoy the luxury of being able to live in order to write, while the majority of authors are forced to write in order to live. Most have to combine other activities with writing to compensate for their limited commercial success, like Brian Castro who teaches in addition to his work as a writer.

The problem is that Australia has gone from a productive culture, reaching its highest point in the 1980s, to a production of culture. And 'production' strongly implies an industrial 'product' that fits into marketing logic. The book market is divided between the aggressive publishers who are fully aware of the economic possibilities of the work and treat it as a commercial product – no more, no less – and the romantic booklovers who maintain the work carries inestimable cultural value, fertile ideas and even a philosophical vision. And what does it matter if the redeemable threshold is not reached?

It would certainly seem these days that book production has declined, but the sales of Australian titles and international titles remain the same. And while in 1970 Australian titles scarcely represented 10% of the business figure for books sold in all categories combined, bookshops can now pride themselves on going beyond 60%. It is true that Nielsen Bookscan (called

Booktrack before 2002) enabled more successful organisation of book sales and a more intimate knowledge of consumer habits. This system, set up in December 2000 to keep reasonably reliable statistical data, collects transaction details from the major book retailers at the point of sale, in contrast to the Australian Bureau of Statistics. Nielsen Bookscan covers only 90% of the market, however. Excluded from the inventory are sales not made in the usual way and those carried out in bookshops that have not computerised their business.

Whether the book sells poorly or not at all, readers and publishers are to be blamed. It has all been heard before: the narrative subtleties are lost on most readers who are now reluctant to buy novels, favouring documentaries and/or non-fiction; the publisher, when not taxed for poorly marketing the work, is accused of making a fortune by exploiting writers, not to mention the fact that book distribution is not widespread enough in an already very limited market. Bookshop owners must also take the blame as even disloyal competition with foreign titles could justify failure! And yet they do the best they can: by placing Australian books in a section marked 'Australiana', bookshop owners allow readers to discover this young literature which is still not well known by the public at large. The only downside of this classification is that it annoys universalistic writers who feel they are victims of being placed in a type of ghetto. However, because of the different activities organised by bookshops (talks, book signings, meetings with the author, literary debates, competitions and so on), the commercial life of a book is more active than ever. And since it is a question of selling reading pleasure, literary bookshops like Readings decorate their shelves with staff book reviews on index cards that promote their favourite reads.

Beyond 2009: New perspectives

In a world increasingly concerned with environmentalism, it can be questioned why publishers are not more interested in multiplying market studies, diminishing their list of titles and carrying out a draconian selection before agreeing to print any physical books. In any case, this is what is indicated by some observers who attribute the drop in production of literary titles to more judicious and informed choices. One suggestion is that potboilers could be made only available through digital books by segmenting them into short reader-friendly instalments for tablets and e-readers.

This challenge implies a merciless sorting of books worthy of printing on paper and those good enough to be viewed on a screen. Other ecological solutions have been tried, or are being studied, and print-on-demand, the ebook and micropublishing could become common practices in the future. Respecting the environment, they would avoid overproduction and the pulping of unsold works and would control the stocking of books by offering good returns. While micropublishing has the inconvenience of not being lucrative (a small print run of 300 copies is scarcely conceivable without a subvention!), it has the advantage of placing quality over quantity. Antoni Jach, who runs a collection with Modern Writing Press, defines this enterprise as 'an act of optimism that brings words out to the light of day rather than leaving them in the bottom of a drawer. This can be seen as a gift.' With the creation in 2008 of a parallel system of distribution (the Small Press Underground Networking Community, now renamed the Small Press Network), these publishers manage to bypass the large established distribution networks whose onerous services put a strain on the budget of Australian publishers.

The quasi-gratuitousness of reading now on the internet, in research centres, with BookCrossing (an online book exchange system), has contributed to the dwindling of book sales and it is getting even harder for novelists to make a living out of writing. To give a clearer picture of the writer's predicament, let us analyse the separation of receipts for a book sold for $20. Firstly, half goes to distribution; that is, $4 goes into the pocket of the wholesaler and $6 goes to the retailer. A portion will then be used to absorb the production costs, so the printer ($4) will obtain nearly double of what the publisher receives ($2.50). It can be said that creation is discredited since only $1.50 goes into the author's pocket. Add to that $2 for the 10% GST imposed by the Australian Government since 2000. Who then makes a profit from this economic activity if publishers and serious writers (meaning those who do not enjoy success with cookbooks or practical guides and manuals of all kinds) cannot play the game correctly? According to publisher Michael Heyward's analysis, the book industry feeds the coffers of the Australian Government nearly 75 million dollars in different taxes from literary production and with utmost leniency only 6% of the gain is redistributed in the form of multiple grants.

Despite the impact of the globalisation of production and the distribution of economic goods, protectionism of the local book industry is rife in Australia, as in many other nations. Attempts to abolish territorial rights in 2003 and in 2009 were backed by major corporations and the Productivity Commission which, in May 2009, recommended the abolition of territorial rights in Australia. They intended to reform territorial rights that protected the Australian book market from the dumping of foreign publications sold more cheaply. The Commission recommended the death of territorial rights a year after publishing the title in Australia – a measure that worried most participants in the book industry. If these territorial rights were to collapse, the ban on parallel imports (controlled by publishers to the detriment of consumers) would be lifted automatically, opening the door to so-called free competition. For some, this was a non-event that would just lower the price of books. For others, there would be plenty to write a book about!

On Wednesday, 11 November 2009, however, the Federal Government went against the Productivity Commission's recommendation and decided to keep the *status quo*, in recognition of 'the importance of preserving Australian culture' (Competition Policy Minister Craig Emerson).

Bonus

1. A word from the translator

The task of translating *Panorama du roman australien des origines à nos jours* has been pleasurable – pleasure derived from a lengthy exposure to and a close involvement with the French language (a passion of mine) and the challenge of coming up with an adaptation that reflects the scriptwriter's intentions. To such delights was added renewed and fresh instruction on the depth and breadth of Australian literature and its filmic (and other) qualities. I discovered authors not familiar to me and re-discovered others as I knew them, but sometimes from a different perspective. Jean-François has come up with a narrative documentary whose centrifugal structure is grounded in time and yet transcends it.

The intimate connection a translator has with a text is, in reality, a virtual conversation with the author. Like a silver screen narrator, Vernay speaks directly to the reader – the 'I' soon becomes 'we'. And this seemingly casual approach continues throughout, in a free-flowing narrative that is not just concerned with giving cold hard disjointed facts (although facts there are), but with involving the reader intellectually and emotionally. One can imagine the reader as part of an audience in a darkened cinema absorbed in exciting action on the silver screen.

For this work, there has been real collaboration – always an advantage for this creative art form. From the outset, it was agreed that there would be close interaction for the shaping of the script. So regular discussions with the scriptwriter/director were held throughout the process and have resulted in ensuring that his original ideas are transposed in the final edited product. This also involved some compromise with modifications to the original script (as is usual for all adaptations). Special thanks to subeditors Xavier Pons, Nicholas Jose and John Ramsland, whose contributions were invaluable.

Panorama du roman australien has a tale to tell. Although it is a sweeping vista of iconic Australia as presented through the eyes of the country's multi-ethnic population, it is in no way superficial. It is a story of Australia, its history (in outline), its people and its ideas as revealed through the rich literary genre of the Australian novel – a story for all Australians to know about and to experience. According to the *Age* (February 2009), the original version 'promise[d] to be uniquely influential in shaping the wider [French reading] world's appreciation and understanding of Australian literature'. I am pleased to have played a role in adapting the original version not only for an Australian audience, but for the wider English-speaking/reading public. This remastered version is available to all zones. Restricting *Panorama du roman australien* to a single zone would be to deprive many of much.

Marie Ramsland

2. Literary milestones

1831	Anonymous publication of the first Australian novel, *Quintus Servinton*, thought to be written by Henry Savery. This is the first colonial novel.
1832	*Woman's Love*, by Mary Leman Grimstone, is the first novel written in Australia; the manuscript was completed in 1828. It is also the first novel published by an Australian woman.
1842	*Legends of Australia*, attributed to John George Lang, the first novelist born in the country, is published.
1859	With *The Recollections of Geoffrey Hamlyn*, Henry Kingsley begins the colonial romance tradition.
1859	*The Broad Arrow* by Caroline Leakey heralds the first of the Australian anti-system novels.
1880	The *Bulletin* is started in Sydney by J.F. Archibald and John Haynes.
1880s–1900s	The adventure novel flourishes.
1886	*The Mystery of a Hansom Cab* by Fergus Hume is the first crime novel published in Australia.
1888	*Robbery Under Arms* by Rolf Boldrewood is the first highwayman novel.
1892–1893	The Lawson-Paterson controversy divides writers.
1901	*My Brilliant Career* by Miles Franklin, the first major novel after Federation, is published.
1911	*Jonah* by Louis Stone launches the tradition of larrikin novels.
1916	Katharine Susannah Prichard's *The Pioneers* appeared in 1915 and is the first Australian novel brought to the screen, the following year.
1920s–1960s	Period of modernism.
1925	Chester Cobb's *Mr Moffat* is published – the first notable Australian example of a stream-of-consciousness narrative.

1929	Arthur Upfield's first novel featuring Aboriginal inspector Napoleon Bonaparte, *The Barrakee Mystery*, is published.
1929	*The Middle Parts of Fortune: Somme and Ancre 1916* by Frederic Manning, one of the most enduring tales of the Great War, is published.
1930s	Many complaints are made about the lack of an Australian tradition.
1932	Katharine Susannah Prichard is nominated for the Nobel Prize for Literature.
1934	J.M. Harcourt's *Upsurge: A novel,* a notable early Australian example of socialist realism literature, is published.
1937	Kenneth MacKenzie, alias Seaforth MacKenzie, scandalously portrays male homosexual desire in *The Young Desire It*.
1938–1955	The most fruitful years for the *Jindyworobaks* take place.
1940s–1950s	Proletarianisation of the novel occurs, due to the rise of social realism.
1944	James Aldrige publishes *The Sea Eagle*, a notable early novel about the Second World War.
1944–1964	The active years of the Social Realist Group of writers take place.
1949–1959	Pulp fiction rises to prominence.
1957	Patrick White is the first recipient of the Miles Franklin Award for *Voss*.
1962	The establishment of the first Chair of Australian Literature at the University of Sydney. Occupied by: G.A. Wilkes (1962–1966), Dame Leonie Kramer (1968–1989), Elizabeth Webby (1990–2007) and Robert Dixon (since 2007).
1963	Publication of the first title in Australian literature by Penguin, which contributed to the

democratisation of the novel.

1965 Christopher Koch's precursor of the Australasian novel, *Across the Sea Wall*, is published.

1973 Patrick White is the first Australian to be awarded the Nobel Prize for Literature.

1974 Christina Stead is the first author to receive the Patrick White Award. Copyright Agency Limited (CAL) is founded to ensure creators' rights and works are respected.

1977 *Monkey Grip* by Helen Garner paves the way for 'grunge' literature.

1978 *Karobran: The story of an Aboriginal girl* by Monica Clare is published, and is later defined as the first Aboriginal novel.

1982 Already a finalist in 1972 and 1975 with *The Chant of Jimmy Blacksmith* and *Gossip From the Forest* respectively, Thomas Keneally is the first Australian novelist to be awarded the Booker Prize (offered each year since 1969) for *Schindler's Ark*.

1986 *Julia Paradise* by Rod Jones is published, a notable early example of an Australian novel with a psychoanalytic plot.

1989 The European Association for Australian Studies is created.

1991 David Malouf is the first Australian to win the Commonwealth Writers' Prize (awarded each year since 1987) for *The Great World*.

2000 The Miles Franklin is jointly awarded to Kim Scott's *Benang* and Thea Astley's *Drylands*. Scott is the first Aboriginal novelist to be awarded the Miles Franklin. Astley is the first writer to be awarded the Miles Franklin four times; with *The Acolyte* in 1972, *The Slow Natives* in 1965 and *The*

	Well Dressed Explorer in 1962.
2001	Peter Carey is the first Australian-born novelist to be awarded the Booker Prize twice (for *Oscar and Lucinda* in 1988 and *True History of the Kelly Gang*, 2001) and the Commonwealth Writers' Prize twice (for *True History of the Kelly Gang* and *Jack Maggs* in 1998).
2003	J.M. Coetzee, born in Cap-Vert, South Africa, receives the Nobel Prize for Literature a year after settling in Adelaide.
2007	*Carry Me Down* (2006) by M.J. Hyland is the first Australian novel to be awarded the prestigious British Hawthornden Prize worth £10,000.
2008	Melbourne becomes the second UNESCO City of Literature, dedicated to pursuing and promoting excellence in literature.
2009	The Federal Government decides not to accept the Productivity Commission's recommendation to lift book import restrictions.
2010	Peter Temple's *Truth* is the first crime novel to win the Miles Franklin Award.
2011	The final issue of the *Australian Literary Review* appears in October.
2012	The centenary of Patrick White's birth takes place. Random House publishes the Nobel Prize winner's unfinished novel, *The Hanging Garden*, while France-based academic journal *Cercles* celebrates the author and his works in a special issue guest-edited by David Coad and Jean-François Vernay.
2013	Copyright Agency launches *Reading Australia*, their Australian literature website, which makes a wealth of teaching resources readily accessible to teachers and educators.

2014	Lily Brett is the first Australian novelist to receive the Prix Médicis Étranger for *Lola Bensky* (2013).
2015	The Boisbouvier Founding Chair in Australian Literature is established.

3. Timeline of writers' birthdates

18th Century

1791 Henry Savery (†1842)

1798 Charles Rowcroft (†1856)

19th Century

1805 Alexander Harris (†1874)

1808 Anna Maria Bunn (†1890) James Tucker (†1888)

1812 Louisa Meredith (†1895)

1815 Mary Vidal (†1873)

1816 John Lang (†1864)

1818 Eliza Winstanley (†1882)

1825 Catherine Helen Spence (†1910)

1826 Rolf Boldrewood (†1915)

1827 Caroline Leakey (†1881)

1830 Henry Kingsley (†1876)

1835 Simpson Newland (†1925)

1843 Joseph Furphy (†1912)

1844 John Boyle O'Reilly (†1890), Ada Cambridge (†1926)

1846 Marcus Clarke (†1881)

1848 Jessie Couvreur (†1897)

1850 John Haynes (†1917)

1851 Rosa Praed (†1935)

1856 J.F. Archibald (†1919)

1857 Barbara Baynton (†1929)

1859 Fergus Hume (†1932)

1861 William Lane (†1917)

1863 Arthur Jose (†1934)

1864 Banjo Paterson (†1941)

1867 Henry Lawson (†1922)

1868 Arthur Davis (†1935), Steele Rudd (†1935)

1869 Paul Wenz (†1939)

1870 Louise Mack (†1935), Henry Handel Richardson (†1946), Ethel Turner (†1958), Aeneas Gunn (†1961)

1871 Louis Stone (†1935)

1872 David Unaipon (†1967)

1874 Ambrose Pratt (†1944), G.B. Lancaster (†1945)

1875 William Gosse Hay (†1945)

1876 Mollie Skinner (†1955)

1879 Miles Franklin (†1954), Norman Lindsay (†1969)

1881 H.M. Green (†1962)

1882 Frederic Manning (†1935)

1883 Katharine Susannah Prichard (†1969)

1885 Vance Palmer (†1959), Grant Watson (†1970)

1890 Arthur Upfield (†1964), James Devaney (†1976)

1891 Marcel Aurousseau (†1983)

1893 Frank Dalby Davison (†1970), Martin Boyd (†1972)

1894 Jean Devanny (†1962)

1895 Doris Kerr (†1945), Leonard Mann (†1981)

1896 Joan Lindsay (†1984)

1897 Helen Simpson (†1940), Flora Eldershaw (†1956), Marjorie Barnard (†1987)

1899 Chester Cobb (†1943), Nevil Shute (†1960)

1900 A.A. Phillips (†1985)

20th Century

1901 Percy Stephensen (†1965), Tom Moore (†1979), Xavier Herbert (†1984), Eleanor Dark (†1985)

1902 John Harcourt (†1971), Dymphna Cusack (†1981), Christina Stead (†1983), Alan Marshall (†1984)

1904 Brian Penton (†1951), Florence James (†1993), John Morrison (†1998)

1907 Gavin Casey (†1964), Ralph de Boissière (†2008)

1909 Ronald McKie (†1991)

1911 Judah Waten (†1985), Walter Adamson (†2010)

1912 George Johnston (†1970), Bertram Chandler (†1984), Kylie Tennant (†1988), Patrick White (†1990), Gus O'Donnell (†1990)

1913 Rex Ingamells (†1955), Kenneth MacKenzie (†1955), Lawson Glassop (†1966), Mary Durack (†1994)

1914 Margaret Trist (†1986)

1915 John Manifold (†1985), David Martin (†1997), Don Charlwood (†2012), T.A.G. Hungerford (†2011)

1916 Jessica Anderson (†2010)

1917 Frank Hardy (†1994), Nancy Cato (†2000), James Macdonnell (†2002), Jon Cleary (†2010), Ruth Park (†2010)

1918 Eric Lambert (†1966), James Aldridge, Amy Witting (†2001)

1919 Olga Masters (†1986), Nene Gare (†1994)

1921 Russell Braddon (†1995), Max Harris (†1995), Jack Beasley

1922 Stephen Murray-Smith (†1988)

1923 Elsie Roughsey (†1985), Dorothy Hewett (†2002), Margaret Jones (†2006), Elizabeth Jolley (†2007)

1924 Monica Clare (†1973), David Forrest (†1997), Walter Kaufmann

1925 Laurence Collinson (†1986), Thea Astley (†2004)

1926 Ian Moffitt (†2000)

1927 David Ireland

1928 Robert Brissenden (†1991), Elizabeth Harrower

1931 Shirley Hazzard, Peter Mathers (†2004)

1932 Sreten Bozic, Christopher Koch (†2013)

1933 Pino Bosi

1934 David Malouf

1935 Giovanni Andreoni, Rodney Hall, Antigone Kefalá, Thomas Keneally, Alex Miller, Thomas Shapcott, Randolph Stow (†2010)

1937 Doris Pilkington (†2014)

1938 Colin Johnson, Don'o Kim, Morris Lurie (†2014), Frank Moorhouse, Les Murray

1939 Barbara Hanrahan (†1991), Clive James, Gerald Murnane, Eric Willmot

1940 Carmel Bird, J.M. Coetzee, Manfred Jurgensen

1941 Murray Bail, Anne Derwent, Beverley Farmer, Roger McDonald

1942 Michael Wilding, Helen Garner, Nicholas Hasluck, Janette Turner Hospital

1943 Peter Carey, Robert Drewe, Roberta Sykes (†2010)

1944 Blanche d'Alpuget, Robert Dessaix, David Foster

1945 Margaret Coombs (†2004), Peter Skrzynecki

1946 Jean Bedford, Lily Brett, Kerryn Higgs, Drusilla Modjeska, Penelope Rowe, Peter Temple

1947 Peter Kocan, Amanda Lohrey

1948 Alan Wearne

1949 Leon Carmen, Steven Carroll, Adib Khan, Jennifer Maiden

1950 Brian Castro, Kate Grenville, Philip Salom, Sue Woolfe, Alexis Wright

1951 Peter Goldsworthy, Angelo Loukakis, Sally Morgan, Ania Walwicz

1952 Nicholas Jose

1953 Rod Jones, Shane Maloney

1954 David Kelly

1955 Linda Jaivin, Gail Jones, Ouyang Yu

1956 Antoni Jach

1957 Tony Birch, Anthony Lawrence, Kim Scott, Archie Weller

1958 Debra Adelaide, Arabella Edge, Michelle de Kretser, Kathy Lette

1959 Merlinda Bobis, Gabrielle Carey, Sophie Masson, Peta Spear

1960 Sallie Muirden, Tim Winton

1961 Richard Flanagan, Simone Lazaroo

1962 Matthew Condon, Luke Davies, Anthony Macris, Sarah Myles

1963 Fiona Capp, Mandy Sayer

1964 Georgia Blain, Elliot Perlman, Eva Sallis, Beth Yahp

1965 Justine Ettler, Kathryn Heyman, Melina Marchetta, Christos Tsiolkas, Charlotte Wood

1966 Terri Janke, A.L. McCann, Andrew McGahan, Dorian Mode

1967 James Bradley, Nikki Gemmell, Melissa Lucashenko

1968 Vivienne Cleven, Dylan Coleman, Sonya Hartnett, Anita Heiss, M.J. Hyland, Sofie Laguna

1969 Larissa Behrendt, Mireille Juchau

1970 Fabienne Bayet-Charlton (†2011), Christopher Cyrill, Norma Khouri, Julia Leigh, Hsu-Ming Teo

1971 Helen Darville

1974 Aravind Adiga

1976 Jared Thomas

1983 Tara Winch

1985 Hannah Kent

4. Select bibliography

Albinski, Nan Bowman. 'A Survey of Australian Utopian and Dystopian Fiction', *Australian Literary Studies* 13.1 (1987), 15–28.

Andrews, Barry et al. *The Oxford Companion to Australian Literature*, New York: OUP, [1985] 1994.

Aschcroft, Bill et al. *The Empire Writes Back: Theory and Practice in Post-Colonial Literatures*, London/New York: Routledge, 1989.

Barry, Elaine. *Fabricating the Self: The Fictions of Jessica Anderson*, St Lucia: UQP, 1992.

Ben-Messahel, Salhia. *Mind the Country: Tim Winton's Fiction*, Perth: UWAP, 2006.

Bennett, Bruce. 'Perceptions of Australia, 1965–1988', Hergenhan, Laurie (ed.), *Australian Literary Studies* 13.4 (1988), 433–453.

Birns, Nicholas and Rebecca McNeer (eds). *A Companion to Australian Literature Since 1900*, New York: Camden House, 2007.

Blake, Ann. *Christina Stead's Politics of Place*, Perth: UWAP, 1999.

Broinowski, Alison. *The Yellow Lady: Australian impressions of Asia*, Melbourne: OUP, 1992.

Burns, D.R. *The Directions of Australian Fiction: 1920–1974*, Melbourne: Cassel Australia, 1975.

Cantrell, Leon. *Writing of the 1890s*, St Lucia: UQP, 1977.

Capone, Giovanna (gen. ed.). *European Perspectives: Contemporary essays on Australian literature*, St Lucia: UQP, *Australian Literary Studies* 15.2 (1991).

Carroll, John (ed.). *Intruders in the Bush: The Australian quest for identity*, Melbourne: OUP, 1992.

Carter, David and Anne Galligan (eds). *Making Books*, St Lucia: UQP, 2007.

Carterson, Simon. 'From little ventures small wonders emerge', *Age*, A2 (24 January 2009), 27.

Clancy, Laurie. *A Reader's Guide to Australian Fiction*, Melbourne: OUP, 1992.

Coad, David. 'Patrick White's Castrated Country', *Commonwealth* 15.1 (1992), 88–95.

Colmer, John. *Patrick White*, London: Methuen, 1984.

Daniel, Helen. *Double Agent: David Ireland and his work*, Melbourne: Penguin, 1982.

Daniel, Helen. *Liars: Australian new novelists*, Melbourne: Penguin, 1988.

Denholm, Michael and Andrew Sant (eds). *First Rights*, Melbourne: Greenhouse Publications, 1989.

Dessaix, Robert (ed.). *Australian Gay and Lesbian Writing: An anthology*, Melbourne: OUP, 1993.

Dixon, Robert. *Writing the Colonial Adventure*, Cambridge: CUP, 1995.

Dose, Gerd and Bettina Keil (eds). *Writing in Australia: Perceptions of Australian literature in its historical and cultural context*, Hamburg: Lit, 2000.

Dudley, Michael. 'Apologia Pro Vita Nostra: Critics and Psychiatrist' in Harry Heseltine (ed.), *Literature and Psychiatry: Bridging the divide*, (Canberra: ADFA, 1992): 67–98.

Duthil, Fanny. *Histoire de femmes aborigènes*, Paris: PUF, 2006.

Esson, Louis et al. *Australian Writers Speak*, Sydney: Halstead Press Ltd, 1943.

Ewers, John K. *Creative Writing in Australia*, Melbourne: Georgian House, 1959.

Ferrier, Carole (ed.). *Gender, Politics and Fiction*, St Lucia: UQP, [1985] 1992.

Flynn, Christine and Paul Brennan (eds). *Patrick White Speaks*, Sydney: Primavera Press, 1989.

Geering, R.G. *Christina Stead*, Sydney: Angus & Robertson, 1979.

Gelder, Ken. *Atomic Fiction: The novels of David Ireland*, St Lucia: UQP, 1993.

Gelder, Ken and Paul Salzman. *The New Diversity: Australian Fiction 1970–1988*, Melbourne: McPhee Gribble, 1989.

Genoni, Paul and Susan Sheridan (eds). *Thea Astley's Fictional Worlds*, London: Cambridge Scholars Press, 2006.

Gerster, Robin (ed.). *Hotel Asia: An anthology of Australians travelling in the 'East'*, Camberwell: Penguin Australia, 1995.

Gilbert, Pam. *Coming Out From Under: Contemporary Australian women writers*, London: Pandora, 1988.

Gibson, Ross. *The Diminishing Paradise*, Sydney: Angus & Robertson, 1984.

Green H.M. *A History of Australian Literature Pure and Applied*, Sydney: Angus & Robertson, 1961.

Halligan, Marion. 'Throwing the book at the critics', *Age* (24 July 1995), 15.

Hassal, Anthony. *Dancing on Hot Macadam: Peter Carey's fiction*, St Lucia: UQP, 1994.

Hawley, Janet. 'Loneliness of the short term writer-in-residence', *Saturday Age Extra* (16 August 1986), 9 and 14.

Healy, John. *Literature and the Aborigine in Australia*, St Lucia: UQP, 1978.

Healy, John. 'The Lemurian Nineties', *Australian Literary Studies* 8.3 (1978), 307–316.

Heiss, Anita. *Dhuuluu-Yala: To talk straight*, Canberra: Aboriginal Studies Press, 2003.

Hergenhan, Laurie. *Unnatural Lives: Studies in Australian fiction about the convicts from James Tucker to Patrick White*, St Lucia: UQP, 1983.

Hergenhan, Laurie (ed.). *The Penguin New Literary History of Australia*, Camberwell: Penguin Australia, 1988.

Heseltine, Harry. *Xavier Herbert*, Melbourne: OUP, 1973.

Heyward, Michael. *The Ern Malley Affair*, St Lucia: UQP, 1993.

Heyward, Michael. 'Word wise, book poor', *Age A2* (8 September 2007), 14–15.

Ikin, Van. 'Dreams, Visions, Utopias', *Australian Literary Studies* 13.4 (1988), 253–266.

Jacobs, Lyn. *Against the Grain: Beverley Farmer's writing*, St Lucia: UQP, 2001.

James, Neil (ed.). *Writers on Writing*, Sydney: Halstead Press, 1999.

Janke, Terri. *Writing Cultures: Protocols for producing Indigenous Australian literature*, Sydney: Australia Council, 2002.

Johnson, Grahame (ed.). *Australian Literary Criticism*, Melbourne: OUP, 1962.

Johnson-Woods, Toni. '"Pulp" Fiction Industry in Australia 1949–1959', *Antipodes* 20.1 (June 2006), 63–67.

Jose, Nicholas (ed.). *The Literature of Australia*, London and New York: Norton, 2009.

Kiernan, Brian. *Criticism*, Melbourne: OUP, 1974.

Kiernan, Brian. *Images of Society and Nature*, Melbourne: OUP, 1971.

Knight, Stephen. *Continent of Mystery: A thematic history of Australian crime fiction*, Melbourne: MUP, 1997.

Kwast-Greff, Chantal. 'Poupées de cire, poupées de sang', *Correspondances océaniennes: L'Australie* 4.1 (octobre 2005), 21–24.

Lamb, Karen. *Peter Carey: The genesis of fame*, Sydney: Angus & Robertson, 1992.

Lidoff, Joan. *Christina Stead*, New York: Frederick Ungar, 1982.

Macartney, Frederick T. *Australian Literary Essays*, Sydney: Angus & Robertson, 1957.

McKernan, Susan. *A Question of Commitment: Australian literature in the twenty years after the war*, Sydney: Allen & Unwin, 1989.

McLaren, John. *Australian Literature: An historical introduction*, Melbourne: Longman, 1989.

McLaren, John. *Writing in Hope and Fear: Literature as politics in postwar Australia*, London: Cambridge University Press, 1998.

McNeer, Rebecca. '"What Might Be True": The diverse relationships of Australian novels to fact', *Antipodes* 18.1 (June 2004), 68–71.

Manne, Robert. *The Culture of Forgetting: Helen Demidenko and the Holocaust*, Melbourne: Text, 1996.

Marr, David. *Patrick White: A life*, Sydney: Random House, 1991.

Marr, David (ed.). *Patrick White: Letters*, Sydney: Random House, 1994.

Mead, Philip. *Australian Literary Studies in the 21st Century*, Maryborough: ASAL, 2001.

Meredith, Peter. *Realising the Vision: A history of Copyright Agency Limited 1974–2004*, Sydney: CAL, 2004.

Modjeska, Drusilla. *Exiles at Home: Australian women writers 1925–1945*, Sydney: Angus & Robertson, 1981.

Moore, T. Inglis. *Social Patterns in Australian Literature*, Sydney: Angus & Robertson, 1971.

Mudrooroo Narogin. *Writing From the Fringe: A study of modern Aboriginal literature*, Melbourne: Hyland House, 1990.

Muecke, Stephen et al. *Reading the Country: Introduction to nomadology*, Fremantle: Fremantle Arts Centre Press, 1984.

Narasimhaiah, C.D. *An Introduction to Australian Literature*, Brisbane: The Jacaranda Press, 1965.

Neilsen, Philip. *Imagined Lives: A study of David Malouf*, St Lucia: UQP, 1996.

Nile, Richard. *The Making of the Australian Literary Imagination*, St Lucia: UQP, 2002.

Nolan, Maggie and Carrie Dawson (eds). *Who's Who: Hoaxes, impostures and identity crises in Australian literature*, St Lucia, UQP, Australian Literary Studies 21.4 (2004).

Pender, Anne. *Christina Stead: Satirist*, Melbourne: Common Ground, 2002.

Petersen Teresa. *The Enigmatic Christina Stead: A provocative re-reading*, Melbourne: MUP, 2001.

Pierce, Peter. *Australian Melodramas: Thomas Keneally's fiction*, St Lucia: UQP, 1995.

Pierce, Peter. *The Country of Lost Children: An Australian anxiety*, Melbourne: Cambridge University Press, 1999.

Pierce, Peter. 'The Solitariness of Alex Miller', *Australian Literary Studies* 21.3 (2004), 299–311.

Pierce, Peter. '"Things Are Cast Adrift": Brian Castro's Fiction', *Australian Literary Studies* 17.2 (1995), 149–156.

Pierce, Peter (ed.). *The Cambridge History of Australian Literature*, London: Cambridge, 2009.

Phillips, A.A. *The Australian Tradition*, Melbourne: Cheshire, 1958.

Pons, Xavier. '"And the Winner is ...": Literary Prizes in Australia', *Commonwealth* 16.1 (1993), 38–45.

Pons, Xavier. 'Dramatising the Self: Beverley Farmer's fiction', *Australian Literary Studies* 17.2 (1995), 141–148.

Pordzik, Ralph. *The Quest for Postcolonial Utopia: A comparative introduction to the utopian novel in the new English literatures*, New York: Peter Lang, 2001.

Reid, Ian. *Fiction and the Great Depression: Australia and New Zealand*, Melbourne: Edward Arnold, 1979.

Riemer, Andrew. *The Ironic Eye: The poetry and prose of Peter Goldsworthy*, Sydney: Angus & Robertson, 1994.

Riemer, Andrew. *The Demidenko Debate*, Sydney: Allen & Unwin, 1996.

Roe, Jill. *Stella Miles Franklin: A biography*, Pymble: Harper Collins, 2008.

Russell, Roslyn. *Literary Links*, Sydney: Allen & Unwin, 1997.

Rutherford, Jennifer. *The Gauche Intruder: Freud Lacan and the white Australian fantasy*, Melbourne: Melbourne University Press, 2000.

Ryan-Fazilleau, Sue. *Peter Carey et la quête postcoloniale d'une identité australienne*, Paris: l'Harmattan, 2007.

Salusinszky, Imre. *Gerald Murnane*, Melbourne: OUP, 1993.

Salzman, Paul. *Helplessly Tangled in Female Arms and Legs: Elizabeth Jolley's fictions*, St Lucia: UQP, 1993.

Seal, Graham. *Ned Kelly in Popular Tradition*, Melbourne: Hyland House, 1980.

See, Carolyn. 'Why Australian Writers Keep their Heads Down', *New York Times* (14 May 1989), 1.

Semmler, Clement. *Twentieth Century Australian Literary Criticism*, Melbourne: OUP, 1967.

Semmler, Clement and Whitelock, Derek (eds). *Literary Australia*, Melbourne: Cheshire, 1966.

Shoemaker, Adam. *Mudrooroo: A critical study*, Sydney: Angus & Robertson, 1993.

Shoemaker, Adam. *Black Words, White Page: Aboriginal literature, 1929–1988*, St Lucia: UQP, 1989.

Stephensen, Percy Reginald. *The Foundations of Culture in Australia: An essay towards national self-respect*, Sydney: W.J. Miles, 1936.

Sullivan, Jane. 'The Power of the Prize', *Age* (22 June 2006), 15.

Tacey, David. *Patrick White: Fiction and the unconscious*, Melbourne: OUP, 1988.

Tacey, David. 'Freud, Fiction and the Australian Mind', *Island* 49 (Summer 1991), 8–13.

Turner, George. 'Parentheses: Concerning matters of judgement', *Meanjin* 48.1 (1989), 195–204.

Turner, Graeme. *National Fictions: Literature, film and the construction of the Australian narrative*, Sydney: Allen & Unwin, 1986.

Vernay, Jean-François. 'The Art of Penning the March Hare in: The treatment of insanity in Australian total institution fiction', *AUMLA: Journal of the Australasian Universities Language and Literature Association* 118 (November 2012), 87–103.

Vernay, Jean-François. 'The Politics of Desire: A psychoanalytic reading of Christos Tsiolkas's *Dead Europe*', *The Journal of the European Association of Studies on Australia* 3.2 (Barcelona), 2012, 80–89.

Vernay, Jean-François. 'Male Beauty in the Eye of the Beholder? Guys, Guises and Disguise in Patrick White's *The Twyborn Affair*'. *Transnational Literature* 4.2, Adelaide, May 2012, 1–11.

Vernay, Jean-François. 'Sex in the City: Sexual predation in contemporary Australian grunge fiction', *AUMLA: Journal of the Australasian Universities Language and Literature Association* 107 (May 2007), 145–158.

Vernay, Jean-François. *Water From the Moon: Illusion and reality in the works of Australian novelist Christopher Koch*, New York: Cambria Press, 2007.

Vernay, Jean-François. 'Only Disconnect – Canonising Homonormative Values: Representation and the paradox of gayness in Christos Tsiolkas's *Loaded*', *Antipodes* 20.1, (June 2006), 7–11.

Walton, Robyn. 'Utopian and Dystopian Impulses in Australia', *Overland* 173 (2003), 5–20.

Ward, Russel, *The Australian Legend*, Melbourne: OUP, 1974.

Webby, Elizabeth (ed.). *The Cambridge Companion to Australian Literature*, Cambridge: Cambridge University Press, 2000.

Wilding, Michael. *Studies in Classic Australian Fiction*, Sydney: Sydney Studies, 1997.

White, Patrick. 'The Prodigal Son', *Australian Letters* 1.3 (1958).

White, Richard. *Inventing Australia: Images and identity 1688–1980*, Sydney: Allen & Unwin, 1981.

Wilkes, G. *Australian Literature: A conspectus*, Sydney: Angus & Robertson, 1969.

Wilkes, G. *A Dictionary of Australian Colloquialisms*, Sydney: Collins, 1988.

Whitlock, Gillian. 'From Eutopia to Dystopia', in Kay Ferres (ed.), *The Time to Write: Australian Women Writers 1890–1930*, Ringwood: Penguin, 1993, 162–182.

Woodcock, Bruce. *Peter Carey*, Manchester: Manchester University Press, 1996.

5. Select sitography

Antipodes: A Global Journal of Australian/New Zealand Literature. Nicholas Birns (ed.), http://www.australianliterature.org/Antipodes_Home.htm

AustLit: The Australian literature resource, http://www.austlit.edu.au

Australian Book Review. Peter Rose (ed.), http://www.australianbookreview.com.au

Australian Literary Studies. Julieanne Lamond (ed.), http://www.australianliterarystudies.com.au

Australian Humanities Review. Monique Rooney and Russell Smith (eds), http://www.australianhumanitiesreview.org/current.html

Commonwealth Essays and Studies. Claire Omhovère (ed.), http://www.univ-paris3.fr/commonwealth-essays-and-studies-16669.kjsp?RH=1226586296353

Heat. Ivor Indyk (ed.), http://giramondopublishing.com/heat/

Island Magazine. Matthew Lamb (ed.), http://www.islandmag.com

JASAL. Joe Cummins, Helen Groth, Susan Lever, Brigitta Olubas, Tony Simoes Da Silva and Jay Daniel Thompson (eds), http://www.nla.gov.au/openpublish/index.php/jasal

JEASA. David Callahan (gen. ed.), http://www.easa-australianstudies.net/journal

Journal of Language, Literature and Culture. Peter Goodall (ed.), http://aulla.com.au/journal-of-language-literature-and-culture-jllc/

LINQ. Ariella Van Luyn and Victoria Kuttainen (eds), http://www.linqjournal.com

Meanjin. Jonathan Green (ed.), http://meanjin.com.au

Overland. Jacinda Woodhead (ed.), https://overland.org.au

Quadrant. John O'Sullivan (ed.), http://www.quadrant.org.au

Southerly. David Brooks and Elizabeth McMahon (eds), http://southerlyjournal.com.au

Sydney Review of Books. Catriona Menzies Pike (ed.), http://www.sydneyreviewofbooks.com

Westerly. Catherine Noske (ed.), http://westerlymag.com.au

Credits

(in alphabetical order)

Wakefield Press is an independent publishing and
distribution company based in Adelaide, South Australia.
We love good stories and publish beautiful books.
To see our full range of books, please visit our website at
www.wakefieldpress.com.au
where all titles are available for purchase.

Find us!

Twitter: www.twitter.com/wakefieldpress
Facebook: www.facebook.com/wakefield.press
Instagram: instagram.com/wakefieldpress